Nuclear Peace

NUCLEAR PEACE

THE STORY OF THE TRIDENT THREE

John Mayer

To my long-suffering wife Lizzie,
my talented son Sam
and his children, as yet unborn.

First published in Great Britain by Vision,
a division of Satin Publications Ltd.

Vision
101 Southwark Street
London SE1 0JF
UK
e-mail: info@visionpaperbacks.co.uk
website: www.visionpaperbacks.co.uk

Publisher: Sheena Dewan
Cover design © 2002 Nickolai Globe
Printed and bound in the UK by Cromwell Press

ISBN: 1-904132-04-9

Contents

Foreword by Robin Harper MSP   VII

Acknowledgements   IX

Introduction   I

Part One Action Stations   3

Chapter 1   All Aboard   5
Chapter 2   The Brief   14
Chapter 3   Cornton Vale Jail   20
Chapter 4   Meeting of the Minds   28
Chapter 5   Planning the Raid   33

Part Two Only the Gods of the Ancient World…   43

Chapter 6   History in the Making   45
Chapter 7   On Target and On Message   51
Chapter 8   The Long and Winding Road to the World Court 66
Chapter 9   The British Government at the World Court   76
Chapter 10   The Judgement of the World Court   84

Part Three Around the World in 80 Cases   97

Chapter 11   That Sinking Feeling   99
Chapter 12   Brothers in Arms   110
Chapter 13   Sisters in Arms   126

Contents

Part Four The Trial of the Trident Three   131

Chapter 14   Much-Needed Inspiration   133
Chapter 15   Delay, Worry and Expense   137
Chapter 16   Call Your First Witness   145
Chapter 17   Voices from Within   156
Chapter 18   All Merry Hell   170
Chapter 19   The Man from Illinois   181
Chapter 20   History 1 Efficiency 0   191
Chapter 21   The Weakest Link   200

Part Five Humanitarian Law Wins the Day   211

Chapter 22   The Strongest Link   213
Chapter 23   Sometimes the Mountain Does Move   226
Chapter 24   They Breathe Another Air   231
Chapter 25   Less Is More   242
Chapter 26   Badge of Office   247
Chapter 27   Judgement Day   257

Part Six The Future is in Your Hands   261

Chapter 28   Boom   263
Chapter 29   Sleep Well   270

Index   274

Foreword

The first half of the 20th century was characterised by enormous bloodshed, untold human suffering and the flattening of cities across Europe and Japan. To make matters worse, the second half of that century was scourged by the threat of nuclear war. The 21st century has opened with an act of terrorism so devastating that it has changed forever the political and moral fate of humanity. However, in all the recent rhetoric it has been largely forgotten that the type of nuclear bombs deployed by the US, France and the UK are the type that can vaporise hundreds of thousands of people in a few seconds whilst leaving their environment uninhabitable for at least 30,000 years.

These are the ultimate weapons of terror. What is not widely known is that these massive indiscriminate nuclear weapons are illegal. In 1996 the United Nations asked the World Court if nuclear weapons were legal or not. In a judgement that will steer the way for the future, the World Court unanimously said that such weapons can never be used within international humanitarian law.

The timing of John Mayer's book is peculiarly appropriate. Not only is John Mayer the Scottish Advocate who won the Trident Three case in court, the three women he defended, Angie Zelter, Ellen Moxley and Ulla Roder have been given a Right Livelihood Award for their contribution to world peace and understanding. These awards are presented in Stockholm as alternative Nobel Prizes. This book takes the reader on a round-the-world investigation of what different peoples have done in their own countries to rid the world of nuclear weapons. The book is written in an informative and engaging style and will give much encouragement to our younger generation to join the cause for nuclear disarmament.

This book gives us a unique insight into the workings of the law when faced with inalienable universal human legal rights against the actions of government. It is a celebration of the right of any individual to challenge any government that threatens the use of weapons that could destroy not only them, but all human life. The children of the 21st century have the opportunity and, as the book explains, the legal rights to lead the world away from the constant dangers of nuclear annihilation and to characterise the third millennium with a peaceful alliance of nations the likes of which humankind has never seen before. In these times, when the new buzzwords for joining the EU or the G8 are 'Human Rights', I wish *Nuclear Peace* every success in enlightening the citizens of the world about their oldest and dearest human rights.

Robin Harper
Member of the Scottish Parliament – Green Party
Scottish Parliament Buildings
Edinburgh
April 2002

Acknowledgements

I firstly extend my grateful thanks to Ulla Roder, Ellen Moxley and Angie Zelter, The Trident Three, for being so dedicated and courageous on behalf of all humanity. I am a better man for knowing them and all at Trident Ploughshares 2000. I am especially indebted to Ulla for her permission to use the material that would otherwise be subject to lawyer and client privilege. Jane Tallents at TP 2000 was a tireless assistant during the trial.

Andrea Longson, Librarian at the Advocates' Library, was of invaluable assistance during my research work for both the trial and the Supreme Court hearing, doing her work with a smile and the ease of an expert.

I am very grateful to Lord Murray for early international law pointers. His work on nuclear weapons and the law was pivotal at trial.

I would also like to thank my agent, Annette Green, for believing in me and this book and for being so dedicated to its publication. My thanks also go to Sheena Dewan at Vision for 'seeing' the book and to Stella Wood, my editor, for all her valuable guidance with the text. Everyone else at Vision knows who they are and how much I value their kind assistance.

My grateful thanks are extended to Anne Battley and her staff at the Cabinet Office of HMSO for waiving all Crown Copyright they may have. The same is due to Frank Cass Publishers for kind permission to quote Lord Murray. I would like especially to embarrass Ian Hamilton QC who is a constant inspiration but was particularly so before the trial

Acknowledgements

of The Trident Three, even though he probably didn't know it. Also, I am grateful to Jackie Elwin for reading early drafts. All errors remain my own.

John Mayer
Edinburgh
April 2002

Introduction

This is not a law book. It's an adventure story. At its core are the actions of three women, designed to uphold certain rules of law. Those laws are called international humanitarian law, the highest laws in the world. What is so remarkable is that it is the world's most powerful nations who are breaking these laws. The women sought to bring the issue of the threat of Trident's nuclear weapons before the Supreme Court in the land where the thermonuclear submarine fleet is kept. That land is Scotland.

The story is about disarmament action by those three women, who, on 8 June 1999, got closer than any ordinary citizen has ever been to halting the threat of nuclear war. Their names are Angie Zelter, Bodil Ulla Roder and Ellen Moxley, and their actions were designed to lead to a court case, which they did. When I met them in Cornton Vale jail they admitted doing the things on the indictment (or charge sheet) but were emphatic that they wanted to plead not guilty. The defence case was to be that in disarming a United Kingdom Ministry of Defence floating computer facility they were not engaged in a criminal act but rather in an act of crime prevention, that is, preventing the United Kingdom from continuing to threaten various nations of the world with use of its Trident 2 thermonuclear weapons fleet, an act that they regard as a modern form of totalitarianism, which could easily lead to global catastrophe.

On 8 July 1996 the International Court of Justice (the World Court) in The Hague had issued an 'Advisory Opinion' to the United Nations General Assembly saying unanimously that to threaten the use of thermonuclear warheads was illegal under international humanitarian law. That body of law contains certain 'intransgressible' rules designed to protect the whole of humanity. Nearly every country in the world had made legal representations to the World Court about the issue but when the Court issued its judgement certain Western nuclear states did not like it one bit. So they simply ignored it.

The women belong to a dedicated group of non-violent, open and accountable activists called Trident Ploughshares 2000 (TP 2000). As the name suggests, their aim is to see swords, or nuclear weapons, beaten into ploughshares, as predicted by the prophet Isaiah in the Old Testament. The group sent copies of the World Court judgement to the Prime Minister, the Lord Chancellor, the Director of Public Prosecutions and the Lord Advocate (the head of the Prosecution Service in Scotland). None of these high officials replied. This book is the remarkable story of what happened next.

ONE

ACTION STATIONS

I

All Aboard

Loch Goil is a tranquil place nestling up the Argyllshire coastline below beautiful hillsides dotted with picturesque farms. In the summertime its waters sparkle in the sunshine and fishermen handle small boats, nowadays as more of a pastime than a living. Occasionally intrepid campers trudge their way up the 'Rest and Be Thankful', the famous West Highland road officially known as the A83 in Argyllshire, which runs up to Beinn an Lochain. But only the hardiest turn into the single-track B828 leading steeply down to the tiny village of Lochgoilhead. When they get there it is obvious that amongst nature's restful contours and gladdening summer colours there is something else in Loch Goil. There in the deepest part of the loch, tethered with four iron chains each as thick as a fisherman's arm, floats the Defence Evaluation Research Agency's most important nuclear laboratory – *Maytime*.

A huge, hard-edged, grey, rectangular steel structure, it rolls in the strong tidal waters like a Lubianka cell block gone AWOL. Accessed from a specially built launching site, it is staffed by highly qualified government scientists and engineers whose work is to keep the British Trident thermonuclear submarine fleet acoustically silent, and thus secret, as it patrols the oceans of the world. *Maytime* has a smaller accomplice, called *Newt*, which lies down the loch a bit. These installations do their work so secretly that the only time the locals notice anything happening is when the guardian hunter-killer submarines come up the neighbouring Gare Loch and peel away, allowing Trident to slip up 'the Goil' to be tested and approved by *Maytime*. Without that go-ahead, the most powerful deadly weapons of mass destruction the world has ever known are useless.

On Tuesday 8 June 1999 at about quarter to seven in the evening Lochgoilhead was closed. The post office-cum-general store and the local garage were shut for the night and the few local residents who work 40 miles away in Glasgow were peacefully at home. The loch was calm and silence reigned because the big boat taking the staff from *Maytime* to shore had long since departed. The tide was fairly high, allowing anyone who might fancy slipping a small boat into the water from the shingle beach to do so quite easily. So no one batted an eyelid when three middle-aged women and a man got out of a car, unhitched a small dinghy from its trailer and did just that. The only oddity was that the women were dressed in bulky clothing and soon unloaded bulging ruck-sacks and tools into the boat. As they got into the boat the man left them to it and drove quickly round the tiny winding road alongside cliff-hanging cottages to one of the few natural vantage points, which, incidentally, cannot be seen from the beach. The noisy single-cylinder marine engine fired up nicely and almost immediately shot the Gemini dinghy forward with a bit of a lurch. Anyone, such as a security guard, who might have looked would surely have wondered why these women took off at such a rate and, even more curiously, where they were going at such speed.

The women were Angie Zelter, Ellen Moxley and Ulla Roder – all members of Trident Ploughshares 2000 and now immortalised as 'The Trident Three'. All three were later to say that years and years of protest at the highest international levels and months of planning this act of disar-mament now rested on what would happen over the next few minutes. For that is all the time they expected to get before being arrested and hauled off by the Ministry of Defence police. They were not to know that their task would be aided by the most mundane omissions of some security guards, who were apathetically lounging in their quarters only a few hundred yards further down the loch.

It took only a few minutes for the dinghy, which had already sprung a leak, to reach the side of *Maytime* that was unseen by the guards in their quarters. But the noise from the engine was horrendous and carried like a First World War machine-gun across the still evening waters. Trepidation set in amongst the amateur seafarers as the foreboding steel structure grew ever larger; so none of them turned back to wave to the man at the vantage point who by now was firing off reels of pictures with a very long lens indeed. Stage one of the plan was completed when the little leaky boat slipped alongside some steps leading from the waterline to the lower deck and the women scrambled aboard.

As Angie tended to the ropes, Ulla, the youngest at almost 45 years old, went up a few steps ahead of Ellen to receive the rucksacks packed full of large white-on-black home-made banners proclaiming 'Stop Nuclear Death Research' and 'Ban Research for Genocide'. Ellen, the eldest at 64, unpacked whilst Angie, a sprightly 48, and Ulla began tying these to the handy railings running the entire length of the upper deck some 20 feet above sea level. When the banners were secured and clearly visible the women drew their breath. Then an astonishing thing happened. Nothing.

Confusion set in as the seconds and then a minute passed. As always and in keeping with the Trident Ploughshares 2000 commitment to openness and accountability, the press had been informed about this daring act. But no one showed up. Perhaps the location was too remote for the reporters or maybe the press release got the details wrong. However, all such misgivings evaporated in another few moments when Ellen, who is slightly under 5 feet tall, peeked her head around a corner. Amazingly, the coast was clear.

The coast was quite literally clear. The western banks of the loch are visible from *Maytime* and it was quite obvious that there wasn't a soul around. Despite that, there was an eeriness in the air because the crushing weight of what happened every day inside this vessel was being overcome by that most fickle of phenomena – opportunity. And when opportunity arrives it can only become indestructible when it is married to a rare human trait – bravery. Fortunately there was an abundance of both on board *Maytime* that evening as the three realised that stage two was waiting. But first they had to get inside.

Angie tried a glass cutter on the window of a laboratory door but to no avail. The glass, being designed to take high seas pounding against it, was far too tough. Vital minutes were wasted in trying to cut through that glass. In the heat of the moment they failed to realise that they were not trying to break into a domestic building. This was a marine installation and there are very special rules about emergency access in and out of such places. That became blindingly obvious when they did a bit of exploring and found a window that could be unbolted from the *outside*. They carefully undid the bolt, squeezed themselves one at a time through the hatch and unceremoniously landed in the most secret laboratory in the UK.

The whole place was pristine. The floor shone like a new pin and the banks of computer terminals around the perimeter were devoid of any Post-it notes or other scribblings so common in offices nowadays. The duty roster hung squarely on the wall and the kitchen area would have been a delight to any health and safety inspector. Now these women were not common vandals. Their intentions were not wantonly to destroy things. Their purpose was not even a political one. You won't hear the name of any particular political party bandied about the Trident Ploughshares 2000 office. They also knew better than most how vital the work of *Maytime* was to the deployment of Trident and they had done their research very well. Their sole purpose was clear – disarmament.

The plan was first to disarm the variable depth hydrophones and vertical line arrays that provide precise measurements of the acoustic profiles so vital for secrecy from spy satellites. These were identified and duly disarmed. The excitement was now rising because surely, in the next few moments, the Ministry of Defence police would be piling in, probably aided by the heavily armed marines who are specially trained to guard Trident. But again, nothing happened. Next the VHF and UHF surface and underwater communications equipment that permits vessel-to-shore communication and tracking information had to be found and safely disarmed. This was pretty obvious, as was the Trisponder tracking system. The radar and electronic warfare calibrators were next, followed closely by the extra-low-frequency emission testing equipment. Much of the computer hardware necessary for these functions was common to other tasks so the decision was quickly made that all such computers were legitimate targets and had to go.

This was easier said than done. The doors were still locked, so everything had to be unplugged piece by piece and handed along that strong female chain gang up to the hatch. The women worked in silence as they unhooked the computers that guard the mathematics and physics of Trident, programs that were developed under the most top-secret of military regimes the world has ever known. As each piece was disconnected it was laid in the chain and only when every offending computer had been isolated did the hard physical work of getting these out on deck begin.

One by one the computers were struggled through the hatch. Ulla's heart skipped a beat when she heard the splash of that first one hitting the lapping waters of Loch Goil. The heavy central control unit sank immediately and sent ripples out over the water. She could not have known how far those little ripples were to pan out across the world, some of them skipping across the very waters under which the Trident thermonuclear fleet was hiding. Gradually more were gaily flung into the water to the tune of 'Hi ho, hi ho, it's off to work we go'. The screens, being vacuum-sealed, simply floated away down the loch, carried by the ripples of their co-dependent units. About an hour later and whilst the women were still on board, locals began to notice these screens being washed up on the shore. Bewilderment was soon followed by the entirely wrong assumption that hooligans from the city had dumped unwanted rubbish from a boat. No one noticed that each piece was clearly marked as MoD property.

With stage two completed, more had been achieved than was ever dreamt of in the planning stages. Curiously though, the press was still absent and nobody was calling from the shore about the large banners that had now been tied to the upper deck of *Maytime* for about an hour. It was as though the world had come to a halt. Where were the shore guards? Where were the boat patrols? Nothing seemed to make any sense. Nothing, that is, except that stage two was now complete and if nothing else was achieved then it was still absolutely certain that the outgoing Trident patrols could not be tested or approved from *Maytime*. There was no other way in the world they could get tested or approved so there was no way they could go out. The incoming patrols were known to schedule themselves to tight limits so they would have to come back on schedule. The inescapable conclusion had been reached: for the moment and the foreseeable future, one half of the UK's Trident thermonuclear fleet was useless and could legitimately be said to have been disarmed. One can only marvel at the consequences if this action had *not* been taken by deeply responsible intelligent citizen interveners but by a destructive international terrorist group.

Obviously, with all the work they had done in the laboratory over the last couple of hours or so, there was a little mess — bits of wire here and there, some dropped documents and that sort of thing — so the women checked that essentials for those who worked on *Maytime* such as the first aid kit and the food in the cupboards were intact before sweeping the floor and tidying behind them. Mission accomplished, one might have thought. But no. These were old campaigners who understood every minute piece of how these gruesome officially held weapons of mass destruction are serviced by the government's Defence Evaluation Research Agency (DERA). The thinking was that now *Maytime* was disarmed there was an unexpected opportunity to disarm its associate vessel, *Newt*, which lay temptingly just a few hundred yards away.

Newt also plays a vital role in keeping Trident secret at sea. Only when these truly enormous submarines are gingerly moored in Loch Goil is *Newt* deployed in a circular course around them, collecting secret data for transmission to *Maytime*, which analyses the data and gives the go-ahead. Also, when there is no actual Trident submarine to test, *Newt* does the same thing with model submarines. This operation is to check the equipment and make any adjustments before the real thing is required. But the women had a problem. Their noisy boat was now only half-inflated and would have sunk had anyone tried to use it. Another big decision was needed — whether it was within their ethical frame of reference to use *Maytime*'s lifeboats for disarmament action. Their instincts and respect for safety equipment prevailed and it seemed a step too far. So the idea was abandoned.

Instead they turned their attention to the equipment used for the essential work of mechanically testing cables and towed arrays. The pull-down winch used to control the model submarines came squarely within this remit, as did the long-baseline experimental set-ups. As they set about making these pieces of equipment useless for approving Trident submarines they actually felt regret and sadness for the people whose time and effort had gone into keeping these things in such good order. 'If only all this work could go into the development of peace; aah, if only.'

This work took about half an hour as it just involved pouring something sticky over certain control valves and chipping away with a masonry hammer at the winch cables so that for safety reasons they would require to be scrapped. How they were not seen doing this disarmament work on the top deck of *Maytime* in full view of anyone paid to watch over the vessel remains a complete mystery. Then, with this bonus work done, the sight of a completely unguarded *Newt* became a temptation too far. There being no 'leader' of this action, they decided amongst themselves that the lifeboats could, after all, be used and should be used.

Disappointment momentarily crushed the three intrepid campaigners when, despite following the launching instructions, the first lifeboat landed in the water upside down and the second failed to inflate properly. It was over. All that could have possibly been done had been done. It was a triumph for nuclear disarmament greater than any other ever undertaken and it was time to celebrate. Hunger and exhaustion now swept through all three women, but they had come prepared.

With *Maytime* now taking on a more foreboding air against the evening sun the women simply went to their rucksacks, unpacked brown-bread banana sandwiches and grapes and went up to the top deck for a picnic. They folded out chairs and, in silence, ate heartily watching the beautiful West Highland sunset. Their feeling of satisfaction was well deserved.

When the wrapping for the sandwiches was folded and put away they all noticed that it was getting chilly. Still not a soul was to be seen, so there was nothing left to do but call the MoD themselves. Others had been trying them for a few hours but Whitehall is very proactive and doesn't respond to anyone. Well, not at that time it didn't.

The MoD initially refused to believe that anyone was aboard *Maytime* and slammed the phone down. It took some persistence to make them realise that what was being reported was true. Then all hell broke loose. Trident's dedicated security team at Coulport naval base, about two miles down the loch from *Maytime*, was alerted, as were the MoD police. It is known that certain spy satellites can look down on *Maytime* and 'see' objects in focus down to half a metre across. This means that, so far as satellite reports were concerned, the MoD could read the banners but the women who put them there remained technically invisible (as they were less than half a metre across).

When the first police boat pulled alongside *Maytime*, Angie, Ulla and Ellen stood by the railings on the top deck waving. The women greeted the police politely, calling down their names and trying excitedly to give a brief explanation of who they were. For the two police officers aboard, it was something of a shock. Constable James Steven Byres was on the deck of Clyde Marine Unit One whilst his colleague, Constable Donald Cameron Blair, attended to the steering. At the point of docking Angie ran down the stairs and took a line from their bow to the stair rail of *Maytime*, assisting Constable Byres in tying up. The conversation was cordial and the police simply asked the women to come aboard their boat. So they did. The women corrected one another along the way as they told the story of the last three hours. When they got to the part about the lifeboats failing to inflate, the police explained why they had got that wrong and pointed out where the oars fitted into pockets on the sides. Concerned for other users of the loch, the three women offered to try to recover the floating lifeboats but the police said there were plenty of other officers on their way who could attend to that. Ulla and Angie then offered to help with casting off but the police told them that, if they didn't mind, they should take a seat below as they could manage that themselves.

The sail, even by the powerful Clyde Marine Unit One, to the naval jail at Coulport took well over an hour. All five aboard sat together as Constable Blair steered the well-known course. After about 15 minutes listening to the women explain why Trident was a weapon of mass destruction outlawed by international humanitarian law, Constable Byres offered tea all round. As he made the tea he reached into a cupboard and brought out some eggs, which he gestured towards the 'prisoners'. Acceptance was by way of polite thank-yous all round and the conversation turned to organic farming and free-range chickens.

And so, as scenes of crime officers and the chief of *Maytime,* Iain McPhee, were arriving at Lochgoilhead, down in Coulport Ministry of Defence jail (or processing centre as it is officially called) the dull procedures of form filling and fingerprinting began their weary course. But nothing could deflate the exhilaration felt by the three proud women standing before the charge bar. Like the others, Ellen just thought it was wonderful. After so many years of hearing about injustice and oppression coming out of our society, there she stood – a dignified human being who refused to be oppressed. She 'felt so terribly, terribly, terribly happy... over the moon'.

2

The Brief

Scotland's supreme courts sit in the regal, ancient and world-famous Parliament House in Edinburgh. However, for all that, Parliament House is known to all who work there simply as 'the Steamy'. That is a reference to the 19th-century steam wash-houses that used to serve every common street and where everyone knew everything about everyone else. I work there and can tell you that, for all the magnificence of Parliament Hall, the white marble statues and well-worn wigs and gowns, it is just like a steamy. The enormous Gothic building sits discreetly behind St Giles' Cathedral in the Royal Mile, and contains the courts and the Faculty of Advocates, whose members practise 'ad voca' in those courts, that is they speak in court. The summer months of July and August are traditionally very quiet because the whole place goes into what we still rather anachronistically call 'the long vac'. That means the judges are mostly in their villas abroad and non-urgent civil cases are being 'punted' into the winter session. However, because crime never sleeps, the criminal courts remain in full flow, meaning that the advocates, solicitors and others who practise in them are similarly busy.

I had been prosecuting for a spell in the spring and, in the last week of June, began defending those charged with drug dealing, rape and other serious crimes in the High Court in Edinburgh. For reasons unclear to me, criminal legal aid work does not generally pay as well as civil legal aid work but at least it pays more quickly. The middle of September 1999 therefore found my wife Lizzie and me at home with, just for a change, some money in the bank and fewer cares than causes to be cheerful as we celebrated her 40th birthday. It was a Saturday night and I had lit the fire early in the evening, not for the heat but more for the feeling of well-being that real flames provide. It seemed daft when half an hour later it became so hot we had to open the living room window but the daftness just lent added good humour to an already joyous occasion. I also made the dinner, chilled her favourite wine and was placing her cards and candles on the table when the phone rang. We looked at each other the way couples do when the world is unwelcome. But these days work comes to advocates in many fickle guises so we both knew I would answer it before she blew out the candles.

'You won't believe this,' said the familiar voice of Matthew Berlow, a brilliant young criminal lawyer in Glasgow with a first-class pass in international law from Strathclyde University. These days he is so busy he spends most of his waking life on a mobile phone and never has time for formalities.

'I'll kill you if this is not top-notch, Matthew,' I said, only half-kidding. 'I told you yesterday how important today is, didn't I? In fact, I told you twice.'

'Shut up. You won't believe this,' he repeated.

Matthew and I treat each other more as nephew and uncle than instructing solicitor and counsel so I went quiet, simultaneously checking the candles and the expression on my wife's face. I figured I had about five minutes at the most.

'I've just been granted legal aid for you to come into the Trident case.'

Silence reigned for a few seconds. We had mentioned the case in passing because Matthew acted in the lower criminal courts for the Trident Ploughshares 2000 campaigners, from whom there was now a stream of appeals coming up to the High Court. I knew their aim was to see the Trident nuclear submarines beaten into ploughshares (or at least decommissioned), as predicted by Isaiah in the Old Testament. I also knew that three women campaigners had recently been arrested and charged with causing criminal damage to a Ministry of Defence acoustic secrecy unit that was floating in the deepest sea-loch in Scotland, Loch Goil. But beyond that I was in the dark.

'We need to consult in the morning,' he said, knowing perfectly well no one ever consults on a Sunday morning. Before I could chastise him he continued, 'I've fixed it. It's a threesome. The first pannel [as accused people in Scotland are technically known] is Angie Zelter. She's the woman who got herself off in the English 'Hawk jets to East Timor' case. She's representing herself. We're for the second pannel, Ulla Roder. I've been reading the international humanitarian law on this and…'

'Whoa,' I commanded. 'I can't do this right now. You know its Lizzie's birthday and you know which one it is. Are you completely insane?'

'I'll call you at 7 in the morning. You won't believe this – the defence is that they weren't committing a crime but that they were engaged in an act of crime prevention. We don't deny the facts on the libel [charge sheet]…'

'Matthew, whoa. I'm not doing this right now, OK?' I said loudly, knowing that I was buying a minute or two.

'Seven am then. Oh, and by the way, it's at Cornton Vale jail,' he yelled, and hung up, no doubt to take another call.

There is only one women's jail in Scotland. It sits in the picturesque setting of Stirling's Vale of Cornton, hence the name. It is also in the shadow of the Wallace Monument, which symbolises the ancient freedoms of the people of Scotland so stirringly pronounced in the Declaration of Arbroath in 1320. The jail is a modern building, erected in the 1970s, and looks like many of the concrete hotels in the area that sprang up to meet the tourist trade around the same time. But it is a jail nonetheless. As a criminal prosecutor in Glasgow I had seen my fair share of women sent there for prostitution, shoplifting and other necessities of life in the sprawling housing schemes of the west of Scotland. I had read of its rising suicide rate and listened with scepticism to the feeble mutterings of politicians on all sides who pretend to have other solutions.

Periodically through our birthday dinner I thought of those three women whom I had yet to meet and pondered their 'crime' of trying to get rid of the world's most powerful thermonuclear weapons – Trident 2

— a weapons system of unimaginable destructive force, which could wipe out large parts of the planet in seconds. I could picture the bare plaster cell walls with the tiny sink in the corner and imagine the noise after lock-down. What I could not figure out was why these women had not been granted bail. It was troubling me to the point where I wanted to ring and ask Matthew but that of course would have brought its own kind of fallout, a price I was not prepared to pay.

That night I couldn't sleep and by 2 am the idea of a defence by reversing the tables on the British government, the Ministry of Defence in particular, and claiming to be acting in crime prevention was still running around in my head. It would certainly take some proving, I thought. Try as I might I could not get over that I had never heard of such a defence, but then again I had never heard of anyone in Scotland being charged with such an unusual crime. I flirted with the idea that the whole thing was just crazy. But I was bedevilled by the case and I hadn't seen a single sheet of the brief papers. We have an old saying in the Faculty of Advocates, which is this: 'Do nothing until you've seen your agent, seen the point and then seen the client.' Despite the wisdom of that unwritten rule, I, not for the last time in this case, tried to get my mind round the whole case. Without more to go on, that was impossible.

I lay awake in the still darkness, my eyes wide open, recalling how in 1964 as a boy of 12 in Glasgow I had done two significant things on the same day. One lunchtime I had combed my hair forward like the Beatles and pinned a home-made 'Ban the Bomb' badge on to the top-left lapel of my school blazer. Walking back to school I shivered as I remembered how, a year or so before, our school playground had been awash with talk of how we were all definitely going to be blown up in what the teachers were calling 'the Cuban missile crisis'. I smiled fondly to myself as I thought back over 30 years, recalling my teacher for the first lesson after lunch. Mr Thomson was his name but all the kids affectionately referred to him as 'Danny'. When he left our East End school to become a scriptwriter at Scottish Television we were bewildered and thought he had been beamed up by aliens, so unreal did that world seem to us. The image of me sitting in class waiting for him to notice my badge was as vivid as any I carry around. Others pupils were getting restless with anticipation but he chose his moment well. He was writing on the black-board and, without turning, said loudly, 'Mayer, if you can tell me what the letters CND stand for, I'll let you wear that badge.' 'Campaign for Nuclear Disarmament, sir,' I called out proudly. 'Correct, Mayer,' was all he replied. I still have that badge.

I felt a deep love for that ragged boy within me and congratulated him on surviving through many tortuous adventures. Against that back-ground life once again seemed fragile as I kissed my sleeping wife's forehead and went quietly downstairs to look up international humani-tarian law. I keep most of the classic sourcebooks for Scots law at home, together with many journals and old books about court cases. I was so impressed by my teachers at Edinburgh University law faculty that I bound my lecture notes. I have even had the honour to contribute to three legal textbooks since being called to the Scottish Bar. The result is that I can usually put a hand on most things when I need to. This time, however, it was different. International humanitarian law is not a 'core' subject at law school; neither is it a required subject for the Bar. I doubt therefore if there are more than a handful of advocates who have ever read anything about it. I searched amongst my favourite books and tried cross-referring a few things to see where that took me. I drew a blank and then, at 3 am, turned to the Internet. Thousands upon thousands of 'hits' popped up. By this time I felt tired and a bit dispirited but fascinated nonetheless by one word that seemed to feature in most of the sites I visited: that word was Nuremberg.

I am originally from a Jewish family some of whom left Byelorussia for the United States in the 1910s and 1920s. Those who remained are gone now, some of them gassed at Auschwitz. But that's another story. However, the chilling sound of those dreadful names, which the world associates with the Nazis, always leaves me feeling desperate and deprived of a lineage I never knew. Nuremberg is one of those names. With its enormity coming at me in waves, I vividly recalled my devil-master (mentor), then Mr Ian Bonomy QC, now Lord Bonomy, telling me that there were three essentials for good presentation of legal argument. These were preparation, preparation and preparation. With that in mind I closed down my computer and crawled into bed feeling trepidation at the scale of what lay ahead. A few troubled hours of sleep passed like a speeding train until the ringing of the phone by my bed woke me.

'Morning. You up yet? I'll meet you at the jail, OK?' said you-know-who.

'OK, Matthew. Nine o'clock at Cornton Vale jail. See you there. Bye.'

3

Cornton Vale Jail

As my new car sped out of Edinburgh up the M9 motorway towards Stirling, I was all too conscious of the fact that, from a legal point of view, my mind was no further forward than it had been the night before. I then did something I have done since my early days at the Bar when confronted with some legal problem about which I knew little or nothing: I called upon a great lawyer for help. More accurately, I wondered what the great chieftain of Scots law, John Inglis, would do. Lord President Inglis reigned for the last quarter of the 19th century over the 'high-water mark' of Scots law. His larger-than-life-sized portrait hangs in Parliament Hall to this day. It is often a source of comfort, at least to me, to know that, whichever court I may appear in, I will not face the likes of him. His approach to fairness was to bring his huge mind to each case unencumbered by any detail in order that it could be systematically filled by the submissions of counsel. I felt much better as on the morning of Sunday 12 September 1999 I pulled into the car park at Cornton Vale jail feeling that to bring an empty but receptive mind was the right thing to do in this case. And so it proved.

It was a bright, tranquil morning and the jail showed no sign of any major incident overnight. I remember birdsong and the distant prattling sound of children from the nearby houses out playing. The only disturbance of the peace was Matthew who was pacing the tarmac and gesturing into his mobile phone. We shared the usual insults that serve as pleasantries between us and he apologised, saying we could not see our client until 10 am at the earliest. In all honesty I was glad to have the opportunity to apply the first two parts of our unwritten rule, namely to see my agent and see the point. Scottish readers will know that our solicitors are properly known as law agents.

We moved away from the high-perched security cameras that penetrate the curls of razor wire and follow anyone who hangs around for more than a minute. There is a pleasant walk nearby along a riverside, and once down a steep bank we were alongside the water and deep into the preliminaries of a criminal consultation. 'What was the exact time and place of arrest? Are any arrest warrants valid in law or flawed by procedural irregularity? Did the police behave themselves under Section 14 of the Criminal Procedure (Scotland) Act 1995?' In short, we covered all the technicalities that might give rise to a later argument in court that any Crown evidence gathered since the error in law is, so far as the prosecution is concerned, 'fruit of the poison tree'. What a sight we must have been: two men in suits, one with a briefcase and the other with a big, old Gladstone bag, heads tilted together in careful discussion, walking along a quiet Stirlingshire riverside at that time on a Sunday morning. We could easily have been taken for spies!

Back at the front door to the jail I was delighted to learn that my learned friend John McLaughlin, Advocate, was instructed for the third pannel, Ellen Moxley. I say 'learn', but no one told me. I could not even see him. But John has the loudest, most genuine laugh of anyone I have ever known and it now rang out across the morning air like a klaxon from around the corner, so there could be no mistake. Scottish advocates, like English barristers, traditionally do not shake hands except in initial welcome to the Faculty and in bereavement. John and I, being originally from the same part of Glasgow, usually slap each other's upper arm and so it was as we all entered reception to begin the signing-in procedure.

'Reception' is a polite way of saying a secure area where all locks on the steel doors are electronically controlled and no two of them can be opened at the same time. Everyone's face is immediately captured on digital camera, from various angles, and these images can be cross-checked against police databases in the blink of an eye. It is a workplace dominated by procedures laid down by Her Majesty's Prison Standing Orders, where there is no room for error. In Cornton Vale, the jailers, or 'turnkeys' as they are known, are of course women, mostly young women who grew up in the environs of Stirling and still live nearby, plus others who can hack the long hours and deal with the commute from Edinburgh or Glasgow. I have always found them to be fully professional, courteous and usually cheery – in short, a great credit to their pristine uniforms. However, as we waited for the message of our presence to be transmitted to the appropriate wings of the building, and the formulaic details of our reasons for the visit to be double-checked, I detected another characteristic in all of them – they were curious. It was almost immediately obvious that our clients were no ordinary prisoners. The usual clientele are young, between the ages of 20 and 30. Our clients were middle-aged. The usual charges are those I mentioned earlier. Our clients were charged with something to do with the UK's Trident nuclear weapons fleet. The usual defence is 'It wisnae me', whereas our clients were spouting stuff about international humanitarian law. Oh yes, they were very curious.

In the few minutes we had, I decided to sit down in an ante-room and have a look at the basics. Now, in any Scottish criminal case the basics are kept to their simplest for two reasons: first, in order that the jury (and the rest of us) can understand what's going on, and second, because less goes wrong that way so fewer appeals get off the ground. Involvement with the criminal law is really a three-stage process. First come the police. They investigate matters of interest to them and decide whether or not to charge a person and, if they do, with which crimes. That is their decision, not the decision of anyone else, such as a victim. If charges are preferred, then these are sent to stage two, to the procurator fiscal. He or she is the local public prosecutor, who decides first whether there is enough evidence in law to secure a conviction and second whether it is actually in the public interest for that prosecution to go ahead. If the prosecution is to go ahead then the next step is to decide at what level of court it should be brought. If the procurator fiscal thinks the matter is serious enough for consideration by the top prosecutor, the Lord Advocate, then the papers are sent to him. In all cases involving a jury, a charge sheet or 'indictment' is drafted and served on the accused person. The next stage is to get that indictment and the accused person before a court of law at the same time so that the judge can read the charges and hear how the accused person wishes to respond to them. Most people are familiar with the question, 'How do you plead, guilty or not guilty?' We were at the point just before trial and I had to know how my client wanted to plead, although I had a very good idea.

I read the indictment looking for both what was in it and what was not in it. It hardly needs saying that, if, for instance, my client turns out not to be the woman named and born on the day that the indictment says, then there is something fundamentally wrong. But it does need saying. I have been in a court in Edinburgh at top level where one of the senators of the College of Justice in Scotland, ie a Supreme Court judge, eventually lost all patience with a junior advocate who wanted to mention his client's case. His client wanted a large sum of money in damages but there was one problem – the client seemed to be dead. The advocate insisted his client wasn't dead but the judge pointed out that if he wasn't then he would be well over a hundred years old and therefore quite obviously not the man who had fallen from a crane whilst in the course of his employment the previous year. Happily the matter was settled when the client turned up, late, and explained that he was the nephew of a crane driver of the same name who happened also to have fallen out of his crane and sued in the same court many years before. So we check these things.

The indictment read as follows:

Sheriff and Jury

Trial Diet: Monday 27 September 1999 (Greenock)

First Diet: Thursday 2 September 1999 (Dunoon)

ANGELA CHRISTINA ZELTER (DOB 5.6.51), BODIL ULLA RODER (DOB 24.8.54) and ELLEN MOXLEY (DOB 12.3.35), all prisoners in HM Prison Cornton Vale, Stirling.

You are Indicted at the instance of The Right Honourable THE LORD HARDIE, Her Majesty's Advocate, and the charges against you are that:

1. On 8 June 1999 on board the vessel '*Maytime*' then moored in the waters of Loch Goil, near Lochgoilhead, Argyll, you ANGELA CHRISTINA ZELTER, you BODIL ULLA RODER and you ELLEN MOXLEY did wilfully and maliciously damage said vessel and did score two windows on board said vessel with a glass cutter or similar object and did attempt to drill a hole in one of said windows;

2. On date and place above libelled you ANGELA CHRISTINA ZELTER, you BODIL ULLA RODER and you ELLEN MOXLEY did attempt to steal two inflatable life-rafts from said vessel and did remove said liferafts from their mountings on said vessel and deploy said life-rafts in the waters of Loch Goil aforesaid;

3. On date and place above libelled you ANGELA CHRISTINA ZELTER, you BODIL ULLA RODER and you ELLEN MOXLEY did maliciously and wilfully damage equipment, fixtures and fittings on board said vessel '*Maytime*' and in particular did cut a hole in a metal wire fence in the laboratory of said vessel, did smash the contents of an electronic equipment cabinet and rip out electric cables in said cabinet, did cut off the main control switch for the winch on said vessel, did damage a padlock on the door to the control room of said vessel by attempting to saw through same with a hacksaw and thereafter covering said padlock in glue or similar substance rendering the said padlock inoperative, did pour glue or similar substance onto the wires and controls of a crane on the upper deck of said vessel, on the controls of the winch aforesaid and onto the cleats securing the hatch on said vessel, did place a chain around the crane on the upper deck of said vessel thereby preventing said crane from operating, did smash a computer monitor on said vessel, did damage a wall clock in the laboratory of said vessel and did damage a cabinet controlling a power supply to an adjacent platform, by forcing said cabinet open and damaging same;

4. On date and place above libelled you ANGELA CHRISTINA ZELTER, you BODIL ULLA RODER and you ELLEN MOXLEY did

maliciously and wilfully damage a quantity of computer equipment, electrical and office equipment, acoustic equipment and amplifier, recording
equipment, fax machines, telephone, tools, documents, records, electronic
components, a briefcase, radio equipment, range finder, books, and a case
and contents, and did deposit said items in the waters of Loch Goil,
whereby said items became waterlogged, useless and inoperable;

OR ALTERNATIVELY

On the date and place above libelled you ANGELA CHRISTINA
ZELTER, you BODIL ULLA RODER and you ELLEN MOXLEY did
steal said quantity of computer equipment, electrical and office equipment, acoustic equipment and amplifier, recording equipment, fax
machines, telephone, tools, documents, records, electronic components, a
briefcase, radio equipment, range finder, books, and a case and contents,
and did deposit said items in the waters of Loch Goil and did thus steal
same.

PROCURATOR FISCAL FOR THE PUBLIC INTEREST
Signed: Mr David Webster, Regional Procurator Fiscal

In other words the prosecutor was saying that they broke into this MoD
installation, wrecked the place and stole a whole lot of expensive things
belonging to the government, making them common vandals and thieves.

I got something of a surprise when I met Bodil Ulla Roder for the
first time. We all form mental images of those we have never met. As
Matthew and I sat in one of the jail's 'consultation rooms', which in fact
was a room so small there was barely enough oxygen in it for 10 minutes'
survival time, I formed an image of a brash, brassy sort who stuck her
nose into other people's business. I was very, very wrong. In fact, some 10
minutes later, the person who slid in the door (that could only half-
open) past our bags and the third chair was a tall, sallow-skinned Danish
woman wearing ultra-thick glasses and a T-shirt so washed-out that the
print was threadbare. She also had a soft voice, warm smile and a gentle
handshake, which, when I got to know her better, seemed to me to sum
up her personality.

The consultation got off to an unusual start. There we were, three adults in a room not much bigger than a lavatory cubicle for the disabled with a table not wide enough to lay a sheet of A4 paper down on, when a young turnkey knocked on the door. As I was nearest I opened it, or rather half-opened it, which was as far as it would go. 'These are for you, sir,' she said very matter-of-factly, pointing to boxloads of paper lined up outside in the corridor. I began to slide the first one towards me but decided this farce had gone far enough and pushed them back out into the corridor again with my foot. 'Why don't we just chat about how you got into all this?' I asked, hoping I wouldn't give the impression of being uninterested.

Ulla was trying her hardest to speak in English but the subject matter was tricky stuff so we were proceeding on the 'three steps forward and two back' principle. What was causing the most trouble was the technical jargon in which she thought we had to speak. When we got past that, we were in easier waters and I gained the impression of a woman who had left her home and family in Denmark to dedicate herself to the cause of ridding the world, or at least the UK, of the horrors of nuclear weapons. She had a tendency to slip into the language of moral crusade, but in the circumstances I thought that was entirely understandable. At one stage I tried to explain to her that the European Convention on Human Rights demanded that she be provided by the Crown prosecutor with an interpreter but she misunderstood me and thought I said 'interrogator' at which point she, naturally, became quite frightened and confused to the point where she thought I was her prosecutor. So quite apart from the tremendous difficulties of learning the international law in preparation for the defence to these charges, whatever that might be, there were worrying problems in communicating clearly with my client. Not an auspicious start.

I decided that more benefit was to be had by listening rather than speaking. But as I sat listening to this courageous woman my mind foresaw difficulties ahead. In any civil court in Scotland, advocates, unlike solicitors, have the authority to settle damages cases on behalf of their clients even if the client disagrees with the sum on offer. This is because the advocate has a good idea what the eventual sum awarded, if any, might be. The client doesn't and might regret making a brave stand for the rest of his or her life. Although the principle seems the same in the criminal courts we have no such mandate. Therefore we cannot plead guilty if the client says otherwise. Throughout the consultation I was very glad of this rule because the more Ulla spoke, the more I could see both sides of this case. On the one hand the women admitted causing tens of thousands of pounds' worth of damage to Ministry of Defence property, namely the computers used for the purposes of keeping the UK's Trident submarines acoustically secret when at sea. On the other hand they wished to argue that this action was necessary to prevent the British government from continuing to threaten many other nations with the use of thermonuclear weapons each about eight times larger than the ones used at Hiroshima and Nagasaki. This, they argue, quite apart from the madness of a nuclear strike, is a modern form of economic totalitarianism. However, most importantly, such threats also happen to be criminal under international humanitarian law, and the International Court of Justice, the so-called 'World Court' in The Hague, unanimously said so in 1996. That simple line of reasoning seemed sensible to me but where private individuals got their legal right to prevent the nuclear states and Britain in particular from continuing to make such threats was another matter altogether. No one, so far as we knew, had ever successfully run such a defence and it all seemed tremendously ambitious, to say the least. As we sat getting to grips with the larger and larger issues I could not keep from glancing out of the single, tiny, barred window to the peaceful hillsides of central Scotland in the distance and wondering what they would look like after a few 100-kiloton thermonuclear strikes. With the power to blast the earth off its axis and a half-life of environmental devastation lasting 30,000 years, any meaningful answer was unimaginable. However, my first certainty in this case was becoming very clear. If the women were convicted, the sentence could be a colossal one. Alternatively, an acquittal would send shock waves of a very different kind around the world.

4

Meeting of the Minds

Matthew and I had just about finished seeing Ulla privately when a message was brought saying that Angie and Ellen would like a joint consultation and that a room was being set up for that. We had expected that to happen because it is quite common when multiple accused have an identical defence. I was now in no doubt that mountains might have to be moved to demonstrate this defence and was glad of the opportunity to float the idea of a division of labour amongst the legal team.

In the intervening minutes I began to get a better idea of just how dedicated and learned these women were when I got the full story as to why they were in jail and had not been allowed bail, as one might expect. Having personally presented hundreds of bail appeals to the High Court I wondered whether the main reason for their incarceration was the seriousness of the crimes with which they were charged. The sheriffs who judge these applications in the first instance in their local courts around Scotland and later the judges of the High Court in Edinburgh are always very reluctant to grant bail when the Crown opposes the application on that ground. The Crown argument is that the public must be protected from any likelihood of repetition of the crime charged or another crime based, for instance, on revenge. Any right-thinking person sees the force of that argument. However, these women did not fit into any of the usual categories.

As Matthew explained, their bail hearing took place in Dunoon Sheriff Court because it was the one closest to the place where, to use a neutral term, the 'incident' took place. Dunoon was once a well-used seaside resort town before Glaswegians discovered the joys of holidaying in Spain. The town lies on the Firth of Clyde and is approached by means of a regular ferry service from Greenock. The town itself still has the trappings of a resort: lights along the waterfront, flower beds, a seaside picture house now busier than ever as a bingo hall and, of course, a working pier. The court is a tiny one by any standards and nowadays deals mostly with the local youths crossing swords with Strathclyde Police and one another. The local Faculty of Procurators (as the solicitors are called) still keeps a respectable working library in its 'agents room', and the sheriffs, who are the judges, seldom find their opinions the subject of attention in the Criminal Appeal Court in Edinburgh. At that time sheriffs in Scotland were chosen by the Lord Advocate, usually for their long years of legal experience and good overall reputation. They still wear a legal wig and gown on the bench, which, to a stranger, might give the impression of being stuck in the past. That is not so. Scottish sheriffs are well aware of current events and indeed are often the very people who shape such events.

On the morning on which the women appeared for their bail hearing, one or two local lads were present for their cases but otherwise the courtroom was packed to its wood-panelled walls with TP 2000 supporters. There was breathless silence as the clerk of court handed up the indictment and the necessary court books. The sheriff took a gold pen from his inside pocket and wrote out the details of the case. When a few moments later he signalled with a nod to bring in the accused, a police constable in shirtsleeves opened the side door to the cells. The sound of the three women and their jailers approaching broke the respectful silence. Then something happened that took the court officials completely by surprise: all the Trident Ploughshares 2000 campaigners in the court stood as a mark of respect for the women. They meant no disrespect to the court. Rather, they wished to demonstrate a principle as old as the hills sitting like a picture postcard in the old window at the back of the court: that an accused person is innocent unless and until found guilty by due process of law. Also, I suspect, in this case they were also

29

silently saying that occasionally there are principles that stand so high and come from so far away that they have to be relearnt by local courts. Unfortunately those principles, such as we find in international humanitarian law, are often thought to be so far above the local law, and local lawyers, that they only apply to those who breathe the air of high office and not among the good folk of the Firth of Clyde and the West Highlands of Scotland. However, it is difficult to overemphasise how wrong it is to forget the high principles upon which civilisation is built. All of those entrusted with the delicate task of keeping society to the rule of law should keep in mind that for evil to triumph it is only necessary for good people to do nothing.

The three accused women were brought into the old wooden dock by police officers and lined up to answer their names. Each accused answered her name in turn and was asked to plead. Matthew sat still, knowing he had taken instructions that he might never get again. The press had been notified and no one wanted a blunder laid at his or her door. An awkward silence then developed and the old gentleman on the bench looked gravely down at Matthew, as there appeared to be no motion for bail, as would be expected at that stage of proceedings. Eventually Matthew rose to explain that this was a most unusual case where the standard bail conditions were, in principle, causing some difficulty.

As the public might expect, there are certain conditions attached to being granted bail. Obvious things are, for instance, promising to turn up at all future court hearings and telling the court if the address given on the day of original appearance has changed. The most important of the conditions is that the accused will not commit crime whilst on bail. Here is where the problem lay. It is every criminal lawyer's instinct to move the court on behalf of the client for bail, when appropriate. Matthew was having more than a little difficulty in explaining that his client's position was that she could not accept the most important condition because as far as she was concerned it was not the women in the dock who were the criminals. On the contrary, it was the British government that, every minute of every day, was threatening to annihilate millions of people and the environment for its own political ends. His client wished to argue that what she had done was not criminal and, if the need arose, then she would have no hesitation in doing it all over again. The other women were asked for their views and both wholeheartedly agreed.

The sheriff seemed bewildered by this argument and was obviously not comfortable with sending three respectable, middle-aged women to jail for months while they awaited trial. In fact he was bending over backwards trying not to send them to jail when he asked, 'Do I understand you correctly? Your client effectively wishes to put the British government on trial for crimes against humanity?' There were audible responses from the public gallery of 'Precisely', which had to be silenced with a look from the clerk of court. When Matthew explained that that was the best way of seeing the case, the sheriff shook his head, realising he was in the presence of a clever young lawyer and some dedicated women who had worked this all out in advance. He had no choice. The clerk read out the ruling of the court, 'Bail is refused for want of insistence', followed by the standard order to the police, 'Take them away.'

Supporters in the gallery, who were mainly silver-haired and well educated, whispered their best wishes as the women were led joyfully out to the prison wagon, which had been reversed right up to the back doors of the court. The women knew they were on their way to the remand wing at Cornton Vale jail for at least three months but any sense of foreboding was trumped by their hopes that they were also on the way to success.

So it was against that background that I completed my first consultation with Ulla Roder and went back to reception whilst special arrangements were made for all three women and their lawyers to meet in a room where they could discuss their common defence. It took the rest of the day and was an occasion I will never forget.

At first sight, it struck me that these three women were not a natural group. By that, I mean that I could not imagine them as having the same personal interests or hobbies. But as the consultation continued at a furious pace, the source of their immense personal power dawned on me and I could see where their inner strength lay: like all extraordinary groups – I immediately think of the Beatles – together they were stronger than the sum of their parts. Now all they had to do was make sure the advocates did no damage as we attempted to come up to speed on the international law aspects of the case. As the days ahead rolled by and that work developed apace, I was happy when Angie put her hand over mine and said, 'We're reaching a meeting of the minds.'

5

Planning the Raid

Anyone strolling along Barrland Street in Glasgow would be forgiven for missing the former shop premises at number 15, which is now a very ordinary-looking office. With three floors of tenement flats above, it is the kind of place that painters and decorators, or plumbers, would find useful. Most days, after school, the local kids kick a football against the front wall whilst their parents come and go up and down the 'close mooths' (stairway entrances). In fact these renovated premises are the home of Scottish CND and the nerve centre for many of the disarmament actions taken in Scotland. There are e-mail and Internet connections, metal filing cabinets carefully stuffed with records of exactly which government departments have done what in promoting Trident and, where possible, expert or official comments on how much this weapons system costs the British taxpayer per year. The wooden floor has been sanded and there is a big pine kitchen table, which serves as the focus for most discussions. The table is also ideal for laying out large maps, should anyone think the time right to plan some disarmament. The whole place is run with boundless energy and expertise by the chair of Scottish CND, John Ainslie. He daily comes and goes in his woolly jumpers, always with a kind word and a broad smile for everyone. A shy man, he gave up full-time ecclesiastical ministry to dedicate his life to the campaign for nuclear disarmament. We all have cause to be grateful to John. However, in the planning stages of Operation *Maytime*, it was Angie, Ulla and Ellen who were most grateful for use of that nondescript office.

Now any local or police officer on the beat who happened to be passing along and saw what was going on in number 15 might have thought that, at these initial stages, a crime was being committed: that of 'conspiracy to commit criminal damage'. And they would have been right to wonder about that. However, The Trident Three had thought of that and would eventually argue in court that their conspiracy was not to commit a crime. Their conspiracy was to prevent crimes. And not just any old crimes. In that back-street office in Glasgow these women sought nothing less than to prevent the British government from committing inhumane acts such as, first, planning, preparing, initiating or waging a war in violation of international treaties, agreements or assurances; second, wanton destruction of cities, towns or villages or devastation not justified by military necessity; and thirdly, murder, extermination and so on against a civilian population in connection with any crime against peace. Put plainly, they were certainly conspiring, but conspiring to prevent government-approved genocide and ecocide. Not everyday goings-on in the back streets of Glasgow.

Trident Ploughshares 2000 pledgers don't believe in state-approved terrorism against people or wanton destruction of property and the environment. They are open, honest, non-violent and accountable at all times. So one might think that would limit their opportunities for disarming something so vastly powerful and well guarded as the British Trident thermonuclear submarine fleet. Wrong. As we saw at the outset, it is entirely possible to disarm such a fleet inside those criteria; but it takes a lot of planning.

Several meetings were required to set out the objectives and methods that Angie, Ulla and Ellen should adhere to. Now it must be kept in mind that theirs was not a political mission. It was humanitarian. On that basis, simply protesting outside Parliament or buttonholing an MEP in Brussels was to miss the point. In any case, as we shall see a little later, they had done all that and more. The infrastructure system that keeps Trident at the ready had to be analysed, understood and targeted. The necessary links in the chain of operation had to be broken – or a good attempt made at breaking them. Nothing less would be capable of justifying the name 'disarmament'. Fortunately (or unfortunately), their choices were many, so classification was required.

What was well known to the women as they began to plan their operation was that the military and governmental infrastructure that supports Trident is spread all over Britain. It is even high in the skies above us. There are the submarine bases and berths at Loch Ewe in the Western Isles, Rosyth on the River Forth, Devonport in the south-west of England, Liverpool and Southampton. Serious consideration was given to the communications and intelligence-gathering sites at Menwith Hill, North Yorkshire, Anthorn, near Carlisle, and Rugby, to mention a few. Investigations were made into the effect of using 300 mobile phones around central communications installations. However, the problem with these sorts of operations is ascertaining exactly what one is dealing with. If a citizen *thought* she was disarming a vital part of the Trident communications network, but was in fact only wiping out an overtime rota or wages record, then that would be futile and not a well-thought-through, responsible act of disarmament. So these were ruled out.

Because the submarine construction site at Derby makes essential parts for Trident it would have made a very worthwhile target, and similarly the warhead assembly plants at Aldermaston and Burghfield. Certainly an easier target would have been to stop one of the nuclear warhead convoys at any point along the 460 miles of roadway between Aldermaston and the Clyde. But public safety might have been compromised and that ruled the idea out immediately. The anti-submarine helicopter base at Prestwick, south of Glasgow, and the Nimrod aircraft site at Kinloss in the Scottish Highlands were too risky, if only to the crews of those aircraft. No; the choice was clear. It had to be the big one: Coulport in Argyll, home of Trident.

As seasoned veterans of many demonstrations at the front gates and various parts of the perimeter, the three women knew the layout of the 3-kilometre by 2.5-kilometre site only too well; but they also knew how difficult it was to get near a Trident submarine when it was in dock. The missile warhead bunkers at the centre of the site are impregnable to three women with hand tools. So too are the re-entry body process buildings.

The explosives handling jetty-cum-Trident berthing site was the obvious choice, but approaching the Trident berths in a noisy boat was almost certainly doomed to failure.

In any case there were well-understood ground rules of their own to obey. All TP 2000 pledgers are warned not to interfere with or damage in any way the main control room, the reactor areas, the warheads, missile fire control computers or bunkers where the warheads are stored.

At Coulport there are dog handlers and armed marines guarding all sensitive areas. The MoD police at Faslane and Coulport have eight very fast launches, which act as special Trident guard boats, plus 13 other support launches and many inflatable boats. Importantly, pledgers swear not to cause any sort of hazard when making an attempt to disarm a submarine. For instance, they are told that if they get near a Trident submarine by boat then they must beware of the suction caused by the hugely powerful water intakes. Sadly, during manoeuvres an MoD policeman has been killed by getting too close to those swirling intakes.

On the submarines themselves the warheads are stored towards the back of the vessel. The front is where the torpedoes are stored ready for firing but the safety-critical components are installed throughout the submarines. Accordingly, pledgers never start fires or cause any electrical disturbance that might start a fire — such as cutting cables or damaging other electrical equipment. This includes any cables from the dockside that are connected to the submarine. This is dangerous and accordingly outside the Trident Ploughshares 2000 remit of always operating entirely safely with respect to everything and everyone.

The planning team knew that all Trident submarines carry around 50 tonnes of high explosive in the form of rocket fuel. Once again, under strict Trident Ploughshares safety guidelines, these cannot be interfered with in any way. Indeed the third-stage warheads are known to be placed in close proximity to a type of rocket fuel that is particularly prone to accidental detonation. The latest torpedoes, called Spearhead, are powered by Otto fuel. Although these are the latest design, they are extremely toxic and more likely to be subject to an explosive hazard than the old design. Again the pledgers take a strict view about the safety of such volatile substances and on no account do they try to disturb the torpedo tubes by hammering or otherwise damaging these in a way that might cause malfunction. The only action allowed against these vital parts is, if possible, to pour something very sticky over the outside, resulting in the whole sub having to be taken out of service and thus 'disarmed' at least during the repair period. This was ruled out because the objective of this particular act of disarmament was to get to the centre of Trident's operational control system.

Similarly, because Trident is supported inside British waters by vastly powerful hunter-killer submarines, these are also considered to be legitimate targets and so can be disarmed in the same way. The same principle applies to all other shipping that provides Trident with necessary support. However, on this occasion, because the tugs and other support vessels could not be said to form part of Trident itself, these were left out of the equation.

Something new was required, something vital at the heart of the operational system. With their combined intelligence and experience it didn't take them long to figure it out. Every system has its soft underbelly and in the case of Trident it is reliance upon anechoic secrecy. That means that, when the submarines are at sea, they are silent and thus cannot be traced by satellites searching the ocean depths for sound patterns that identify each submarine as though it were sailing in broad daylight. Bingo. If the system controlling that secrecy could be deactivated then there would be no way the submarine commanders, or for that matter those in Whitehall, could be certain that Trident was presenting an 'invisible sound signature at sea'.

The planning team knew this vital function was performed by DERA, now trendily rebranded as 'QinetiQ'. The bad news was that, like most military operations, DERA was spread all over the country. It didn't take long for the good news to arrive that all the sound secrecy work for Trident was done at Loch Goil, the deepest sea-loch in Britain. It was imperative that there was no back-up system, no shadow system that could seamlessly take over from *Maytime* as the disarmament work was being carried out. It was soon confirmed that no such system existed.

Also, at that time, it was known that those who worked aboard *Maytime* were seen by the armed marines who guarded the actual submarines as a 'boffin squad'. No one wore a uniform, or saluted anybody. They fiddled about as and when they liked with computers and satellite control programs. They had their own schedules and reported to Whitehall. So the marines must have figured there was not much to worry about there. Lastly, it was not lost on the women that this vital work was all done an hour away by sea from the main activity at Coulport. The soft underbelly had been identified. Now all they had to do was figure out a way of striking at a time when they could effect the maximum impact.

The precise operational schedules of each Trident submarine going in and out of the waters around the West Highlands are known to Trident Ploughshares, and records are kept up to date by the keen observations of pledgers who give their time voluntarily to the cause. The best vantage points are just opposite the Finger Jetty on Loch Goil and another just south of the big north gates at the main entrance to the Coulport base. With a good pair of field glasses one can even get an accurate sense of the vastness of these beasts from up on the road that leads out from the base towards Glasgow. Also, from the data that are regularly gathered about the comings and goings of the staff on *Maytime*, it was possible to calculate with some precision just when Trident's soft underbelly would be most exposed. Obviously the ideal time to strike was when the whole place was peaceful.

I remember Ulla Roder describing to me the churning in her stomach as the plans took shape. She had previously taken political action in Denmark against the threat from Britain's nuclear weapons, reaching ministerial and ambassadorial level with some success. She had given up her job in a bank in protest at the amount of money it invested in the nuclear industry. Now she had disposed of her house and left her grown-up children in their homeland and was resident in Scotland, all with the single purpose of planning and executing the most effective disarmament action the anti-nuclear movement had ever seen. She was dependent upon the charity of other pledgers who were often little more than strangers. Her eyes misted over as she struggled for the English words to express how their affection never wavered and how grateful she was for their charity.

Ellen Moxley is a life-long Quaker who, as a young woman, had done her best to help the victims, on both sides, during the Vietnam War. She has crawled under napalm clouds to rescue children. She has administered practical and spiritual help to the burnt, shot and dying. She, perhaps more than anyone (with the exception of her life-long friend Helen Steven who has more often than not been by Ellen's side in these exceptional acts of human kindness to their fellow human beings), had seen people's inhumanity to other people at close range and accordingly felt the need for action most acutely. One has to qualify such accolades because it is impossible to measure the depth of commitment and influence that Angie Zelter has had on peace campaigns of all kinds over the last 30 years. A veteran of Greenham Common and a world-wide ambassador in the cause of peace amongst humanity, Angie has always had her sights on the highest possible targets. She is not a woman who accepts that anything should be said or done half-heartedly. Her snow-white hair and hearty complexion make her a beacon when the press need a focus or the police need a target. But as striking as she is to look at, it is her razor-sharp mind that calls all around her to task when there is important work to be done. And in John Ainslie's office important work was indeed being done.

With the site chosen and the schedules worked out it became necessary to look in more detail at exactly how this operation was to be carried out. One of the objectives was simply to bring to the attention of the press and public just what *Maytime* did and what significance that work had for the continuing threat from nuclear weapons. However, important as awareness may be, it is not per se disarmament. That requires a giant step into the world of specially written computer programs, top-level coded access regimes and inside knowledge of *Maytime* in order to distinguish between the harmful and the mundane. Secrecy and certain other confidential restrictions demand that I cannot go any further into those matters here but suffice it to say that the three women spent long hours ensuring that their skills were up to the task. Of course others with specialist skills, from more than one country, helped a great deal. But at the end of the day it was up to Angie, Ulla and Ellen to ensure that they disarmed the might of the Trident thermonuclear weapons system without risking the health or safety of themselves or anyone else, including the staff of *Maytime*. As they planned their operation they were conscious that there are five live, armed (Polaris) nuclear submarines lying at the bottom of the world's seas, lost with all hands, rusting away in the salt waters, one day to come back to us with all the terror that unknown perils from the sea can bring. And these are just the Western ones. No one knows how many Russian nuclear weapons submarines are also lying at the bottom of the seas, nor in what condition they are. According to John Ainslie, it is probably more than five. Against that background, the women could not afford a mistake. Nothing was to be done that even carried a risk of setting in motion any course of action that might frighten anyone, let alone harm them.

Accordingly, preparations had to be made to ready their boat for service. Decisions were taken about the precise time of arrival at Lochgoilhead, which hand tools would be required to effect entry to the vast steel floating laboratory and, importantly, which literature and videos to take for leaving on board after the disarmament work was done. We have seen how the Crown Office ultimately reacted – they indicted the women for common burglary, vandalism and theft. However, one has to ask what kind of burglars take with them on a job a video showing themselves in plain view saying who they are, what their purposes are and where to contact them. But in accordance with their policies of openness, non-violence and accountability, that is exactly what the women decided upon.

Amongst the planning group an air of some relief was descending because plans were almost finalised, but their relief did not last long. Word came through that a nuclear arms crisis was brewing on the other side of the world, and for the Trident Ploughshares pledgers an old lesson was being relearnt: just when you think the world is safe from nuclear explosion or accident, something new arises. The planning group heard that Rebecca Johnson, an old friend of Angie's from their Greenham days who was now the head of a think tank called the Acronym Institute in London and a United Nations permanent observer to the Geneva Conventions, had just come out of a hurriedly convened meeting in Vienna trying to defuse the India–Pakistan dispute over which one would be first to resume nuclear weapons testing. That top-level meeting was also attended by representatives of the United Nations Security Council, and the two quarrelling nations were not mincing their words. They stated quite bluntly that whilst Britain, their former colonial master, had nuclear weapons they would also have them. Rebecca tells me that such quarrels are often resolved, not by the intervention of United Nations politicians, but by the parties negotiating through trusted third parties like herself. The top brass of the Ministry of Defence met in Whitehall as simultaneously the joint chiefs of staff met in the Pentagon. All concerned agreed that it was a close-run thing but the fragile peace was eventually, if narrowly, maintained and the Security Council representatives scuttled off to London and New York. The front pages of broadsheet newspapers such as the *Washington Post* and the *International Herald Tribune* reported that the Indians were enraged at being told by the British how to run the largest democracy in the world. Rebecca was widely quoted as the authority figure who could be relied upon to tell the truth. Months later, at the trial of The Trident Three in Greenock Sheriff Court, that is exactly what she did.

And so, on the summer's evening of 8 June 1999, before they left Barrland Street, Glasgow for Loch Goil, as the diplomatic world held its breath over that serious nuclear escalation, The Trident Three uttered prayers of thanks for Rebecca and her skills as a woman who proudly serves the citizens of the world every day of her working life. Others added their prayers, asking that these three precious women would not spend the next 10 years rotting in jail. Then finally, with those firm, holy words of prayer hanging like protective shrouds in the atmosphere around them, The Trident Three ate a good dinner before the last rucksacks were loaded, tight hugs and warm kisses exchanged and it was time to go disarming.

TWO

ONLY THE GODS
OF THE ANCIENT WORLD...

6

History in the Making

It is worth repeating that The Trident Three are not political activists. They are humanitarian activists. Supporters of all political parties would agree that apathy amongst the general public is the real enemy of vibrant democracy. One only has to count the tiny number of devotees who voluntarily turn out to assist at local or European elections to have that amply demonstrated. One can therefore only marvel at the dedication it must have taken to get as far as marching to Downing Street in London and the Crown Office in Edinburgh carrying a copy of every word of the World Court judgement of 8 July 1996 for presentation to the Prime Minister and the Scottish Lord Advocate. However, to see such a procession passing by in the street and to be told how long these people had been dedicated to getting this far is only to appreciate the quantity of time taken without appreciating the quality of their work – a case of 'never mind the quality, feel the width'.

The Lord Advocate is historically the Queen's presence in Scotland. Accordingly he sits in the Crown Office in Edinburgh and is responsible among other things for all prosecutions in Scotland. He is often referred to as the Keeper of the Queen's Peace. So if anything is being done to upset that peace, he ought to be told about it. In November 1991 Scottish Christian CND wrote to the incumbent Lord Advocate, The Right Honourable Lord Fraser of Carmyllie, pointing out to him that something was going on in the west of Scotland that was of grave importance to him as public prosecutor.

What was going on, according to Archie Hamilton, the armed forces minister, was the largest construction programme in Europe. The locations were Coulport and Faslane in Argyllshire. These sites were owned by the British government and were employing 3,300 people. So far, apart from the sheer scale of the works, there was nothing of concern. However, it was the nature of the works that CND said was of grave concern. They pointed out to Lord Fraser that both the commissioning by the government and the building work itself rendered both the government and the workers liable to criminal prosecution for crimes against humanity. It cannot have been every day that his lordship got such a letter.

The basis of these astonishing claims was that the works were part of planning and preparation for the deployment and use of weapons of massive indiscriminate human destruction, which, they said, was against the law. Particularly, this was a contravention of the Genocide Act 1969 as well as other laws and, just in case his lordship was unaware of these laws, they included a full citation of where these laws could be found in well-known textbooks. They concluded by reminding the Lord Advocate that such laws applied to everyone, including him, and asked him to investigate this illegal activity and to prosecute those guiding hands in London who were responsible.

In Scotland, it doesn't take long for word to get about. By 26 November 1991 there was such widespread interest in that letter to the Lord Advocate, that an open letter signed by hundreds of individuals and organisations was posted. This effectively took the form of a petition and was presented as a matter of legal obligation, moral duty and urgent business. As always, CND relied upon the rule of law as the basis of their argument and pointed out to the Lord Advocate that, when previous attempts had been made in England to bring this illegality to the attention of the courts, the prosecution service had done everything it could to hush up the matter or the government had claimed Crown immunity. As these works were ongoing in Scotland, CND wondered if the independence of the Scottish legal system might be more robust in protecting the rule of law. Mention was made of the ongoing work in getting the International Court of Justice (World Court) to give its opinion on the legality of nuclear weapons. The petition ended by urging the Lord Advocate to act within international humanitarian law by putting a stop to the beginnings of atrocities unimaginably worse than those described to a sickened world during the Nuremberg trials. Oh, and one last thing, they wanted a meeting.

As 1992 slipped in, correspondence between Scottish Christian CND and the Crown Office trundled on. The letters sent on behalf of the Lord Advocate were civil in tone but had the familiar air of doing what usually happens when the government is in trouble – stalling for time. A church service was arranged for Ash Wednesday, 4 March 1992, appropriately the first day of Lent, in dedication of the open letter. This was no ordinary service. It was held in St Giles' Cathedral at the top of the Royal Mile in Edinburgh and was conducted by The Revd Maxwell Craig, General Secretary of Action of Churches Together in Scotland. The lesson was from John 18 verses 33 to 38, which ends with Jesus saying to Pilate, 'Everyone on the side of truth listens to me.' The open letter and the supporting legal documents sat on the holy table throughout, and a moment of particular poignancy came when Revd Maxwell Craig said the prayer of dedication: 'Holy God, source of wisdom and truth, we bring before you these documents gathered from around the world as evidence to support our request for an inquiry into the legality of the activities taking place at Faslane and Coulport. Bless those who prepared them; bless the hands that carry them now; bless your servant the Lord Advocate, to whom we will present them today; fill his heart and mind with light and with your Holy Spirit; lead him to truth through your son, our Saviour Jesus Christ, the Prince of Peace and the Light of the World. Amen.'

The Lord Advocate was personally invited to attend the service, but, just in case he could not do so, CND arranged for the service to end at 12.30 pm and to march from the cathedral's west door in Parliament Square to the Crown Office to present the open letter formally at 1 pm. And so, as the open letter was carried at the front of the procession, the congregation sang the blessing: 'The Lord bless you and keep you. The

Lord make His face to shine upon you and be gracious unto you. The Lord lift up His countenance upon you and give you peace.'

The long procession then began to file out of the west door into the Royal Mile, which had been closed by the police for the occasion. Edinburgh city centre then took on an air of peace as the long line of marchers, led by Revd Maxwell Craig in full ceremonial dress, walked in complete silence to the door of the Crown Office. There they were met by Mr W. A. Gilchrist, the assistant with whom they had been corresponding these past few months. No one got so much as a glimpse of The Rt Hon Lord Fraser of Carmyllie, Her Majesty's Advocate.

By 30 April 1992 things had changed. Well, at least the personage of the Lord Advocate had changed. However, because these high legal offices are occupied by political appointees, Lord Fraser had been succeeded by his second-in-command, the Solicitor General for Scotland, Mr Alan Rodger QC, who now became Lord Rodger of Earlsferry, Her Majesty's Advocate. Whilst still in academia, as Dr Rodger he had the highest possible reputation as an academic lawyer, particularly in the field of Roman law. Whilst in practice, Mr Rodger QC played his part in developing the law from the Bar of the Court. You may be wondering what happened to his title of 'Dr' when he became an advocate. The answer is that we don't use academic titles at the Scottish Bar because all advocates are members of the College of Justice in Scotland and (theoretically) that trumps everything done before achieving the office of advocate. Now, whereas Lord Fraser had been rather shy of the glare of the political stage, Lord Rodger had been carefully noted as having enthusiastically shared every political platform on which Margaret Thatcher ever set foot in Scotland. North of the border it was 'weel kent' (well known) that things were indeed about to change.

On 30 April 1992 Scottish Christian CND wrote to Lord Rodger congratulating him on his appointment, reminding him of the open letter and inviting him to attend a forthcoming conference organised by the World Court Project in Geneva on 14 and 15 May that year. Lord Rodger replied by returning the open letter together with all of the legal support documents, saying he was refusing to investigate the matter of the legality of nuclear weapons. He gave no reasons, nor even any hint of reasons, for his decision. Coincidentally, around the same time the English Attorney General sent the national coordinator of Christian CND a similar reply.

By the summer of 1992 the pattern was clear. To no one's surprise the government wasn't listening. But if it thought that those who had so carefully compiled the open letter and researched the international humanitarian law on the subject would just go away, they were wrong.

On 24 June 1992 Scottish Christian CND wrote back giving the first clue about what would happen if the government did not begin to listen. They mentioned the words 'Nuremberg Principles'. This must have sounded a chord somewhere because on 4 August 1992 Lord Rodger wrote to Dr W Arthur Chapman, the chair of Scottish Christian CND, setting out the government's legal position. This was progress – well, progress of a sort. Lord Rodger's job as Lord Advocate, apart from running the prosecution service, was to advise the Prime Minister and the Cabinet on Scottish legal issues. Given that Polaris nuclear submarines were about to be succeeded by Trident in Scotland, their legality or otherwise was very much an issue for the Lord Advocate. So we can only assume that he considered the matter very carefully.

Nevertheless, the government's legal position was stated in a six-line reply simply saying that it rejected the assertion that the government was deliberately pursuing a policy (of deployment and use of weapons of massive, indiscriminate human destruction) that it knew to be illegal. Lord Rodger pointed out that there was no general treaty that outlawed nuclear weapons and that the use of such weapons would have to be judged as lawful or not in the light of the particular circumstances in which they were used. In other words, with all due respect, he did not deal with the point. He did not mention any of the evidence sent in support of the open letter that nuclear weapons were illegal. These of course had been returned to Scottish CND months before. He further did not mention the points that make such weapons illegal per se, namely that they are too massive to be targeted solely against military targets and thus are indiscriminate as to how many millions of people they wipe out and which territorial borders they cross as the wind blows the thermonuclear gas clouds around the world.

The last shot in this correspondence went to Scottish CND, who wrote on 4 October 1992 expressing dismay at the attitude of the most senior legal officer in Scotland. They pointed out that this latest result was curiously similar to what the United Kingdom delegation to the World Health Assembly had done in May 1992 when the matter of sending the whole question of the legality of nuclear weapons to the World Court was raised: it did everything in its power to prevent that. What Lord Rodger could not have known at the time he was defending the indefensible was that, despite the British government's best efforts to prevent them, the World Court would soon be considering the matter.

And so when the World Court convened to hear legal submissions from every nation that cared to make its case for or against nuclear weapons, it was the quality of the work done by such dedicated citizens of the world that was striking. Their understanding of international law and of the machinations of the United Nations, put together with an action programme to use these entities for the ultimate benefit of the people of the world, was truly impressive. At that point the people of the world owed these dedicated souls their deepest gratitude and ought to have expressed that gratitude very publicly. Of course, that did not happen because most people were far too busy with 'real life'. But even if some recognition had been given, that does not get at the core strength of The Trident Three and all the others in the World Court Project and Trident Ploughshares 2000. Their core strength lies in what happened when, armed only with printouts of the World Court judgement and an unshakeable belief in the rule of international law, they were politely refused entry to those august chambers of power in London and Edinburgh.

7

On Target and On Message

You may imagine that some of the best brains in the country together with mountains of information from the highest sources would go into such a fundamental decision as how best to develop Britain's place in the future and its relationships with the rest of the world. It is fair to say that sometimes that is the case. But not always. The plans to replace Britain's ageing Polaris nuclear fleet started in the late 1970s. By 1977 a committee had been formed and we all know what that means. People start justifying their existence and importance with reports, conclusions and recommendations. Well, this committee was no different. Sir Ronald Mason was the chief scientific adviser to the Ministry of Defence (MoD) from 1977 to 1983. By the late 1970s he was chairing a small group that was examining three questions. First, did Britain need nuclear weapons? Second, if we did, then against whom should these be directed? Third, what type of nuclear weapons do we need? We should note carefully that the third question did not ask which weapons we 'might' need; it asked which weapons 'do we need'. The so-called 'answers' reached by that tiny committee led directly to Prime Minister Margaret Thatcher making a deal with US President Ronald Reagan and ordering that the outdated Polaris system should be replaced with the US Trident system. The die was cast. In late-20th-century Britain, the ideas of the awesome Professor Friedrich August von Hayek provided the economic and political basis for the capitalist theories on continuous economic growth. These theories were being spoon-fed to Mrs Thatcher by her special economic adviser, Professor Patrick Minford, and, like Britain's economic growth, the weapons that protected the West's wealth just had to keep getting bigger.

Since those desperate days, Sir Ronald Mason has conceded that his committee overestimated the need for Britain to have nuclear weapons at all and rushed to answer the second and third questions. In typical fashion for those who talk of nuclear weapons as though they are the largest catapult in the playground, Sir Ronald said that, in answering the first question, his committee had 'over-egged the pudding'. Thanks a lot. And so, with that ill-thought-out 'decision', 'answer' – it's hard to know what to call such a botched job without dignifying those feeble efforts – the British were off and trundling down the road of posturing to destroy the world with overgrown schoolboys in charge of our survival. Then the situation got worse.

The House of Commons defence select committee, no doubt in full justification mode, described the replacement of Polaris with Trident as 'a significant enhancement of Britain's strategic nuclear capability'. Enhancement? They talked as though these weapons of mass human and ecological destruction were works of art. The schoolboys were out to play again. Across the Atlantic (you've guessed it) things were no better. The US military were overjoyed at Mrs Thatcher's decision to take Trident. Her decision was taken in the teeth of opposition from virtually all quarters, which were advising her, as a world leader, to take the high ground by *not* replacing Polaris at all. Their joy stemmed from what lies at the root of modern US culture: making money. Trident's thermonuclear warheads are eye-wateringly expensive and their maintenance alone would lock the British into buying the latest top-up technology, renting intellectual property rights and generally playing the role of the small child in the playground who buys friendship with the big children at the expense of lunch money and by skipping classes. The result is time and money wasted that ought to have been spent on health and education. I trust the analogy holds that far.

It is at this point that critics of nuclear disarmament usually say, 'Ah, but these submarines are just standing by. They are not really in a war at all, so how can you say that they pose a threat to world security?' The answer comes from the mouths of those who knew only too well about the state of preparedness of Britain's older nuclear weapons and lately of the Trident fleet. In the old days of the V-bombers, which were designed to drop nuclear weapons, Air Vice-Marshal Bobby Robson said publicly that 'the V-bombers are permanently on a war footing'. So that's plain enough. When Britain had Polaris nuclear weapons, Commander Jeffrey Tall, captain of HMS *Repulse* from 1989 to 1991, said, 'There is no doubt that when we went to sea we went to war.' So that's equally plain.

It has to be remembered that nowadays families don't crowd around the big, brown, bakelite wireless in the front parlour to listen to the Prime Minister coming on to a background of solemn music and then announcing in sombre tones that it is with the greatest of care and after full dialogue around the Cabinet table that he must inform the nation that Britain is at war with another nation. It's just not like that any more. Britain fights wars constantly but nowadays it is usually under the NATO umbrella and only seldom alone, such as in the Falklands. Every minute of every day at least one of Britain's Trident submarines is on active patrol. Very few people know where they are but it is thought, for reasons connected with their targeting range, and the limit of their fuel and supplies, that they patrol the dark depths of the North Atlantic. There is of course another factor in the determination of where they go. It is that all-important factor mentioned earlier – the relationship with the United States. In other words they are told where to go.

The lessons of these daunting quotes has been hard learnt by the Ministry of Defence, and nowadays everyone is 'on message' so no one says anything about the operational details of Trident – except, that is, when they are legally cited by solicitors to the likes of Greenock Sheriff Court and they swear before sheriff court judge Margaret Gimblett to tell the truth, the whole truth and nothing but the truth. But more of that later. Suffice to say for the moment that the missile guidance computers are kept empty of their software programs as Trident glides a few feet above the ocean floor. This fact is often held up as Britain having made significant steps forward towards world peace by taking its nuclear weapons 'off hair trigger', a fact that supporters of Trident say should assure us in our beds at night. However, what the strategic defence reviews that trumpet such 'progress' don't tell us is that these programs can be loaded up on to these very sophisticated computers in less than 15 minutes. Some assurance.

Before moving on to Trident's targets, let me take a moment to demonstrate that it is not just The Trident Three, CND and their many armchair supporters who think that a war with nuclear weapons would be global madness. It certainly surprised me to learn from just how high up in the British and US military the cries for sanity came. An observer from another planet who took but a few minutes to peruse the television news from around this world might conclude that there were two camps in this debate: those who marched the streets wearing brightly coloured woolly jumpers with bare legs and Doc Marten boots and those who lived their lives in palaces and the Pentagon. The big surprise is that the most reasoned and authoritative calls for nuclear peace come from the latter.

Opponents of nuclear weapons of course come from all walks of life and from all age groups. Some though surprise us more than others. On 11 May 1979, the year in which Mrs Thatcher took office as Prime Minister, it was no less an Establishment figure than Admiral of the Fleet the Earl Mountbatten of Burma on the occasion of the award of the Louise Weiss Foundation prize to the Stockholm International Peace Research Institute at Strasbourg who took the world by surprise. These are extracts from what he said:

> Do the frightening facts about the arms race, which shows that we are rushing headlong towards a precipice, make any of those responsible for this disastrous course pull themselves together and reach for the brakes? The answer is 'no'.

> I know how impossible it is to pursue military operations in accordance with fixed plans and agreements. In warfare the unexpected is the rule and no one can anticipate what an opponent's reaction to the unexpected will be.

I cannot imagine a situation in which nuclear weapons would be used as battlefield weapons without the conflagration spreading.

Einstein was asked to prophesy what weapons would be used in the Third World War. He replied, 'On the assumption that a Third World War must escalate to nuclear destruction, I can tell you what the Fourth World War will be fought with – bows and arrows.'

I say in all sincerity that the nuclear arms race has no military purpose. Wars cannot be fought with nuclear weapons. Their existence only adds to our perils because of the illusions they generate. There are powerful voices around the world who still give credence to the old Roman precept – 'if you desire peace, then prepare for war'. This is absolute nuclear nonsense. I repeat, it is a disastrous misconception to believe that by increasing the total of uncertainty one increases one's own certainty.

These words are well delivered when one stops to think that it was only in October 1962 during the Cuban missile crisis that we came so close to world annihilation. The former US defence secretary Robert McNamara, having now had meetings with his Soviet counterparts from that time, reminds us that the United States completely misjudged the situation in Cuba at that time. Discussion took place in the White House that seriously considered an all-out attack on Cuba, not realising that there were already Soviet nuclear weapons installed, ready and waiting for the order to fire. That order wasn't a theoretical or prospective possibility. The Soviet generals had given the order that if the United States attacked then the nuclear response was to be immediate.

Let us now consider the views of the man who was at the top of the US military establishment and who for years had his finger on the nuclear trigger. General Lee Butler was in overall strategic command of United States nuclear weapons from 1992 to 1994 and therefore in the best position to understand things like kill ratios, compound eco-damage and after-strike political realignment. Now retired, he has reversed his opinions on all of the nuclear strategies he once believed in and is now a tireless opponent of nuclear weapons. He says:

> The policy of nuclear deterrence is based on a litany of unwarranted assumptions, unprovable assertions and logical contradictions. It suspends rational thinking about the ultimate aim of national security to ensure the survival of the state. The Cold War lives on in the minds of those who cannot let go of the fears, the beliefs and the enmities born of the nuclear age. They cling to deterrence, clutch its tattered promise to their breasts, shake it wistfully at bygone adversaries and balefully at new or imagined ones. They are gripped still by its awful willingness not simply to tempt the apocalypse but to prepare its way.

Against that background one would be forgiven for thinking that 'Things can only get better'. And so it appeared. In July 2001 US President George 'Dubya' Bush and Russian President Vladimir Putin agreed in Genoa amid much fanfare and photo ops to 'reduce the number of nuclear warheads they have between them'. Since 11 September 2001 they have agreed even further reductions. However, you will understand that the familiar story is what they didn't say. In fact the US and Russia still have 13,000 nuclear warheads between them, let alone those of Britain, France and several other nations. That US/Russian figure is down from 20,000 during the Cold War; but we can be sure that the main reason for reduction is not a change of policy but the expense of keeping these volatile warheads under control. Despite such promises of 'reduction', there will easily still remain enough nuclear firepower to destabilise the orbit of the planet should a few warheads be fired into a concentrated area, like around China's major cities. The key point is that nowadays there is no opportunity for a Hiroshima or Nagasaki scenario. The bombs are too large. Exploding only one of these would be so catastrophic that there would be a new world order immediately after it was fired. New political alignments would occur. The General Assembly of the United Nations would be powerless to stop all such political landslides after such an explosion.

In the wintertime in Britain we often see television reports of farming folk and their animals snowed-in or police officers sailing up a main street in a lifeboat taking hot tea to elderly villagers. There are always complaints that the power lines are down over such-and-such an area and won't be back up again for a week or more. The United States sees exactly the same news from this or that state. Occasionally the President orders special aid to be sent in and usually salutes those in the worst-affected areas. So if Trident, by accident or design, fired one missile, the question arises, 'What might the world look like?' Many people and organisations, civil and military, have been trying to imagine that for decades and using what platforms they had to get the message across. Years ago Count Basie's jazz album entitled E=MC2 had a photo of a mushroom cloud on the front cover. Movies have been made and computer programs have been built to 'extrapolate' (read 'guess') how the physical landscape would have changed. I can tell you that the legal landscape would be in smithereens.

The exercise of imagining a post-nuclear explosion first involves knowing what the missiles are capable of and where they are targeted. I said at the outset that this is not a law book. Neither is it a nuclear technical manual. There are already plenty of those in the world. So please forgive me if I draw only a sketch from information I got from John Ainslie but which we were not allowed to use at the trial of The Trident Three.

We are constantly lulled into a false sense of nuclear peace because there is no mention of the warheads exploding (thank God) nor anyone being killed by them. But these warheads nearly go off all the time and people are killed by them. The idea that humans can keep such a system in perfect safety, for ever, is obvious nonsense. A glance at the accident record reveals that the whole system is an accident waiting to happen. Let's now take a look at those incidents that might be called 'off target and no message'.

Such accidents, blunders, mishaps and misinformation are, as you can imagine, closely watched by CND, Greenpeace and other such respectable organisations. Their revelations are enough to make the blood run cold. It is tempting, and very comforting, to think of the potential for nuclear accidents as belonging to a world before computers ran everything, where men with big spanners and dirty overalls arrived to fix all problems, and whacked things with hammers if they didn't work first time. In such circumstances something was bound to happen sooner or later. But it can't happen now, surely? Well, guess what?

Only about 20 per cent of all nuclear-related accidents are reported into the public domain. Sometimes, despite the best efforts of the Ministry of Defence, reports only come out many years after the event happened, when the effect on the public is one of, 'That was years ago. Everything will be all right now, surely?' Such was the case when HMS *Sheffield* sank in the Falklands War. Certainly, the *Sun* had the report the following day. So did many other papers. What no one was told for 14 years was that the *Sheffield* was carrying nuclear weapons when she was hit.

Then sometimes the government's left hand doesn't know what the right hand is doing. In 1996 the MoD finally admitted to seven nuclear accidents since 1966. What they didn't realise was that the people who wanted to know about these accidents had taken the precaution of asking someone else who was in a position to know the answers. They had asked the chief scientific adviser to the MoD the same question. He was honest and said the number in that period was actually more like 20.

It is true that the control systems for all nuclear weapons' containment and firing functions have become more reliable. But that wouldn't have been very difficult. It is now widely known that, at the height of the Cold War, when primitive computer systems were at the heart of nuclear control systems, some 1,250 nuclear weapons were involved in accidents involving handling, transporting and storing warheads. The University of Bradford's highly respected department of peace studies informs us of many incidents, but let us look at just two, one from the United States and one from the Soviet Union.

On 26 May 1968 the nuclear submarine USS *Scorpion* collided with a barge in Naples harbour. The USS *Scorpion* 'made a run for it', no doubt to avoid those pesky photos that get into the papers on such occasions. However, she was fatally damaged and sank a day later. She was manned by 99 sailors, all lost at sea. The nuclear reactor and all the weapons went down to rest with the men. The dead men do us no harm; indeed we mourn their loss. But the reactor and the weapons are gradually rusting to the point where they will, one day, be back to harm our ocean, our fish, our air and us.

Years later, on 4 October 1986, a USSR Yankee-class nuclear submarine caught fire at sea. It sank off the eastern coast of Russia with all hands lost and the same terrible fate awaiting us, just as soon as the rust can do its final penetrating work. Then there are the plane crashes. The giant B-52 bombers, which often carry around the plutonium needed for nuclear warheads, have not done their work without incident. One crashed near Polmares in Spain in 1966. Another crashed at Thule, Greenland, dispersing plutonium over an area many miles wide. Well, Greenland? No one would be harmed in that one, surely? Well, yes, they were, and not just in Greenland. Of approximately 800 Danish people who worked long hours to help clear the contaminated soil and ice, about 500 soon reported sicknesses of various degrees. But the real crime is that over 90 of those volunteers soon got cancer.

Everyone who was at Greenham Common, and many who weren't, know about the fire in the B-47 bomber that caused a nuclear bomb on board to release its plutonium and uranium over an area of several miles around the base. In 1980 a Nimrod plane with nuclear depth bombs on board crashed at RAF Kinloss in Scotland. On 20 June 1985 two lorries carrying Polaris warheads collided with each other. Well, you may say, these incidents are minor compared with an all-out war and have been contained so that shows the government knows what it is doing. Doesn't it?

Guess what? It doesn't. The problem of safe and permanent disposal of outdated nuclear weapons is one for which no government has a solution. In Britain these decommissioned submarines with their highly radioactive materials inside lie in the ports of Rosyth and Devonport awaiting the day when someone finds a solution to their existence and then the government finds the money to implement that solution. My advice when near these things is, 'Hold your breath.'

I want to return to our friends with the big spanners and dirty overalls for a moment and mention some well-known accidents involving nuclear weapons being hoisted into and out of their positions. Now if these incidents were not so horrendous I would invite you to imagine the Marx Brothers running a naval base where nuclear submarines go to be maintained and have their weapons loaded. Not very long ago, in 1991, at the Holy Loch in Scotland, a Poseidon missile containing 10 warheads was being winched into the USS *Holland*. So far so good. Then the winch failed and ran out of control, allowing the missile to drop 17 feet and roll, crashing into the side of the USS *Los Angeles*. (Groucho to Harpo: Hey, watch what you're doing with that thing. Your missile almost ran over my toe and these shoes cost 12 bucks each!)

Then in 1997 a Harrier jump jet crashed at RAF Wittering only a hundred yards or so from a fully loaded Trident convoy waiting to roll for Loch Goil. In January 1998 the nuclear submarine HMS *Torbay* was abandoned to its own devices in the River Tamar by an overtired tug master and risked running aground. Can you imagine the embarrassment of asking a few locals with 4x4s to lend a hand pulling a nuclear submarine off the riverbank? Then later in 1998 we know of a power failure aboard HMS *Vanguard* that caused the giant nuclear submarine to go into an uncontrolled dive. There were 96 warheads loaded into their firing positions and 135 crew aboard. A major catastrophe was averted with only about a minute to spare.

As if that wasn't bad enough there was the late-1998 debacle of the Russian teenager hijacking a submarine, killing nine crew and threatening to blow the thing up. With Russia's command and control systems well out of date for want of funding, one asks, 'How long before they respond to an incoming attack that is no more than the northern lights confusing the early warning system?' Some may scoff, but that really happened.

So much for accidents. Let us turn now to firing these weapons. Each Trident warhead must be fired from a Trident submarine. We know that these submarines depend upon acoustic secrecy for their survival. We can assume that gliding around the bottom of the world's oceans in silence is relatively easy for Trident because these submarines have been well designed to do that and have had a lot of practice. But the firing of a nuclear warhead shatters that bizarre form of peace and immediately betrays the submarine's position. That means that in order to avoid an enemy retaliatory strike that would blow up all of the live nuclear warheads on the first submarine, it has to fire all of its 14 missiles in the shortest possible time, that is in under 10 minutes. The missiles rocket out of the earth's atmosphere and then each one releases five armed nuclear re-entry vehicles. Each of these comes back to earth at an astonishing rate, containing a 100-kiloton targeted nuclear warhead that lands almost precisely on its target. The idea is that one missile causes five explosions and there are 14 missiles per submarine. So our question becomes, which people would they incinerate and which parts of the planet would these weapons of unimaginable ecological destruction destroy for a half-life of 30,000 years? The obvious answer is they would destroy the whole planet, either directly by incineration, radiation or the effects of buildings and other infrastructure collapsing, or indirectly by sending poisonous gas clouds swirling around the world to fall as rain wherever the wind might take them. It is worth recalling that the wind patterns of the world would be altered unpredictably. I have heard arguments that not the whole surface of the planet would be affected by such explosions. Well, OK. My only response is that it would be 'life, Jim, but not as we know it'.

One would be forgiven for paraphrasing Earl Mountbatten and General Lee Butler and thinking that the idea of setting such an irreversible train of events in motion ought to be abhorrent to any government's policies. Unfortunately, it's not. For the official British government position we must first go back to those strategic defence reviews. These recognise that Russia is no longer the threat it once was. Fair enough. But to recognise that fact and to do anything about it are two different policies. The latest reviews say:

No threat on the [previous] scale is in prospect. It would, however, be unwise to conclude that one could never re-appear but the conventional forces required to threaten such an attack would take many years to create. The Mission therefore provides for longer term insurance through a credible nuclear deterrent and the retention of essential military capabilities on which we could rebuild larger forces over a long period, if circumstances were to radically worsen.

Insurance? Well, so much for Earl Mountbatten's warning of the folly in trying to increase one's own certainty by increasing the total amount of uncertainty in the world. But there's worse. There always is. The reviews go on to say:

very large numbers of strategic and shorter range nuclear weapons… remain as a potent potential threat to the security of Britain and our Allies should current circumstances change for the worse. In present conditions nuclear deterrence still has an important contribution to make in insuring against the re-emergence of major strategic military threats, in preventing nuclear coercion and in preserving peace and stability in Europe.

There's that word 'insurance' again. Don't they know that insurance does not prevent anything? It never did because it cannot. Insurance gives you something comfortable to call upon when a damaging event occurs. British government defence policy therefore amounts to nothing more than 'If they hit us, we'll hit them back.'

The mention of 're-emergence of major strategic military threats' is a thinly veiled reference to Russia. Despite all that was said in Bonn in 2001, the Old Black Bear is still the West's No 1 target for its nuclear weapons. In 1994 an agreement was signed saying that Britain and Russia would no longer 'target' each other with nuclear weapons. However, all that means, as we saw above, is that the computer programs are not live in the guidance computers. They are kept by the side of their host computers in readiness for uploading. So it's a case of yet more money spent on junkets to Russia, more platitudes about 'steps towards world peace'… (you know the routine). The British government is quite open about admitting that the main threat to the UK would come from anti-ballistic missile defences. The only place in the world protected by such defences is the greater Moscow area. Such defences could, if used in attack mode, easily reach the Trident submarine base at Faslane in the West Highlands of Scotland. There is no way of knowing with any certainty just how well these old defences are maintained nor even if they are still live. From the British side of the equation it can therefore be concluded that the nuclear planners in Whitehall remain locked into the Cold War mentality. That mentality holds to the old-fashioned view that war is a collective activity for a collective purpose. Those purposes have traditionally been about land grabbing or self-protection, the latter being done both offensively and defensively. That is historically the way in which empires have risen and fallen. The 20th century was characterised by two world wars, the latter being absolutely necessary to resist the rise of the Third Reich, and nuclear annihilation. Thus, humankind having barely survived the last century, at the beginning of this new millennium the question arises: to what extent can any society that calls itself increasingly multicultural in substance and international in outlook maintain a global posture that threatens the world with annihilation?

Everyone will have their own answer to that question, some clearer than others. However, the British government's two-faced position could not be clearer. Against a background of toothy smiles and talk of ethnic harmony, there are two plans setting out the targets for Britain's nuclear weapons. The first is the NATO nuclear planning system and the second is Britain's independent nuclear target plan – which is not really independent at all, as it is approved by the United States. Additional information can be transmitted to the submarines by old-fashioned radio; however, this assumes that acoustic silence has been broken and that means a missile has been fired and that means... yes, you've guessed it.

Now let's consider the situation in Russia. Anyone who has been to Russia will tell you that the people are, on the whole, all right. They love their poetry (no one loves poetry like a Russian). They love their vodka – especially the types kept exclusively for the Politburo. They love to sing and dance at weddings and they love to learn. But they are repressed by bureaucracy and decades of corruption. A bit like us really. Now just imagine those armed nuclear re-entry vehicles hurtling eastward. One 100-kiloton warhead (eight times larger than Hiroshima) strikes central Moscow and there are plenty more on the way. Dozens of them. The number of civilians incinerated immediately would depend upon whether the warhead exploded above ground or upon impact. Either way it would also depend upon the wind speed and direction. Then there's the strength or weakness of the buildings, gas pipes, electricity stations, etc. The whole city would be flattened in seconds and over the next few hours the mushroom cloud would take care of everyone else, their pets and every other living thing (except cockroaches). A few seconds after the first strike the other warheads will be raining down on their targets. Let's take one pretty sure bet as an example – Polyarny Shipyard.

Polyarny is a medium-sized town in northern, really polar, Russia, near the Norwegian and Finnish borders. Its 30,000 population work mainly in the shipyards, some of which are used to repair nuclear-powered submarines. If one of our raining warheads exploded above the town, the superheated fireball would be nearly 1,000 metres across and everyone under it, including approximately 7,000 children, would be incinerated. For up to 4.5 kilometres away from the centre of town, everyone under the explosion would suffer from third-degree burns. Most would not survive because the emergency services would be unable to cope with them in time. Even 10 kilometres away, in the town of Severomorsk, there would be extensive blast damage and probably hundreds of deaths from both radiation poisoning and collapsing buildings. Neither the BBC nor CNN would be able to get close. No more weddings. No more learning. Nothing would grow in the soil for a half-life of 30,000 years. There would be no more anything there.

That was the scenario with just one warhead. Let's now have a look at one missile with, say, five of its warheads targeted at: 1) Nerpicha submarine base near the town of Zaozersk, which has a population of 30,000; 2) Gadzhiyevo submarine base near the town of Skalisti, the population of which is unknown because it's a secret; 3) Shkval naval shipyard near our friends in the town of Polyarny (population 30,000); 4) naval head-quarters in the town of Severomorsk (population 76,000); and 5) Safonovo naval shipyard near Murmansk (population 468,000). So that's 604,000 people plus the unknown amount in Skalisti. It is not my intention to be gory, so please forgive me if I leave these people in peace. In any case, I'm sure you've got the picture. What I will say is that the amount of radioactive material that would be scattered downwind would be eight times greater than that after the Chernobyl accident. On that occasion it skirted the north-eastern and south-western parts of Scotland where some farms are still badly affected. If the poison gas clouds from our new five-town scenario hit London, then there might conceivably be a greater public outcry about the matter.

In a strategic attack the Trident submarine on patrol at the time would be ordered to fire all of its nuclear weapons. This is the most horrific scenario, dragging with it the highest numbers and 'best' television images. Up to 20 million people would die instantly or soon after the explosions. Millions of animals would die too. Cities would be flattened and the poison gas clouds would be swirling over you and me, wherever we were in the world. The legal point to note here is that both military personnel and civilians would indiscriminately die. There happen to be quite a number of international humanitarian laws against that kind of thing, but we'll get to that when we arrive at the trial of The Trident Three.

8

The Long and Winding Road
to the World Court

Everyone gets it now and then. I used to find it arrived during examinations, Roman law in particular I seem to recall. It's all-consuming and won't go away no matter what you try. A song or image in your head that shoves all else aside. For days after meeting The Trident Three I had a scene from one of my favourite movies in my head and it just would not budge. I was acting in an important international child abduction case, at an early procedural stage I hasten to add, and I could not shift from my mind the scene from *Butch Cassidy and the Sundance Kid* where Butch and Sundance (Paul Newman and Robert Redford) have been on the run for days from a posse whose pace and formation never change – they just keep coming. Our heroes decide to get away from the savannah and climb into some high rocks where they are absolutely sure they cannot be tracked. They send Sundance's empty horse off to the east as a decoy and double up on Butch's horse, which scrambles up the rocks carrying the two riders. Butch and Sundance, from a high vantage point in the rocks, are looking down at the pursuing posse in the distance when they identify the leader. It's Joe LeFores. You can tell by his white skipper hat. And the man on the ground who is tracking them over streams, bush and even rock? He's Native American but with an English name, Lord Baltimore. He is known to be able to track anything and anybody, day or night. Bewildered and deeply worried, Butch turns to Sundance, saying, 'I couldn't do that. Could you do that? I couldn't do that. How can those guys do that?' Then whispering, 'Who are those guys?'

66

Over the previous week what I had learnt of The Trident Three, but Angie Zelter in particular, was an exact parallel to that scene, the main difference being that it was the women who were in pursuit. What Angie and her dedicated group of friends were pursuing was as old as the hills around Athens or Rome where great civilisations got their first sparks of life. They were pursuing their rulers with a cry from the people in their throats, reminding us that the rulers were not almighty – not above the law. Their cries were that high crimes and misdemeanours were being committed in the name of the people and that these should cease forthwith. For years, however, their cries fell on deaf ears. But that did not discourage them. Far from it.

Popular uprisings are often started with great enthusiasm in pursuit of a single ideal. The formation of CND in the late fifties was no exception. However, such movements are often seen by their originators as being 'hijacked' by lawyers who come in with an explanation here, a shake of the head there or at worst an ultimatum that if things are not run their way they will leave and the movement will collapse into internal anarchy. The great strength inherent in the cause, which those who sought to disarm Trident built into their strategy, was that every move would be designed to uphold the rule of law.

To that end the first significant step towards the World Court Project was taken in London in January 1985. The Ecology Party organised a nuclear warfare tribunal chaired by the legendary Sean MacBride, former assistant UN secretary-general, Nobel peace prizewinner and president of the International Peace Bureau. The idea was to set out the arguments for and against the deployment and use of nuclear weapons and see, impartially, which arguments stood up and which fell flat. The 'tribunal' was a big success and focused the international legal community's attention on the issue of nuclear weapons. Two years later MacBride launched the historic lawyers' appeal that called for the legal prohibition of nuclear weapons. Astonishingly, that appeal was signed by 11,000 lawyers from 56 countries who agreed that the use of nuclear weapons would constitute a crime against humanity.

In October 1991 the World Court Project UK was launched. Keith

Mothersson's 'Declaration of Public Conscience' was translated into 36 languages and collected a staggering 3.6 million signatures world-wide. By May 1992 the World Court Project went international with its launch in Geneva. Its sole intention was having the legality of Trident decided at the highest legal level without the obstacle of national jurisdictions being interpreted by clever-clever lawyers to mean that the ruling of a supreme court of one country could be reinterpreted or ignored by another. That meant getting to the International Court of Justice in The Hague – the World Court. Easier said than done.

One might think that the people at the World Health Organisation, itself an organ of the UN, would be able simply to talk to the people at the World Court, a sister organ of the UN, about nuclear weapons. Indeed the ordinary person in the street would be forgiven for thinking that such important people must drink in the same pubs or, at the very least, ski on the same slopes. Alas that seems not to be the case. The World Health Organisation began investigating the health and environmental effects of thermonuclear explosions in 1981. In December 1994, conscious of its mandate to all nations to provide medical opinion and certain amounts of practical assistance, the World Health Organisation adopted a resolution asking the World Court, 'In view of the health and environmental effects, would the use of nuclear weapons by a state during a war or other armed conflict be a breach of its obligation under international law including the constitution of the World Health Organisation?' This time, the ball was well and truly rolling.

So, it can fairly be said that for 10 solid years that dedicated band of ordinary, faithful, concerned citizens printed leaflets, spoke at local gatherings and wrote to their MPs – all very familiar and usually dispiriting stuff. But the World Court Project also had friends in high places. It is just a law of nature that people get older and usually their views mellow as they do so. But we children of the 1950s and 60s seem to have held dear to our ideas of love and peace, and these are powerful tools. We only have to look as far as Vaclev Havel for confirmation of my point. If some enterprising PhD student would trace the women from Greenham Common I'm sure the point could be reinforced. And so it was that a

kind of old girl network was used to get at those who could make a difference – a real difference. They were after the ambassadors to the United
Nations – and they got some.

Early research was assisted by the use of fax machines and then e-mail.
It was easy to spot the obvious targets. These were the countries that had,
by way of referendum, asked their people whether to adopt nuclear
power as their main source of electrical energy. Denmark is one such
country, and New Zealand is another. Now you don't just walk up to
ambassadors in the street outside the UN in New York with a banner.
Not if you want to be taken seriously. For that you need insiders, usually
the permanent observers to the Geneva and Vienna Conventions. And
guess what? If you look hard enough you can trace a direct link from
Greenham Common to those exalted heights. So an encouraging start
was made.

For the last 20 years not a plenary session has gone by where some
nation has not laid down an official protest at the UN complaining that
Britain's nuclear weapons are a threat to that nation's people and environment. All such protests are ignored and nothing is ever done because
all of the permanent members of the United Nations Security Council
have nuclear weapons. These are the United States, the United
Kingdom, France, Russia and China. Japan, by contrast and for rather
obvious reasons, is a non-nuclear state. However, these protests serve to
keep the nuclear issue very much alive, and eventually enough ambassadors were minded to approve a motion to send a question of law to the
legal organ of the United Nations – the World Court in The Hague.

What the General Assembly of the UN wanted to know was whether
the threat or use of nuclear weapons was legal or illegal under international law. Everyone knows that nuclear weapons have been in 'service'
for decades so it seems amazing that they even had to ask.

Now this exercise of asking the World Court to advise the UN is not
new. The first 'advisory opinion', as these are officially called, was issued
in 1949 and arose out of the assassination of the UN peace negotiator,
Count Bernadotte, in Jerusalem in 1948. The questions on that occasion
were about whether Israel, which was not then a state within the UN,

would have to pay compensation for the loss of Bernadotte. Israel paid up and soon afterwards joined as a full member of the UN. In 1971 the World Court advised the UN that South Africa had breached the trust of a mandate about South West Africa. The ruling eventually led in 1990 to the creation of the independent state of Namibia. In 1975 the Court ruled on the Western Sahara question, over whether it was part of Morocco or Mauritania. The World Court has also settled dozens of international disputes across a wide range of issues involving one state against another. Such cases illustrate how the Court's opinions, if not instantly acted upon, eventually lead to a legal solution to international disputes. The thorny question about the legality or illegality of nuclear weapons has been the UN's longest-running dispute.

And so, after a decade of effort by that small group of concerned citizens that came to be known as the World Court Project, during a fairly ordinary day's business at the end of 1994, a most extraordinary result was achieved. Resolution 49/75 K was adopted by the General Assembly of the United Nations on 15 December 1994. The resolution was communicated to the Court by the secretary-general on 19 December 1994. A ball had begun to roll. Being such a historic document, Resolution 49/75 K bears repetition. It read:

The General Assembly,

Conscious that the continuing existence and development of nuclear weapons pose serious risks to humanity,

Mindful that States have an obligation under the Charter of the United Nations to refrain from the threat or use of force against the territorial integrity or political independence of any state,

Recalling its Resolutions 1653 (XVI) of 24 November 1961, 33/71 B of 14 December 1978, 34/83 G of 11 December 1979, 35/152 D of 12 December 1980, 36/92 I of 9 December 1981, 45/59 B of 4 December 1990 and 46/37 D of 6 December 1991, in which it declared that the use of nuclear weapons would be a violation of the Charter and a crime against humanity,

Welcoming the progress made on the prohibition and elimination of weapons of mass destruction, including the Convention on the Prohibition of the Development, Production and Stockpiling of Bacteriological (Biological) and Toxic Weapons and on their Destruction (1) and the Convention on the Prohibition of the Development, Production, Stockpiling and Use of Chemical Weapons and on Their Destruction (2),

Convinced that the complete elimination of nuclear weapons is the only guarantee against the threat of nuclear war,

Noting the concerns expressed in the Fourth Review Conference of the Parties to the Treaty on the Non-Proliferation of Nuclear Weapons that insufficient progress has been made towards complete elimination of nuclear weapons at the earliest possible time,

Recalling that, convinced of the need to strengthen the rule of law in international relations, it has declared the period 1990–1999 the United Nations Decade of International Law (3),

Noting that Article 96, paragraph 1, of the Charter empowers the General Assembly to request the International Court of Justice to give an Advisory Opinion on any legal question,

Recalling the recommendation of the Secretary-General, made in his report entitled 'An Agenda for Peace' (4), that the United Nations organs that are authorized to take advantage of the advisory competence of the International Court of Justice turn to the Court more frequently for such opinions,

Welcoming the resolution 46/40 of 14 May 1993 of the Assembly of the World Health Organisation, in which the organisation requested the International Court of Justice to give an advisory opinion on whether the use of nuclear weapons by a State in war or other armed conflict would be a breach of its obligations under International Law, including the Constitution of the World Health Organisation,

Decides, pursuant to Article 96, paragraph 1, of the Charter of the United Nations, to request the International Court of Justice urgently to render its advisory opinion on the following question: 'Is the threat or use of nuclear weapons in any circumstances permitted under International Law?'

So the legal question that had been posed by the opponents to Mrs Thatcher's unilateral decision to bring Trident to Britain in the early 1980s was now official. The nuclear states didn't like it but they were stuck with the fact that the legality of their activities when patrolling the world's oceans, targeting other nations for thermonuclear incineration, was about to come under a level of scrutiny they could not have dreamt of in their worst nightmare. Furthermore, the question for the Court was about nuclear weapons in general, not Trident in particular. So the Court had scope to examine everything from so-called low-yield weapons through to the massive 100-kiloton Delta 5 thermonuclear warheads of mass indiscriminate destruction carried by Trident. So they did what those under legal pressure usually do. They played for time.

A tension thus arose because the secretary-general in his letter had asked for an 'urgent' opinion. The Court, very conscious that this question was the most politically loaded question it was ever likely to be asked, decided that it would be necessary for all 14 judges to hear 'submissions' from each interested state in order fully to understand what each had to say in favour or against the 'threat or use of nuclear weapons'. But, mindful of the request for urgency, the Court set deadlines for these initial statements. The date for receiving each initial written statement was set as 20 June 1995 and the date for receiving comments on one another's written statements was set as 20 September 1995. Then the Court did something that no one expected: it decided to hold public meetings.

There was a flurry of activity leading up to these public sessions, as each participating state knew only too well that the eyes and ears of every international lawyer would be upon them. And then there were these troublesome people at the World Court Project who somehow had their oar in at top levels. In all, 28 states submitted detailed written legal statements; these included small countries such as Nauru and Qatar. The public hearings opened on 30 October 1995. However, when it came to sending top international lawyers to appear personally before the Court, some of the tiny countries were so poor that they could not afford the fares to send anyone, never mind hire an international lawyer to appear for an unspecified period of time. So special arrangements were made for them to phone in their views. We don't know why, but for some reason, by letter dated 20 October 1995, the tiny state of Nauru wrote to the Court asking to withdraw its statement entitled 'Response to submissions of other States' and the Court allowed that to happen. It is not known whether the two incidents are related but the Court then decided to do something else no one expected: it made the statements and comments made to the Court accessible to the public with effect from the opening of the oral proceedings.

Those who were playing for time and betting that the public would not be very interested in the subject matter before the Court must have been delighted to see the top-level legal teams arriving from around the world. Professors of international law galore poured in, followed by QCs, foreign ministers and ambassadors. The UK sent Sir Nicholas Lyell QC MP, the English Attorney General, whilst the United States sent Conrad K Harper and other top brass from the State Department and the Department of Defense. Between them, with tens of billions of dollars spent on Trident every year, they had no trouble finding the air fares for their august legal teams.

The World Court consists of 14 judges appointed by various states large and small around the world in order not only to provide as wide a range of legal expertise as possible but also to demonstrate that justice is being seen to be done to all nations. The president for this advisory opinion was Judge Bedjaoui. The names of the rest of the judges show what I mean. These were Judges Schwebel, Oda, Guillaume, Shahabuddeen, Weeramantry, Ranjeva, Herczegh, Shi, Fleischhauer, Koroma, Vereshchetin, Ferrari Bravo and Higgins.

The Court deals with international law, not any domestic system in particular. The judges questioned the legal teams that came before them and had a few surprises for the nuclear weapons states. Obviously, if there was an international law somewhere, anywhere, that said in any language that the use of nuclear weapons was legal under international law then none of the legal teams need have taken the trouble to show up at all. They could simply have picked the youngest law student they could find, set that person the task of finding this law and, when the smiling student slapped it down on the table, simply faxed it to the World Court and told them to stop wasting everybody's time. However, as every top-brass lawyer who appeared before the World Court knew perfectly well, no such law existed.

So naturally, the lawyers first tried the first trick in the book – attack the roots of the question. They argued that the UN had included the word 'permitted' in the question and could be said to have done that deliberately. Quite true, they had. Then they tried to argue that *permission* under international law is not the same as permission in a domestic legal system, where you have to point to a statute or a case or in some other way demonstrate you have a legal right to do what you did or are pro-posing to do. The Court would have none of it. The nub of the issue was: *is it legal to threaten to use nuclear weapons or indeed actually use them?* and that is where the Court wanted to start. Eventually, the Court noted in its final judgement, at paragraph 22, that 'the nuclear weapons States appearing before [the Court] either accepted, or did not dispute, that their independence to act was indeed restricted by the principles and rules of International Law, more particularly Humanitarian Law, as did the other States which took part in the proceedings'.

Later in their judgement, at paragraph 85, the Court went further saying:

> Turning now to the applicability of the principles and rules of humanitar-ian law to a possible threat or use of nuclear weapons, the Court notes that doubts in this respect have sometimes been voiced on the ground that these principles and rules had evolved prior to the invention of nuclear weapons and that the Conferences of Geneva of 1949 and 1974–1977 which respectively adopted the four Geneva Conventions of 1949 and the two additional Protocols thereto did not deal with nuclear weapons specifically. Such views, however, are only held by a small minority. In the view of the vast majority of States as well as writers there can be no doubt as to the applicability of humanitarian law to nuclear weapons.

At paragraph 86 the Court went on to say:

> The Court shares that view. Indeed, nuclear weapons were invented after most of the principles and rules of humanitarian law applicable in armed conflict had already come into existence; the Conferences of 1949 and 1974–77 left these weapons aside, and there is a qualitative as well as quantitative difference between nuclear weapons and all conventional arms. However, it cannot be concluded from this that the established principles of humanitarian law applicable in armed conflict did not apply to nuclear weapons. Such a conclusion would be incompatible with the intrinsically humanitarian character of the legal principles in question which permeates the entire law of armed conflict and applies to all forms of warfare and to all kinds of weapons, those of the past, those of the present and those of the future. In this respect it seems significant that the thesis that the rules of humanitarian law do not apply to the new weaponry, because of the newness of the latter, has not been advocated in the present proceedings. On the contrary, the newness of nuclear weapons has been expressly rejected (by New Zealand) as an argument against the application to them of International Humanitarian Law. None of the statements made before this Court in any way advocated a freedom to use nuclear weapons without regard to humanitarian constraints. Quite the reverse; it has been explicitly stated by Russia, Britain and America that the laws of armed conflict (called the *jus in bello*) apply to nuclear weapons.

One can but speculate on the extent to which those simple concessions reverberated around the corridors of the MoD in Whitehall and the top table at NATO headquarters in Brussels. What was certain was that the concerned citizens making the most of the public access to such legal submissions got every word down in writing, verbatim.

9

The British Government at the World Court

It was Sir Nicholas Lyell, the English Attorney General, who had the job of putting the position of the United Kingdom on record before the World Court, which he did on 15 November 1995. The UK is a member of the Security Council at the UN so one would reasonably have hoped, because it was the UN that had asked the question about the legality of nuclear weapons, that the UK would have a good deal to say about the subject. However, those who had such hopes were about to have them dashed.

It wasn't as though there was nothing to say about the matter. Britain has a long history of involvement in building and testing nuclear weapons. It also has a long history of legal brinkmanship when it comes to international law restricting the use of such weapons. For instance, on 5 August 1963 in Moscow, the British signed a treaty banning nuclear weapons tests in the atmosphere, in outer space and underwater. 'Great, what a start,' one might think. Wrong. The British government even went so far as formally to ratify the treaty but it never formally incorporated it into English or Scottish law. That meant that, despite the pomp and ceremony, the photo opportunities and the handshakes all round, the treaty was a dead duck in the country whose people had paid for a whole lot of diplomats and civil servants to go to Moscow, talk at top international level about the future of the world's security, write it all out in a formal treaty and come home to trumpet how well they had done.

'Oh, come on, the British government wouldn't do a thing like that, would they?' the sceptic might say. Wrong. They did exactly the same four years later with the treaty governing the activities of states in exploration and use of outer space, including the moon and other celestial bodies. That one was ratified in London, Moscow and Washington on 27 January 1967. 'OK, so they did it twice – big deal.' Wrong. It was exactly the same story with the treaty on non-proliferation of nuclear weapons, 1 July 1968, and with the treaty on the prohibition of the emplacement of nuclear weapons and other weapons of mass destruction on the seabed and the ocean floor, dated 11 February 1971.

So the pattern was clear. As far as successive British governments were concerned, it was all right for us to have nuclear weapons and to continue to work in close partnership with the United States on developing the technology for larger and more destructive weapons but we didn't want anyone else having them and we would not bind ourselves in law to restricting their use, even on the moon.

It was against that background that Sir Nicholas opened his speech to the World Court. The theme of his speech can be summed up as, 'These hearings involving every country in the world about the future security of the planet are all a waste of time.' 'Strong stuff,' you may say. But it was true. Instead of fully participating in the legal debate, as one might expect of the senior English law officer, he pulled an old stunt, one that if tried by any student sitting an exam would normally result in a fail. It is the old trick of, 'I don't know the answers so I'll attack the question and see if I can come out of this without too much embarrassment.'

Sir Nicholas began by putting a lot of platitudes on record. He said, 'The United Kingdom has had nuclear weapons for over 40 years. As a member of the Security Council of the United Nations, the United Kingdom has a special responsibility for maintenance of peace and security amongst nations. And lest anyone think otherwise, the United Kingdom is a staunch supporter of this Court.'

It is plain that there is nothing of any substance in these opening remarks, no hint of where his argument was going and equally nothing to suggest that he was not about to embark upon an analysis of the UK's legal position on the threat or use of nuclear weapons.

Sir Nicholas then politely said that his primary argument was that the International Court of Justice should decline to answer the UN's question because there was no need to answer it. Given the background of enormous concern at the UN about the future of nuclear war, this was nothing less than an astonishing act of arrogance before the highest court in the world. But there was more.

Sir Nicholas said that the policy of deterrence was a warning to any would-be aggressor not to embark upon an attack of the UK. If that seems like a dressed-up version of the kind of thing a hard man might say on the streets of Glasgow or Liverpool then we only had to wait until 8 July 1998 to learn that it was in fact government policy. On that day in the House of Commons the then secretary of state for defence, George Robertson (now Lord Robertson of Port Ellen, secretary-general of NATO) is reported in Hansard as saying, 'making absolutely certain that people know the [nuclear] deterrent is still there, still credible and no one should mess with us as a consequence'. Street-fighting talk if ever I heard it.

I hope it is fair to say that to any rational person that looks like the language of threat. It could certainly be construed as such by any jury in the land listening to evidence about the jostlings of a big bunch of heavies in any city centre. These remarks were not made about a real fight in a real city centre, but they degraded Britain's standing in the rational world in the centre of the law and development of civilisation, the World Court. Sir Nicholas seems to have forgotten that the World Court was examining precisely the question of 'threat' as well as 'use' of nuclear weapons. So like the student, unaware of how much ignorance he betrays by trying to be clever by avoiding the question, Sir Nicholas, without citing a single precedent, statute or any other piece of law, revealed exactly the UK's position. It was that of aggressor.

Schoolchildren of the world no longer learn that Britain has an empire. But Britain of course does still have an empire. The difference between the old images of crowds of 'coolies' staring at white men in white military uniform with white feathered plumage in their tall hats and the image of the modern empire is that nowadays power comes in economic and political form rather than physical dominance over all those expensive territories. And, just in case the world's poor should somehow revolt in their billions against such dominance, Britain, the US and France have Trident.

The question arises, 'Isn't the daily deployment of thousands of tons of thermonuclear explosives aboard Trident submarines a form of military imperialism to the point of totalitarianism?' Sir Nicholas didn't think so. He went on to say that to call into question the legality of the system on which so many states have relied for so long, that is since the end of World War II, could have 'a profoundly destabilising effect'.

Sir Nicholas did not elaborate but one has to wonder, 'profoundly destabilising what?' The answer to that simple question is to be found in successive British strategic defence reviews since the issue of the World Court judgement. As we shall see, at the last gasp of its opinion the World Court said that it might be legal to use a nuclear weapon if 'the very survival of a state was at stake'. The World Court did not distinguish between a physical place as a 'state', like the island nation of Britain, and the cultural centres or political institutions of a nation as making up a 'state'. We can only assume that the World Court took the view that ordinary people know exactly what is meant by the phrases 'the very survival' and 'at stake'.

So it was in those extremely limited and virtually inconceivable circumstances that the World Court said it left open a theoretical possibility of 'using' nuclear weapons legally. What it most certainly did not do was leave open a possibility that nuclear weapons could be used to protect, say, economic interests in oilfields or the destruction of rainforests for the production of hamburgers. But, nevertheless, that is exactly the position the British government takes.

The purpose of the UK strategic defence reviews is to report to Parliament on how well the military is placed from time to time to protect the nation. A good example is the strategic defence review presented to Parliament by the secretary of state for defence in July 1998. It says at paragraph 60:

Deterrence is about preventing war rather than fighting it. All our forces have an important deterrent role but nuclear deterrence raises particularly difficult issues because of the nature of nuclear war. The Government wishes to see a safer world in which there is no place for nuclear weapons. Progress on arms control is therefore an important objective of foreign and defence policy. Nevertheless, while large nuclear arsenals and risks of proliferation remain, our minimum deterrent remains a necessary element of our security.

The government says it 'wishes to see a safer world in which there is no place for nuclear weapons'. All well and good. They then go on to talk about 'prevention' of war. But how? By threatening other nations with nuclear weapons? Of course, it must be. Against the background seen above of refusal after refusal to incorporate treaties into UK law, one has to gasp at the sheer two-faced way in which such a statement is made. At this point I suggest that our answer to the question asked earlier about military imperialism to the point of totalitarianism is coming more clearly into focus. However, it is about to become crystal clear.
Paragraph 61 goes on:

The Strategic Defence Review has conducted a rigorous re-examination of our deterrence requirements. This does not depend on the size of the nation's arsenals but on the minimum necessary to deter any threat to our vital interests. We have concluded that we can safely make further significant reductions from Cold War levels, both in the number of weapons and in our day-to-day operating posture. Transparency about nuclear weapons holdings also plays a part in arms control and, although we cannot give precise details of all aspects of our deterrent, we intend to be significantly more open in some areas.

The key phrase here is of course 'the minimum necessary to deter any threat to our vital interests'. What vital interests? Oil? Tele-communications? Hamburgers? No mention is made of 'the very survival of [our] State [being] at stake'. It is as though the advisory opinion of the World

Court did not exist. Perhaps the most worrying statement of all is that paragraph 62 goes on to say that Trident will be with us for at least another 30 years. What a prospect.

Whilst these statements for the strategic defence review were being drafted, Sir Nicholas was getting himself, not for the first time, into a tight corner. Anyone who has ever questioned a child about the disappearance of another child's toy, let alone sat on a jury, will tell you that there is a host of body signals and speech patterns that betray when people move from fact into fiction. It is that basic human skill in recognising these signs that keeps the jury system at the heart of justice in so many countries in the world. Unfortunately these pages cannot show you the video, so we have to imagine the hapless Sir Nicholas as he faced a mostly silent full bench of the world's highest judges. As an advocate of the Scottish Bar who has faced his share of hostile benches, I can tell you that to appear in such a place with such a specious argument is not a prospect I relish. Shoved by one's masters into the front line to do the dirty work is never a pleasing prospect and, lawyer to lawyer, I sympathised with the poor man.

Faced with such a simple question and all the time and legal resources in the world at his disposal I expect the judges were rather disappointed when Sir Nicholas got a bit bogged down and resorted to saying that the UN's question, far from being simple, was too abstract and speculative for a meaningful response. I could understand that argument if there had been a normal 'case' with one side against another. In such cases we stick to what is relevant to the areas of dispute between the parties and try, by means of sufficient evidence, to demonstrate that our case is to be preferred to the other side's case. But this was not a normal case. It was the UN seeking the advice of its own legal organ, the World Court. So, with respect, I see no force in Sir Nicholas's approach.

Then he gave the real game away again when he said that, in any case, to answer the question 'may even do harm'. He seems to have ignored the fact that the question had the approval of the UN in General Assembly and thus reflected the wishes of the majority of states and not just those who controlled the Trident thermonuclear fleet. Once again he did not say to exactly which British interests the answer might do harm.

Once he had embarked on this line he had to follow it through. 'The Court', he said, 'ought to leave disarmament to the various nations. There are Conferences for these things. We don't need a Court to tell us why we should disarm our nuclear weapons.' We are now seeing, ad nauseam, this old chestnut preferred by the British – the modern spin, I suppose, would be, 'We are engaging in meaningful dialogue with our friends in many other nations about this important matter and expect these fruitful discussions in the fullness of time to become the subject of a treaty, which we will sign in due course.' There's not a lot of substance here from which to derive reassurance.

It was no surprise to see the World Court ignoring the poor man's submissions. The Court was quick to point out that the nuclear nations involved had been called upon for decades to disarm these weapons of mass destruction and had failed to do so. The Court did not go into the issue that the USA, the UK and France, in order to get around the test ban treaties and all other legal requirements to stop inflicting the threat of nuclear winter upon the earth, have developed the National Ignition Facility in the Nevada desert. This military installation is paid for by those three nations and is there to explode tiny nuclear weapons that release radiation clouds the size of real mushrooms. The idea is then, using super-computers linked to environmental projection programs, to 'extrapolate' the effects so that real-world consequences can be predicted. To my mind this is not only the height of legal arrogance but is a blatant disregard of all that international humanitarian law has striven to achieve in the cause of protecting humankind from dictators.

As his parting shot, Sir Nicholas said that the position under international law was clear: there was no prohibition against either the 'use' or 'the threat of use' of nuclear weapons. No customary law or treaty actually banned these weapons and no judge had ever ruled them to be illegal. Five years later this was exactly the line taken by Duncan Menzies QC (now Lord Menzies) in Scotland during the hearing before the Scottish Supreme Court. However, what this line of argument ignores is that the opposite is also true. No treaty has ever, as a matter of law, specifically approved nuclear weapons nor have the methods of threatening humankind used in their deployment ever been given lawful authority. So it was quite appropriate for the World Court to reject all of what Sir Nicholas said. And that's just what happened.

10

The Judgement of the World Court

International law is the greatest idea mankind has ever had. Its purpose is to civilise the global community by ensuring the most basic of principles amongst human beings: that all over the world 'right' prevails over 'might'. To that end it searches for more and more fundamental ideas with which to unify us and seeks to apply these ideas universally.

The greatest weakness of international law is that it is made and operated by humans who run individual countries. These humans have been warring with one another over the way lives are lived ever since humans crawled out of the sea and began to organise the space round about them. Against the millennial span of humankind's presence on earth, international law can be thought of as being about five minutes old and a tiny part of the sum total of human development. However, let us imagine an enormous dinosaur named 'might over right', with a tiny wart on the top of the brain. That wart is humankind's secret weapon that ought to ensure people do not go the way of the dinosaurs. That weapon is of course 'the power of reason'.

We know that the most basic human instinct is to *survive*. However, in life we all make mistakes, particularly mistakes of judgement, which occasionally place us in peril. But if we were starting the last 60 years over again would we really place ourselves in peril of blasting off weapons that could easily poison the oceans for thousands of years or knock the planet out of orbit? Professor Hindsight would say we would not, but his great failing is that he only exists in the future.

So because international humanitarian law is so important it may surprise you to learn that no law student ever need pass an examination in it. It's just not required in order to be able to practise law. Indeed many law students don't even need to understand the vital distinction between the *law* and the *laws*. The former is an intellectual construction whilst the latter is simply a written list. The *law* begins with a decision by a community that 'right' is preferable to 'might'. The *laws* are the rules written down by that society, such as prohibiting murder or driving above the speed limit. You could say that the law is the rule (*why* we do or don't do certain things) and the *laws* regulate us (*how* we do or don't do things).

The great Roman law scholar Gaius reduced all legal control to three constituents: persons, things and actions. By that he meant that, for civilisation to advance, all living creatures, including those entities created by people, like governments, and all pieces of property in the country or even empire, are subject to legal action, that is to say legal control. The main thing is that good ideas are written down and applied over and over to new situations like running a country after a war or the operation of a satellite television company.

Given the importance of international humanitarian law I hope you will agree that the greatest task ever taken on by anyone on behalf of others must be to sit on the World Court. To decide not only about person versus person or corporation versus corporation but state against state, even groups of states like NATO versus the Soviet bloc. Neither Pharaohs nor emperors knew what that was like. Such power is comparable to the omnipotent, albeit mythical, power of the gods of the ancient world.

Who therefore would have blamed the judges of the World Court if they had said, 'You are asking us if one way of life on earth, let's say a vaguely Christian notion of how we should live, is preferable to say, Islam, or whether capitalism is preferable to egalitarianism. If more than half of the people on the planet want it one way and are prepared to risk a nuclear winter to get it, then who are we to stop them? Have your nuclear weapons and do your worst with them. We are mere lawyers. Now let me go home.' With the label 'democracy' slapped on to that speech, some people might just shrug and say, 'Yes, that seems democratic. Problem solved.'

But it is not 'problem solved'. That superficial analysis ignores the fundamental good idea I mentioned above, that is, continuous civilisation: not just for now, but for all time coming. The superficial would be wrong to say that whatever the majority want, they can have. If the majority of shareholders in a corporation want to dissolve their company then that is fine but when the very survival of the species is at stake we need to think a little more deeply. And that is precisely what the World Court judges did.

It is worth reminding ourselves of the question the UN asked the World Court. It wasn't very long or even very complicated, but it allowed for speculation as opposed to doing what courts usually do: establish the facts and apply the relevant law. The question was, 'Is the threat or use of nuclear weapons in any circumstances permitted under International Law?'

Next it is worth a moment or two to tease out the bits. We understand 'International Law'. We also know what nuclear weapons are. The terms 'threat' and 'use' also present us with little difficulty. Threats come first from having such weapons, then from having the secretary of state for defence (George Robertson) using platforms like the Westminster Parliament to talk up the weapons' devastating effects should anyone 'mess with us' and lastly from directing attention to such weapons in circumstances of international conflict, like during the Gulf War or the height of the war in Kosovo. Happily we have no real-life conception of what the word 'use' really means in this context. That leaves us with the phrase 'any circumstances permitted', and that's where the lawyers come piling in.

For the 'permitted' part we have to turn to the task of looking up the whole law on the subject to see what is and is not 'permitted' under international law. Then we turn to what we are dealing with to see if any of it is permitted under the laws we now have in front of us. Easy, really. 'Nothing to this international law stuff,' I hear you say. Well, as you have come to expect, it's not so easy.

The problem is with that word 'any'. How was the Court to know what all the possible circumstances were in which 'threat' or 'use' may be employed at the time it answered the question? It did get some input from the submissions of each country before it sat down to consider its answer to the question. But, as you will recall, these were not always useful. Remember our friend Sir Nicholas? If the World Court had followed his advice the judges would have been taking 'the early bath', as they say in football circles. There were no helpful lists from the Internet entitled, 'All the ways to threaten or use a nuclear weapon' or 'Circumstances in which using your nuclear weapon will be legal under international law'.

Furthermore, to embark upon an analysis of specific scenarios, like the British responding to a rogue state, would have been to fall into the abyss. Why? Because there is no end to that road and in any event it might have led the judges into criticising some particular nations for particular acts or omissions, and there is already a legal remedy for those things. It's litigation, and litigation was not the Court's business on this occasion. So that's where the speculation comes in.

You will also have noticed that the word 'Trident' does not appear in the UN's question. Nor does the word 'Delta' referring to the Delta 5 warheads that Trident carries. However, these can easily be implied as part of the whole body of 'nuclear weapons' available in the world, but not all of it. The judges also had another problem. They were aware of the existence of experimental nuclear weapons and the tiny nuclear weapons in the Nevada desert.

I'm sure you see their problem. The judges just couldn't draw a line and say, 'We'll answer the question up to here and no further.' This was the World Court being asked by the UN for guidance and that doesn't happen every day. It took over 10 years to get the question to The Hague in the first place. To answer the question partially would have been of little use to anyone. Even Sir Nicholas's suggestion would have been better than a partial answer.

So, with that task before them, the judges of the World Court couldn't be what they try their whole professional careers to be: they could not be 'objective'. Neither could they rely on any particular law with certainty because they had no real factual basis upon which to proceed. In other words, they had to do what lawyers are taught to detest – they had to enter the arena of the abstract.

To keep some grip of reality the World Court focused on the biggest factor that makes nuclear weapons like Trident illegal under international law. Since we started to make laws about war, a clear distinction has been drawn between soldiers and civilians. We hear a lot about that nowadays but it is not a modern idea. The Romans did it a lot, though not all the time. The idea is that 'battle lines' are drawn and both sides know whom and what they can target and what they can't. Most people now agree that to target civilians is an uncivilised thing to do. You may be surprised to learn that there has in fact been an international law against wantonly killing civilians since the late 19th century. It was made in St Petersburg and remains the law to this day.

The whole idea of protecting civilians is summed up in the term 'discrimination'. Basically, if a weapon is so massive that when used the effects do not discriminate between military and civilian people and property then that weapon is described in international law as a 'massive' weapon. Another way of measuring whether something is massive or not is to measure its capability for destruction. Put the two together and you have a 'weapon of mass destruction', a phrase with which, unfortunately, we are all too familiar these days.

The next big rule of international law that the World Court kept in mind is the rule on 'proportionality'. Again the idea is to keep a legal restriction on warring nations so that, as far as possible, events do not escalate into all-out conflict spreading to other nations. International law does not leave countries defenceless. Far from it. If attacked, any country has the legal right to defend itself. There is absolutely no question about that. But if country A is attacked on its north-eastern border by country B with its marines and rocket launchers, country A cannot legally carpet-bomb the whole of country B with kilotons of high explosives.

We can see that there are two things that are illegal about the response of country A. First, its carpet-bombing is indiscriminate, landing on everything and everyone in country B. Second, the carpet-bombing is out of proportion to what country A is suffering. If the attack is by say a dozen marines and three rocket launchers and the country under attack is the size of Russia or China, then the attack is little more than a fleabite and could be contained without resort to breaching international law with a 'massive' response.

Here I think it is worth recording the exact wording of what the World Court had to say about territorial integrity, forcing another state to follow certain economic paths and the principles of proportionality and self-defence.

46. Certain States asserted [before the Court sat to consider its answer] that the use of nuclear weapons in the conduct of reprisals would be lawful. The Court does not have to examine, in this context, the question of armed reprisals in time of peace, which are considered to be unlawful. Nor does it have to pronounce on the question of belligerent reprisals save to observe that in any case any right of recourse to such reprisals would, like self-defence, be governed [amongst other laws] by the principle of proportionality.

47. In order to lessen or eliminate the risk of unlawful attack, States sometimes signal that they possess certain weapons to use in self-defence against any State violating their territorial integrity or political independence. Whether a signalled intention to use force if certain events occur is or is not a 'threat' [under international law] depends upon various factors. If the envisaged use of force is itself unlawful, the stated readiness to use it would be prohibited [under international law]. Thus it would be illegal for a State to threaten force to secure territory from another State, or to cause it to follow or not follow certain political or economic paths. The notions of 'threat' and 'use' of force stand together in the sense that if the use of force itself in a given case is illegal – for whatever reason – the threat to use such force will likewise be illegal. In short, if it is to be lawful, the declared readiness of a State to use force must be a use of force that is in conformity with [international law]. For the rest, no State – whether or not it defended the policy of deterrence – suggested to the Court that it

would be lawful to threaten to use force if the force contemplated would be illegal.

48. Some States put forward the argument that possession of nuclear weapons may indeed justify an inference of preparedness to use them. In order to be effective, the policy of deterrence, by which those States possessing or under the [protective] umbrella of nuclear weapons seek to discourage military aggression by demonstrating that it will serve no purpose, necessitates that the intention to use nuclear weapons be credible. Whether this is a 'threat' contrary to [international law] depends upon whether the particular use of force envisaged would be directed against the territorial integrity or political independence of a State, or against the Purposes of the UN or whether, in the event that it were intended as a means of defence, it would necessarily violate the principles of necessity and proportionality. In any of these circumstances the use of force, and the threat to use it, would be unlawful under [international law].

What the World Court is getting at here is the idea that say, Britain, cannot hide behind its nuclear weapons by simply saying 'Aha, we only have them in case we are attacked, in which case we'll use them in self-defence.' We are back to the fleabite again whereby Britain could not legally use its nuclear weapons against the attacker because Trident, due to its massive and indiscriminate effects, at the very least breaches the international laws of discrimination and proportionality.

Whilst we are on the subject of proportionality a little must be said about so-called 'small-scale clean-strike' or 'tactical' nuclear weapons. Some states argued that relatively small nuclear weapons could be used without causing the kind of 'collateral damage' to civilians and domestic property that, say, Trident would be bound to cause because of its weapons' massive scale. They argue that it would be possible to use such a nuclear weapon, say, on a ship in the middle of the ocean without breaking international humanitarian law. So such a weapon must be legal.

The counter-argument is that there was no evidence before the World Court that such a weapon even exists. Moreover, even if it did, there is the risk, first, that using it would escalate the conflict into full-scale nuclear war and second, that any nuclear explosion would cause unacceptably high amounts of damage to the sea and atmosphere. Last, in these days of pinpoint-accurate conventional weapons, using a nuclear weapon is a breach of the international humanitarian law of proportionality. So using one of these weapons would, in fact, be illegal.

The World Court obviously regarded the arguments that 'You can't apply the Geneva Conventions, which are designed to save the world from the horrors of another world war, to our nice, new, shiny nuclear weapons' and 'We promise we'll only use little nuclear weapons in remote places' as a source of irritation. So it dug in a little deeper and said:

78. In conformity with the aforementioned principles, humanitarian law, at a very early stage, prohibited certain types of weapons either because of their indiscriminate effect on combatants and civilians or because of the unnecessary suffering caused to combatants, that is to say, a harm greater than that unavoidable to achieve legitimate military objectives. If an envisaged use of weapons would not meet the requirements of humanitarian law, a threat to engage in such use would also be contrary to that law.

79. It is undoubtedly because a great many rules of humanitarian law applicable in armed conflict are so fundamental to the respect of the human person and 'elementary considerations of humanity' as the Court put it in its Judgement of 9 April 1949 in the *Corfu Channel* case, that The Hague and Geneva Conventions have enjoyed broad accession. Further, these fundamental rules are to be observed by all States whether or not they have ratified the conventions that contain them, because they constitute intransgressible principles of international customary law.

80. The Nuremberg International Military Tribunal has already found in 1945 that the humanitarian rules included in the Regulations annexed to the Hague Convention IV of 1907 'were recognised by all civilised nations and were regarded as being declaratory of the laws and customs of war'. (International Military Tribunal at Nuremberg, Trials of the Major War Criminals 14 November 1945 – 1 October 1946)

Heady stuff, I'm sure you will agree. From a legal point of view there is one word in paragraph 79 that we seldom, if ever, see elsewhere in the law. It is that word 'intransgressible'. In that paragraph the World Court was on the subject of war and breaches of the code of neutrality. Now please remember that we don't have formal declarations of war any more. In those circumstances, what clearer message could the World Court send than to say that, during times of conflict, no state, anywhere, any time or in any way, may transgress the laws of humanity?

Then the World Court did something quite surprising. It repeated itself. Repetition is frowned upon in legal circles as being unnecessary and a sign that the point repeated is masking the weakness of the rest of the argument. I'm sure you've come across the same sort of thing yourself. There is a shouting match at home or in somebody else's home. One party is shouting that he or she is insulted or owed something by the other. The other party simply shrugs and quietly rebuts the claim by saying that no insult was meant or that for some good reason nothing is owed. The shouting party ignores what is quietly said and shouts his or her point again. And again. And so on. Well, being practised at stating our cases, we don't shout in court and we don't repeat ourselves.

What was so surprising was that the World Court did not repeat itself once. It did it twice. The World Court first (at paragraph 81 of its judgement) saw fit to remind everyone that the report of the secretary-general of the UN discussing Security Council Resolution 808 (1993), with which he introduced the statute of the international tribunal for the prosecution of persons responsible for serious violations of international humanitarian law committed in the territory of the former Yugoslavia since 1991, and which was unanimously approved by the Security Council, stated: 'In the view of the Secretary-General, the application of the principle *nullum crimen sine lege* [there is no crime which is not covered by the law] requires that the international tribunal should apply rules of International Humanitarian Law which are beyond any doubt part of customary [international] law.'

Then second (at paragraph 85), just in case anyone was in any doubt about the applicability of international humanitarian law to nuclear weapons, the World Court reinforced the point. It said:

> Turning now to the applicability of the principles of Humanitarian Law to a possible threat or use of nuclear weapons, the Court notes that doubts in this respect have sometimes been voiced on the ground that these principles and rules had evolved *prior* to the invention of nuclear weapons and that the Conferences of Geneva of 1949 and 1974–77 which respectively adopted the four Geneva Conventions of 1959 and the two Additional Protocols thereto did not deal with nuclear weapons specifically. Such views, however, are only held by a small minority. In the view of the vast majority of States as well as writers there can be no doubt as to the applicability of Humanitarian Law to nuclear weapons.

I emphasised the word 'prior' to highlight that, although nuclear weapons were clearly used in 1945 in Hiroshima and Nagasaki, the principles and rules that went into the Geneva Conventions after the war were worked out many years before, the earliest being in the 19th century. That passage was the Court being kind to that tiny group of states (guess who?) that argued that nuclear weapons were not in the contemplation of those who drafted the principles and rules of international humanitarian law. So when the nations of the world sat down in Geneva to save humankind from the horrors of another world war by applying these principles and rules, these could not apply to nuclear weapons. Have you ever heard anything so daft?

I have. Absurdity is the last resort of the desperate lawyer. It is one thing to construct a logical argument, however remote it may be from serving the people whom it will affect. It is quite another thing to suggest such a daft idea and (conveniently) forget the purpose of the law, which is fundamentally about providing justice to the community that decided it wanted 'right' over 'might'.

So there we have it: the World Court stating on numerous occasions in the same passage that international humanitarian law applies to nuclear weapons and that such laws are 'intransgressible'.

The World Court decided, despite the protests of Sir Nicholas, that it would issue a judgement. However, before rushing to pronounce on this or that, the judges unanimously took the opportunity to remind all states that have nuclear weapons of their legal obligations to the UN and the rest of the world to speed up the negotiations to rid the world of these terrible devices.

Then the Court, which was down to 14 members due to the ill health of one judge, got down to the real stuff: the judgement.

THE COURT,

A. By thirteen votes to one, Decides to comply with the request for an advisory opinion.

B. Unanimously says: There is in neither customary nor conventional International Law any comprehensive and universal prohibition of the threat or use of nuclear weapons as such.

C. Unanimously says: A threat or use of force by means of nuclear weapons that is contrary to Article 2, para 4, of the United Nations Charter and that fails to meet all the requirements of Article 51, is unlawful.

D. Unanimously says: A threat or use of nuclear weapons should also be compatible with the requirements of the International Law applicable in armed conflict, particularly those of the principles and rules of International Law, as well as with specific obligations under treaties and other undertakings which expressly deal with nuclear weapons.

E. By seven votes to seven, the President's casting vote: It follows from the above-mentioned requirements that the threat or use of nuclear weapons would generally be contrary to the rules of International Law applicable in armed conflict, and in particular the principles and rules of Humanitarian Law:

However, in view of the current state of International Law, and of the elements of fact at its disposal, the Court cannot conclude definitively whether the threat or use of nuclear weapons would be lawful or unlawful in an extreme circumstance of self-defence, in which the very survival of a state would be at stake.

IN FAVOUR: President Bedjaoui, Judges Ranjeva, Herczegh, Shi, Fleischhauer, Vereshchetin, Ferrari Bravo.

AGAINST: Vice-President Schwebel, Judges Oda, Guillaume, Shahabuddeen, Weeramantry, Koroma, Higgins.

F. Unanimously says: There exists an obligation to pursue in good faith and bring to a conclusion negotiations leading to nuclear disarmament in all its aspects under strict and effective international control.

Big stuff, indeed. The most controversial of these judgements is of course (E) where the votes were tied. We just do not know how the vote would have gone had the Court been up to its normal 15 members. What we do know is that the President, Judge Bedjaoui, said in a note he appended to the judgement that the ruling was not to be seen as a 'door half-open to the nuclear States'. In fact, quite the opposite. The Court's last word was to remind the nuclear states of their obligations to 'bring to a conclusion' the negotiations on nuclear disarmament. Against that background, the door was decidedly to be seen as half-closed.

Well, we began this chapter with enigma and some may say, given the split vote, that we end it there too. I disagree. The World Court was careful to outlaw anything done in anger, whether threat or use, that breaches the 'intransgressible' laws of humanity. That in itself is a huge step forward for humankind. Then there is the ruling that threat or use of nuclear weapons would only be lawful under international law in the most extreme circumstances imaginable. So threatening other nations with Trident's weapons of unimaginable mass destruction in protection of, for instance, oil interests, is absolutely illegal under international law. That is another great stride forward. Furthermore, even within the split vote, the judges are careful to insert that 'the threat or use of nuclear weapons would *generally* [my emphasis] be contrary to the rules of International Law... and in particular the principles and rules of Humanitarian Law'.

That leaves one remote circumstance in which threat or use of a nuclear weapon would be legal – 'where the very survival of a state would be at stake'. The World Court did not tell us whether it meant

'State' as a geographic piece of land, the political institutions or the people who live in it. However, any way round, it would *always* be illegal under international humanitarian law to use a weapon that was incapable of discriminating between soldiers and civilians and does unnecessary harm to soldiers. So turning to Trident, we can clearly see the World Court saying that any use of even one of its massive indiscriminate warheads would be illegal under international humanitarian law. We know that if use of such a weapon would be illegal then so is the threat to use it. Done deal. Trident must be illegal at all times. The World Court says so.

THREE

AROUND THE WORLD IN 80 CASES

II

That Sinking Feeling

Justice is not automatic. It has to be won. Sometimes hard won. It doesn't matter how much law you have on your side, nor where you happen to be in the world, to bring a recalcitrant person, organisation or government around to your way of thinking you have to win your case in court. The Parliament at Westminster is a court and I've also seen a court function in a mud hut. The Scottish Land Court once convened on a hillside in the Highlands with a very suspicious crofter barricaded inside his house (croft) shouting his answers to counsel's questions out through the letter box. The judge, who was standing in his overcoat and heavy country brogues, having heard the man, then made a ruling without actually laying eyes on him. So you see, courts come in all shapes and sizes. What you don't see is that courts also come in an equally wide range of quality.

Criminal trials are conducted through 'adversarial procedure', that is, the two sides are presumed to be adverse to each other's point of view. The prosecution says the accused is 'guilty' whilst the defence says 'not guilty'. This leads to what the lawyers of ancient Rome called 'litis contestasio' (litigation as contest) and, indeed, what the best criminal advocates do in court is positively gladiatorial. In Scotland, it is the prosecutor who decides in which court a particular case will be called. In the case of The Trident Three there was no question that their case would be shoved in amongst a pile of manila folders, glanced at quickly over a lunchtime sandwich by an overworked parochial junior procurator fiscal depute (prosecutor). Oh no, it was Crown counsel in Edinburgh who 'marked' their case and I imagine it must have been a difficult one.

Over the previous 10 years or so, there had been hundreds of summary prosecutions, usually in Helensburgh District Court, for minor offences involving Trident-related protests. These in the main were petty breaches of the peace. You know the kind of thing: singing at busloads of workers going into Coulport naval base, chaining oneself to the gates or the fences, and even praying for those inside. Yes, believe it or not, praying can be a crime in Scotland if you happen to be doing it outside a naval base and obviously asking God to intervene on the side of peace. By praying in those circumstances the peace is breached, and that's a crime. So there in the august chambers of the Lord Advocate of Scotland the decision had to be made. Which court do we put these women in?

Because of the value of the damage to MoD property that the Crown was trying to prove (nearly £100,000), there was no question but that, if convicted, the three women faced a sentence far more severe than the few months in jail that any sheriff, sitting without a jury, could impose. So it had to be a jury court. In Scotland we have two jury courts: the sheriff and jury courts, which can sentence up to three years, and the High Court of Justiciary, where the sentence is unlimited. Given the background of the women waiting on board *Maytime* to be caught and leaving printed material for the police and staff to see, it was clear that they wanted to bring as much awareness about Trident to the public attention as possible. So for the prosecution to put them in the High Court was playing into the hands of the whole peace movement on the publicity issue. To put them in the sheriff court with a jury would risk them getting a sentence far less than they 'deserved'.

As you might expect, the Scottish criminal justice system has a way out of this dilemma. It lies in a little-used mechanism that allows the sheriff to send a convicted accused to the High Court for sentence. So the Crown could get out of playing into the women's hands by putting them for trial in a sheriff court. Also, because the 'crime' was committed in the remote West Highlands, the sheriff court into which they were placed for trial would be in the sleepy town we visited earlier: Dunoon.

Bingo! Being remote from the big cities of Glasgow and Edinburgh would ensure that the trial passed off with as little fuss as possible. There was only one problem the Crown hadn't foreseen. It was that these women had their trial well planned in advance. They had a list of expert witnesses as long as your arm ready and waiting to come to Scotland to give evidence about Trident for as long as it took. They also had many piles of A4 documents about a metre high standing ready and waiting to lodge with the clerk of court as defence productions.

Now clerks of court are civil servants and anyone who has ever tried to challenge the decision of a civil servant knows what that means. When the clerk of Dunoon Sheriff Court saw the mountains of materials coming into his court he pulled the plug on the prosecution. Well, at least he pulled the plug on the Crown bringing its case in Dunoon Sheriff Court. The single courtroom would be swamped for weeks. No other cases could be dealt with and the appeals resulting from that scenario could just not be allowed to happen. There was no option. It would have to be the mainland and that meant the nearest court to the locus of the 'crime' – Greenock.

So while these procedural shenanigans were weaving their tangled web I was left in the Advocates' Library in Edinburgh with the unenviable task of putting the defence case together. The Faculty of Advocates takes enormous pride in the materials it keeps in its law library. It has books from the pre-Reformation of Scotland. It is the legal depository in Scotland so it gets everything published from everywhere. It has all the British Commonwealth law reports and acres of space devoted to European law on everything from tax to termites in buildings. And it has a fantastic library staff of very highly qualified and equally helpful people. So, a few white slips to be completed, a few computer locations and a squint at a few encyclopaedias ought to dredge up some kind of defence, mustn't it?

In every criminal case the prosecution has to do two things. It has to establish, beyond reasonable doubt, first that a crime was committed and second that the accused did the crime. In the serenity of the library I looked at the indictment and the statements of my client and quietly sniggered at the audacity of the raid. Eyebrows were raised and one or two coughed but no one actually said anything to me about this questionable conduct.

In our joint consultation at Cornton Vale jail the women had been adamant: no tactics on their behalf. Nothing was to be done that might distract the court from the central issue – the legality of deploying Trident in order to threaten millions of people around the world with annihilation. I respected their wishes but could not help feeling that the women could well be convicted and sent to the High Court for sentence – and that meant jail, for a very long time. However, against that background and in all professional responsibility, I could hardly claim that this was, for instance, a case of mistaken identity. There was just no question of the Crown witnesses getting a fleeting glance at a man running from a bank pulling off a Tony Blair mask. There was no argument that the women broke into *Maytime*. No question that they threw the Defence Evaluation Research Agency's anechoic testing computers into the dark depths of Loch Goil, one by one. No question that these computers were damaged beyond repair and very little argument over how much these might cost to replace. What I had to come up with was something a bit more subtle than a Tony Blair mask.

I said earlier that I was delighted to see my learned friend John McLaughlin appearing at the jail to represent Ellen Moxley, and I was. Angie always represents herself. As I began to read the mountains of defence papers it quickly became obvious that a few library slips would not do the trick. To mount a defence of 'We were not committing a crime, we were involved in *crime prevention* – namely the British government's planning, preparation or initiation of a war of aggression, wanton destruction of civilian populations and their cities, towns and villages, etc', I needed some help. Luckily those lawyers around the world who have been involved in peace campaigns since ever we needed them are very approachable and helpful people. I had sent out an open e-mail to the effect that I was instructed in this case and would anyone who had run similar defences in other countries please get in touch. For a while there was stony silence but then an e-mail came through from the World

Court Project. What these people didn't know about the law and practice of all the US states, England, New Zealand, etc would not fill the back of a bus ticket.

But there was one problem. They were all Anglo-American thinkers. The more I read from those lawyers the more I knew their kind assistance would lead me into trouble in a Scottish court. All of the charges on the indictment were Scottish common law charges. There wasn't a breach of statute amongst them and that meant no convenient pegs on which to hang arguments used in the English or US courts. At that moment I was at the lowest emotional point I had reached so far. We come to the Scottish Bar to do big cases and in all big criminal cases there are emotional moments. Indeed, our top criminal QCs tell those training for the Bar (called 'devils') that if they stop becoming nervous and excited about appearing in the criminal courts, then it's time to pack it in and go and sell houses or something. Then, as usual, things got worse.

The word had spread around the library like wildfire that these women had put the security of NATO at risk and, with that, the whole world. Over morning coffee in our splendid reading room I heard Angie, Ulla and Ellen described as everything from lunatics to victims of PMT. I approached a few members of Faculty asking if they were interested in coming into the trial. I was not prepared for the shock of hearing the venomous personal reactions of some of my fellow advocates. For the first time since I was called to the Bar I felt isolated amongst colleagues in my belief that everyone is entitled to a defence and that only by applying that principle to its maximum extent can any civilised society claim it has the moral and legal rights to convict and punish one of its own citizens. These were dark days indeed.

My instructing solicitor, Matthew Berlow, was in almost constant touch with Ulla so I knew that being on the remand wing of a Scottish prison whilst awaiting trial was a lonely, frightening experience for this courageous Danish woman whose only intention was to rid the world of nuclear weapons. It was no better for Ellen or Angie, though Angie had done it before in England. In the course of preparing the defence I would sometimes walk around Arthur's Seat, the hill in the centre of Edinburgh, and recall the day's reading. Was there an argument that…? Was there a better argument that…? The charges contained the key phrase 'you did wilfully and maliciously damage'. I couldn't argue away the 'wilful' part. But what about the 'malicious' part? Anyone (anyone with an open mind, that is) who has ever met these women would agree that there is not a malicious bone in any of them. Well, that may be all right in the coffee shops and churches, but in court, as I said at the outset, you have to win your case using evidence and mechanisms like 'legal presumption' and 'onus of proof'. Not so easy when you're up against the military and legal establishments.

I would go into Parliament House each morning with the sole aim of achieving an acquittal. Nothing else could be allowed to cloud that issue. All political and media scrutiny had to be avoided because none of it was any use in court. Happily, each morning I was greeted by our senior librarian, Andrea Longson, with the day's tomes on international law, Protocol this, Treaty Ratification that. It was all a bit daunting, to say the least. Then, at the bottom of a box of papers, I found something that would begin to make the wind blow the other way. I was still alone in the case and my research was taking me to more and more obscure laws from more and more obscure places. But this crumpled bundle of papers told me something I did not know, but perhaps should have known. It was the name at the top of the front page that caught my eye – Lord Murray. The next thing to catch my eye was the title of this piece. At first I hadn't noticed it because the paper looked like, and indeed was, a retype of an article from a learned journal. The syntax looked awry and the paragraphing was too bulky to be a learned piece of legal sculpture. But all that didn't matter. It was the title that jumped out at me – 'Nuclear Weapons and the Law'.

I remember Lord Murray as a snow-white-haired judge with the sharpest of legal minds and a deep Scottish voice untainted by his time in Oxford and high government office. He also had a pleasing manner on the bench. I never once saw him berate junior counsel nor lose his temper, as so often happens in the Scottish Supreme Court nowadays. As

Ronald King Murray he took a first in philosophy from Oxford. Then he got his law degree. He was called to the Scottish Bar in 1953 and became a QC in 1967. A career in politics saw him become Member of Parliament for Leith from 1970 to 1979. In 1974 he became a Privy Counsellor and was Lord Advocate of Scotland from 1974 to 1979. Thereafter he was elevated to the Supreme Court Bench in Scotland (that is, became a senator of the College of Justice), often sitting as chairman of the Scottish High Court of Criminal Appeal. He is now retired but without question remains one of the best Scottish legal minds of the 20th century, so I couldn't help but wonder what his name was doing on a ragged piece of paper beside a lot of well-intentioned but legally irrelevant materials supplied by the clients.

I scanned this coffee-stained and badly stapled bundle of papers and could not believe what I was reading. If what I had in my hand was in any way accurate, it appeared that Lord Murray had delivered a lecture to a massed audience in Oxford Town Hall in 1998 entitled 'Nuclear Weapons and The Law'. But that sinking feeling came back as I turned to the back page. No footnotes. No references. Not even a precise date. Nothing to indicate that this wasn't a bootleg paper cobbled together by some well-meaning Trident Ploughshares 2000 pledger or supporter who might have pasted together the bits of Lord Murray's lecture that suited the cause and left out the nasty bits – like where to find the law that says Trident is actually perfectly legal and the British government can therefore legally sail it in and out of the deep waters of the West Highlands of Scotland, or anywhere else for that matter, any time it likes.

I read the paper. No question about it. This was a bootleg. Even the spelling left a lot to be desired. So no. It almost certainly had little or nothing to do with Lord Murray. My sinking feeling changed to one of being hopelessly sunk. I got up and did a 'walk'. That is, I walked up and down the length of our ancient and very grand Parliament Hall trying to figure out why someone would bootleg something like this. Surely, if the intention was to use it in the lowest courts (Helensburgh District), any judge or even an overworked parochial junior procurator fiscal depute would see straight through this 'reconstruction' – or whatever it was.

I read it again, this time concentrating more on the legal scheme than on the typing mistakes and coffee stains. The legal logic made excellent sense. Much better sense than could be cobbled together by anyone who had not studied the subject matter for some considerable time. And also, what, I wondered, could be the counter-argument that was left out? I was intrigued and was (to stretch my metaphor) gaining some buoyancy to the point where I decided to do a bit of detective work.

I showed the thing to Andrea but she hadn't seen anything like it before. Without a frontispiece, a date or any other clue as to the source I decided to take the bull by the horns and make use of my status as a member of the College of Justice. I decided to phone Lord Murray. This was not just a case of looking up a number and dialling. Counsel do not ring up retired chairmen of the High Court of Criminal Appeal seeking help with preparation for a defence case. It's unheard-of. However, if my research so far had told me one thing it was that these were uncharted waters and, in any case, I would be the height of politeness and I only had one question – 'Sir, is this your work?'

I figured that if this was Lord Murray's work then I was on solid ground in seeking to lay my hands on an authentic copy of the text of the lecture. If Scottish advocates keep one thing in the forefront of their minds it is always to act with complete integrity. The courts and the public in Scotland demand nothing less and in us they are not disappointed. Where there is very occasionally any substance in a complaint, the Dean is swift to act. This was exactly what was going through my mind as I heard the ringing tone. The voice that answered with repetition of the number I had dialled was unmistakably that of Lord Murray. We address our judges off the Bench as sir, unless they happen to be your dad or some pal who has been elevated. In this case it was strictly by the book. I imagined myself appearing in front of him as I had done so many times before, and that made it a lot easier for me. But apparently not for him.

'Do stop calling me sir. I'm retired, so please use my first name,' he said with a real softness. 'I think you are John, aren't you?'

'Yes, sir.'

'Do stop…'

When I got the hang of addressing him informally we got down to business. Yes, he had delivered such a lecture and yes, he was aware not only of Trident Ploughshares 2000 but also that they couldn't afford to buy many copies of the published article, so they typed some out themselves.

Published article? 'Yes, you'll find it in the *Journal of Medicine Conflict and Survival*, Volume 15 (1999).' I couldn't believe it.

'What are the counter-arguments, the bits left out by the Trident Ploughshares typist?' I asked.

'Oh, they don't do that kind of thing, you know. Far too honest. No, if I know them they will have tried to type the thing out as accurately as possible. No, I'm pretty sure it will all be there.'

I will go into Lord Murray's conclusions and how he arrived at them in the trial section of the book later on, but for now suffice it to say that his conclusions were fully on our side. Yippee. I had the international law part of my defence. Now all I had to do was flesh that out with good old Scots criminal law and the picture would be complete. Alas, you've guessed it; it wasn't that simple.

When I got off the phone with 'himself', I arranged for Matthew to ring Jane Tallents, one of the Scottish Trident Ploughshares core group organisers. She was our point of contact outside Cornton Vale prison and was in daily touch with the clients. I wanted to know whether the substance of this essay, as I was now calling it, had ever been used in the lower courts. Apparently it had, but only by activists who represented themselves before being fined the usual £30 (never paid) and sent on their way. The local volunteer magistrates (often retired bank managers and the like who are on the local council) simply pooh-poohed the argument and explained to the pledgers that international humanitarian law did not apply in the town of Helensburgh. That was news to me but I was getting the picture. No one at local court level was listening to this argument. I smiled quietly to myself and figured that, for the moment, that suited me fine.

The light showing where this defence was headed had well and truly dawned and it was time to 'get my ducks in a row', as US lawyers say. It was complicated by international humanitarian law and swathes of treaties, some in force and others not in force, but essentially this defence was simply one of self-defence, which includes defending others. The law has a special word for it – necessity. In other words it was necessary to do the damage in order to prevent a greater crime from happening or continuing.

Let's take an example of a child having fallen into a swollen stream. Now it may well surprise you to learn that in Scotland there is no legal obligation on anyone, including the parents of that child, to reach in and try to save the child from drowning. It is not that Scots law is intellectually backward or draconian in this respect. There are good reasons why this principle is also applied in many other countries around the world. The basis of the argument is that no one can be obliged by the law to put him- or herself in danger for another person, no matter how close a relative the person already in danger may be. If the law were otherwise, then parents and passers-by all over the world would be in jail for not going into burning buildings or swollen streams to rescue others and that would be preposterous. So there may be a moral obligation to get in there and do something but there cannot be a legal obligation, making it a crime not to help. However, if you do try to help by grabbing the passing child by the hair and, in the course of attempting to save it, you pull out some hair and perhaps damage an eye, in Scotland you are not guilty of assault because you had no intention to harm. Your intention was to save – and by any means possible in emergency circumstances. It follows that you could not be found guilty of wilfully and maliciously doing damage because, although you acted wilfully, you did not act maliciously.

As I began to look at previous cases from around the world of people acting out of necessity I was struck by just how undeveloped Scots law was to deal with the situation in this case. Our law only went so far as to cope with drunken drivers trying to get people to hospital and irate shopkeepers lashing out at robbers in an attempt to save their stock. The United States had a lot of cases, mainly arising out of the activities of the Lockheed Corporation, which makes parts for nuclear weapons. In some of these cases juries had given the peace protesters on trial a 'sympathy vote' but these were no use to me. There were also Dutch, German and Canadian cases but these were either too old or did not involve the same arguments that were now forming in my mind. The more I read the more I could see that the opportunity was lying in front of me to go for a legal first. I was after the big one – having an argument saying that deployment of Trident was illegal under international law and having that argument upheld by a judge who had reviewed the legal materials in order to reach that conclusion.

I will come to these arguments when we reach the dock in Greenock Sheriff Court. Suffice to say for the moment that new law would be made by this case. There was no doubt about it. What was concerning me was the legal route down which I would have to take the court for it to be made. I was reading material that sometimes seemed to be bang on point and sometimes seemed to be completely irrelevant. However, as with my research on that first Saturday night, what kept coming up from Web site after Web site, law book after law book, was one word – Nuremberg.

Time and again I saw the parallel being drawn between the kind of totalitarianism that nuclear weapons bring and the aspiration for a Nazi Third Reich. Total control. Ultimate power. Over everything and everyone. It made my blood run cold, so for comfort I turned to the famous words of Pastor Martin Niemoeller: 'When the SS came for the Communists I did not protest because I wasn't a Communist. When they came for the trade unionists I did not protest because I wasn't a trade unionist. When they came for the Jews I did not protest because I wasn't a Jew. Then they came for me and it was too late.'

Every day as I walked home from the Advocates' Library down the Royal Mile, through the glorious natural colours of Arthur's Seat and past the Salisbury Crags to Duddingston, I thought of Angie, Ulla and Ellen in jail. That caused me to hold my freedom very dearly indeed. And with each day's research I grew in confidence that this defence could be properly stated in court and, if successful, would be a truly awesome event.

Brothers in Arms

Bob Dylan was right. 'The times they are a changin'.' More accurately they have changed since Bob inspired the young of the world to think the unthinkable. Since the auspicious day when the first woman arrived and pitched camp at Greenham Common, the military authorities might have known it would not be military-trained, combat-clad, super-fit men but plumpish white-haired women who would get behind their battle lines and disarm the deadliest weapon ever invented. And, on 8 June 1999, so it proved. You may well ask, 'Didn't the Ministry of Defence see it coming?' Don't they monitor the efforts of the peace movement? Well, no actually, they didn't see it coming and they don't seem to monitor the world-wide efforts of the peace movement, the main reason being that each country is jealous of its own jurisdiction so there is no international task force winging e-mails about the movements to and from number 15 Barrland Street in Glasgow, for instance. It appears very much that to the nuclear nations there is no 'movement', just isolated incidents by a lot of lefties wearing pixie hats and tie-dyed T-shirts. Funny, isn't it? No one thinks of Earl Mountbatten or the US chief of staff wearing a pixie hat.

But there certainly is a world-wide movement working for nuclear peace, and Trident Ploughshares 2000 is only a small part of it. There are some countries, like New Zealand and Denmark, that wouldn't allow anything nuclear within a centimetre of their coastal waters. This is despite the best efforts of the French secret service to sink the

Greenpeace ship, *Rainbow Warrior*, whilst she lay in harbour in New Zealand, and the US navy's best attempt at sailing nuclear submarines through Danish waters after being expressly told that they could not. And we are not talking here about some kitchen-table letter sent in the vain hope that it would be read and acted upon by some senior official in the State Department. Denmark laid an official complaint about the incident in the UN during plenary session.

My research into the world-wide efforts of that nuclear protest movement often saw me working very late into the night, usually slumped in the Advocates' Library, being woken only by the sound of the night staff's industrial vacuum cleaner munching its way through acres of our finest Wilton. However, the smell of fresh polish on old hardwoods was always welcome. And once awake it was a swift return to whichever part of the world I had been visiting that night. What I mean of course is that once I had found the necessary casebooks from the particular part of the world that I happened to be focusing on that week, they had to be analysed for case reports that could be of use. This would not be a case of a retired bank manager sitting as a local magistrate and saying, 'You women and those who support you, many of whom I see again sitting in the public benches, are habitual offenders at the Coulport naval base. So I fine you £50 this time in the hope that this will be a lesson to you not to try this sort of thing again. That is all.'

My initial surprise that there were so many cases from so many countries over so many years soon dissipated as it became clear that there was little that I could apply directly to the case of The Trident Three. That was too bad because most of them were very interesting. So please hop aboard as I take you to these oases of nuclear peace.

I first figured that the United States was likely to be the place where my efforts might bear most fruit. And so it proved to be. What I was not expecting was just how long they had been applying the defence of necessity (ordinary people doing extraordinary things in times of imminent or constant danger). Let us keep in mind that an essential element of the defence of The Trident Three was to be that the UK's permanent deployment of Trident put the world in 'constant danger' of being incinerated or injured by nuclear explosion – either by accident or design. So that put the women in exactly the same position as someone attempting to save a child who had fallen into a swollen stream.

One of the United States' earliest such cases was in 1834, *United States* v *Ashton*, and involved a mutiny in circumstances where the ship's crew was justified in disobeying orders because they had a 'bona fide reasonable belief' that the ship was unseaworthy. The crewmen's evidence established in court that they were indeed in impending peril so they acted to prevent that peril. I was delighted. That was just the kind of thing I needed more of.

In 1810 another US case, again involving a ship, the *William Gray*, demonstrated the point very well. The Embargo Act banned the importation of certain goods. The captain and the owner of the *William Gray* were prosecuted for coming into port with exactly these goods aboard. The law was strict. There were no exceptions to the ban on importation, and that was that. The captain and the owner were allowed to lead evidence demonstrating that a severe storm had forced them into port and that such an act of saving life did not mean they were illegally 'importing' the goods at all. They were acquitted, but it was lucky for them they were on trial in the United States and not Scotland, where at that time the defence were not allowed to demonstrate anything.

As many people know, in 1853 a large fire threatened to burn down the then small town of San Francisco. A public official ordered the destruction of houses to create a firebreak and was subsequently sued by one of the unfortunate owners for his actions. The case (*Surroco* v *Geary*) went all the way to the California Supreme Court where the official's actions were upheld as proper because:

> The right to destroy property, to prevent the spread of a conflagration, has been traced to the highest law of Necessity and the natural rights of man, independent of society and the civil government. It is referred to by moralists and jurists as the same great principle that justifies the exclusive appropriation of a plank after a shipwreck, even though the life of another

be sacrificed… It rests upon the legal maxim 'Necessitas inducit privi-
legium quod jura privat' [Necessity leads to legal privileges].

I trust the point about necessity is making itself clear. Basically it is a
principle of law that protects those who act for the good of another or
many others, even if some other people's rights get trampled on in the
process. Those other people's rights can be their property rights. So what
this law does is create a hierarchy of rights. It puts saving human life
above someone else's right to protection of private property. I was really
getting somewhere with this. I saw immediately that the Scots law of
necessity applied to The Trident Three, but guess what? Scots law was
woefully inadequately developed to deal with three women destroying
the property of the Defence Evaluation Research Agency in order to
save the people of the world from extermination by nuclear weapons.
This was all good stuff and I was enjoying the exploits of the people
saving San Francisco, so I read on, into the modern age, glad to see that
the legal principle of necessity had found its way into the criminal statute
codes of 22 US states. My heart stopped. Only 22? What about the rest? I
am delighted to report that my heart started again when I read that the
rest do not restrict themselves to their own wording; they apply the
written statute codes of other states. Sheesh, that was a close one!

In the law we often use the mechanism of 'analogy' to flesh out the
bones of our arguments. In other words, if some line of argument holds
good in a number of legal areas then it has a good chance of survival in
one more. It was hard to keep a straight face when I got to the unfortunately named Mr Lovercamp and his case (*People* v *Lovercamp*). What
happened here was that Mr Lovercamp was in jail in California where he
was not having the easiest of times. In fact, to be serious, he was facing a
daily ritual of sexual abuse and other horrible physical attacks. He com-
plained to the prison authorities (anything coming back to you about
The Trident Three here?) but they ignored his plight and said he wasn't
in any danger. So he broke out of jail at the first opportunity.

The California Supreme Court was prepared to forgive his felony and
said:

Where there is no time to resort to the authorities or there is a history of futile complaints which makes any results from such a complaint illusory: and there is neither time nor opportunity to resort to courts: and the escape did not involve violence to another person: and the prisoner immediately reports to the authorities (on the outside) then he is acting out of necessity and cannot be guilty of the crime of jailbreaking.

Yippee. These were exactly the kind of circumstances in which The Trident Three found themselves. The constant danger from nuclear accident or strike; the World Court saying indiscriminate nuclear weapons were contrary to international humanitarian law; the history of complaint to the authorities; being ignored by those very authorities and taking remedial action by intervening to save themselves and others. I remember dropping my head on to the stack of big, infrequently used law books and saying under my breath, 'Aahh, if only we were on trial in California.'

With some basis for expectation I then turned to the US body of law on cases involving the principle of necessity in the nuclear age. These include cases about nuclear power plants as well as nuclear weapons, but the same laws apply, so I got to it.

The state of Oregon provided a good example of citizen intervention at the Trojan nuclear power plant. On 5 August 1977 a large group calling themselves the Trojan Decommissioning Alliance had had just about enough of complaining to the authorities about the dangers of this plant to the local people and many more much wider afield. They were also sick of being ignored by the state authorities and the futility of attempting to get legal remedies. So they took 'citizen intervention action' to try to shut the plant down. With several hundred people watching from the visitor centre, 82 people got into position outside the main gates, letting nothing in. It took two days to clear them and then charge them all with criminal trespass. At their trial the judge would not dismiss the prosecution on the legal ground that they had a legal right to do what they did, based on Oregon's 'choice of evils' statute. Neither would he allow the accused to lead expert evidence to demonstrate that the plant wasn't safe in a number of ways. However, the jury found that the protesters were not guilty on the ground that, after much investigation and complaining, they understood exactly why the plant was not safe and were not intending to do criminal damage; in fact they were intent on saving life and property.

Following the Oregon Trojan case, similar cases soon followed in Illinois, Wisconsin and California. In the latter the Rancho Seco facility was the subject of citizen intervention because the plant was built to exactly the same specifications as another plant in Pennsylvania with the resounding name of Three Mile Island, where in 1979 a failure in a nuclear reactor led to the release of radioactive water and gases, and thousands of people leaving the area.

Turning to the issue of preventing nuclear war and further nuclear weapons proliferation, I again found a wealth of material. Let's begin with *People* v *Aldridge*. What happened was that on 1 March 1979, the 25th anniversary of the Bikini hydrogen bomb test that contaminated Marshall Islanders and Japanese fishermen, more than 200 people assembled to prevent a 'grave harm' at Lockheed's naval industrial reserve ordnance plant in Sunnyvale, California. At that time the plant was the central management facility for the US Trident missile programme. Much of the design and manufacturing was also done there. Hundreds of citizens paraded a 560-foot-long Trident monster that was a replica of the real thing, made out of bamboo poles and hung with 408 black flags, being one for every hydrogen bomb on board the real thing.

Twenty-eight people carried the replica on to Lockheed property and were arrested. At their trial they raised a necessity defence but were not allowed to lead expert evidence about the dangers from Trident as a first-strike aggressive weapon. The case got complicated on appeal but I could see the pattern beginning to emerge. Few, if any, judges were independent-minded enough to uphold the laws against planning, preparing or initiating a war of aggression using weapons of mass destruction but they would allow the juries to acquit on those grounds because the public perception would be that the defendants got a 'sympathy vote'. This was worrying.

But hope was on the horizon. In *Commonwealth* v *Berrigan*, the so-called 'Ploughshares 8' trial, I was spirited to the early morning of 9 September 1981 when eight people got into the General Electric re-entry systems plant at King of Prussia, Pennsylvania, where nuclear warhead shells were made. Some of them carried blacksmith's hammers to make an attempt at bringing true the Old Testament prophecy of Isaiah that 'swords will be beaten into ploughshares and spears into pruning hooks'. The police hadn't heard of Isaiah and would have none of it, arrested and charged them with conspiracy, criminal mischief and burglary. How ironic is it that it is always the citizens who are trying to save the planet from the huge evil of a nuclear explosion who are charged with conspiracy and criminal actions, never those who are actually in control of such mass extermination? Ah well, that's life in the government for you.

At their trial the eight accused did not deny their actions but pleaded the Pennsylvania form of necessity, which is in their Justification Statutes 501, 503 and 510. The usual pattern at trial emerged. Yes, you've got it: the judge refused to allow them to lead expert testimony to demonstrate the danger… But this time the jury found all eight guilty. Oh no, I thought! Things are going into reverse here. However, help was at hand in the form of the State of Pennsylvania Appeal Court. Previous cases showed that people were not guilty of a crime where they caused damage during natural disasters. So what was different about this case?

On appeal the convictions of all eight were reversed for several reasons, including the appeal judges saying:

> [The judge in the trial court] seemed to say that to avail themselves of the defence, those on trial had to demonstrate that their actions could *totally* avert nuclear war. We will not hold them to such a burden. All [the appellants] have to do is show that their actions could *reasonably* have been thought necessary to avert a public disaster… Surely the use of the weapons, the components of which were damaged by the appellants, would cause a public disaster on the order of a 'conflagration, flood, earthquake or pestilence'.

Judge Spaeth added:

> Whenever a person pleads 'justification' for his actions the court should
> ask 'What value higher than the value of compliance with the law is the
> defendant asserting?' In this case the trial court failed to ask that question.
> Here the appellants are pleading the danger arising from nuclear missiles.
> One who does not understand that danger, does not understand the
> defendants' pleas. No peril is greater, indeed no peril even approaches the
> peril of nuclear war. It is in the light of this peril that the reasonableness of
> the appellants' belief must be judged.

Game, set and match to the Ploughshares 8 you may think. Well, as usual,
alas not. The California Supreme Court reversed the appeal court judgement and any lawyer worth his or her salt would understand why. The
appeal court judges were right to say that the defendants need not
demonstrate that their actions would *totally* avert nuclear war; no one
could say with any certainty that they would. However, they were wrong
to say that the simple exercise at trial is just to add up the factors in favour
of the action and those against and see which side weighs heaviest. That is
too simple an approach, too subjective and too open to sympathetic
manipulation. What the Ploughshares 8 needed was the opportunity to
present objective facts alongside their objective understanding of the situation and drive any reasonable judge or jury member to measure their
case against the law, international humanitarian law if need be. And they
were a long way from doing that.

A citizen intervention action that got closer to the objective approach
based on the government committing crimes under international law
was the *Winoosky 44* case from the state of Vermont. But it wasn't a
nuclear case. It involved US citizen intervention to prevent government-
approved atrocities in Central America. On Friday 23 March 1984, only a
few days prior to a major debate in the Senate on US Central American
policy and after repeated attempts to have Senator Robert Stafford hold
a public meeting on the issue, more than a hundred citizens went to the
senator's office in Winoosky. They implored the senator to withdraw

support from the administration's Central American policy, to vote against supplementary military aid to El Salvador and to hold a public meeting on the subject. The senator refused all of their requests. So the citizens occupied the senator's office over the weekend, holding workshops on the topic attended by over 400 people.

On the Monday morning they were asked by the police to leave and, naturally, when 44 of them refused, those 44 were arrested and charged with various crimes. At the trials of 18 of the protestors the judge refused to entertain the introduction of a defence of necessity. However, for reasons of rotation of district judges, the judge who had disallowed the defence any opportunity to put its case properly was replaced. In making the replacement the superior court said that serious judicial errors had occurred in these trials and ordered that the remaining 26 trials be appointed to Judge Frank Mahady who was entrusted to ensure a fair (communal) trial. Which he did.

Expert witnesses were allowed to be called and, at the end of the trial, Judge Mahady, who held the reputation of the best jurist in the state, instructed the jury that 'the defence of necessity is well recognised by the law and has been used in our Supreme Court within the past year'. He then instructed the jury on how properly to weigh up the factors involved in a defence of necessity and it did not take them long to find all 26 defendants not guilty.

So the expert evidence to demonstrate the objective facts and a full understanding of the situation, including the imminent danger to life, was all brought out in court. What the judge did not do was to find that as a matter of law there was 'no case to answer'. Obviously, when a case goes to the jury for their consideration, there is a case to answer. The question for the jury is: has the accused answered the prosecution case? So from the point of view of getting Trident on trial, as it were, the citizens were still a vital step away from turning the tables on the government. Then someone had the bright idea of using international law instead of state law.

In *People* v *Ann Jarka* that was just what they did. For a week following the re-election of Ronald Reagan to the presidency, a series of citizen intervention actions was mounted at the Great Lakes naval training centre in Illinois, the purpose being to save lives – not North American lives, but Central American lives. The action was on two flanks: to stop the US naval activities, including nuclear activities, in Central America and to stop the navy assisting in supplying nuclear-capable artillery to the region. On 13 November 1984, 22 people were arrested for blocking the main entrance to the base and charged with mob action. The charges were dropped against some of the citizens but seven people went to trial and relied on both the necessity defence and international law, saying that lives in Central America were at severe risk and in all probability there would be lives lost if this military action were allowed to continue.

The associate judge, Alphonse Witt, said, 'Let them have their day in court. The jury may, or may not, buy their story.' He went on: 'International Law is binding on the United States of America and therefore on the State of Illinois. The threat or use of nuclear weapons is a war crime because such use would violate International Law by causing unnecessary suffering, failure to distinguish between combatants and non-combatants and poisoning its targets by radiation.' This was probably the first time any judge in the United States had mentioned international law in a citizen intervention case. He did not mention Nuremberg by name but he discussed every Nuremberg crime in the book. However, he did not rule that as a matter of international law the defendants should be acquitted. He left it to the jury, who did 'buy it' and found all seven not guilty. Therefore, from the point of view of using international law as a defence, I guess those from the USA would say this case was one of 'close, but no cigar'.

A very similar case, again with nuclear parallels and again from Illinois, was that of *Chicago* v *Allen Streeter*. The eight defendants included a preacher, a union official, a community organiser and students from ethnic minority groups. Their purpose was to see an end to apartheid in South Africa. On 15 January and 7 February 1985 they packed the doorway of the Chicago offices of the South African consulate and remained there until Consul General Willie P N Lotz abandoned his long-standing refusal to discuss killings, detentions and overall disrespect for human rights in South Africa. They raised the defence of necessity to prevent lives being lost in South Africa, saying the damage they caused, if any, was minuscule by comparison with the 'greater evil' of apartheid. Once again the judge did not rule on the case as a matter of international law. He left it to the jury, which took two and a half hours to find all eight defendants not guilty. It was the United States' first big case on South African anti-apartheid but there were many more to follow, right up to that historic day when Nelson Mandela walked free and the pressures from around the world for real political change brought down that murderously oppressive regime.

I learnt a great deal from reading the voluminous reports of these important US cases but I was left with a feeling of foreboding because even in the United States, with their constitutional protections so jealously guarded by the courts, no judge had gone the final yard and turned the tables on the government, ruling that as a matter of international law the US government was committing crimes against humanity.

At such weighty moments in legal research we advise our younger lawyers that it is always advisable to 'look over your shoulder' to see what the English might have said or done about a particular topic – from their own peculiar legal point of view, of course. So that's what I did at this point, although, because I had been in the USA, I looked over my shoulder to Canada.

There I was to find that the best attempt at disarmament via the courts came in the form of *Operation Dismantle Inc* v *The Queen*, which got as far as the Canadian Supreme Court. You may be wondering what Queen Elizabeth II has to do with anything in Canada. The answer is that she is the head of state and head of the Commonwealth, of which Canada is a member, and the Canadian legal system still sends its ultimate appeals to the Privy Council in London.

This was an overambitious attempt to change government policy, a type of challenge that is almost certainly doomed to failure in a court of law. Courts interpret legislation when governments are successful in distilling ideas into a form of writing that can be understood, at least by lawyers. Courts also keep governments, central and particularly local governments, from doing anything *ultra vires*, that is 'beyond their statutory powers'. Which isn't much these days.

What courts do not do is tell governments what ideas they can have and what ideas they can't have. So when the bottom line of a case is that the government should change its policy, it's time to change to a lawyer who knows the difference between what a court can give you and what it can't. However, that is not to say the lawyers in *Operation Dismantle* didn't know what they were doing. Quite the opposite. I have taken the same legal approach in Scotland when, on behalf of unpopular clients, I was locked into a five-year battle against the Law Society of Scotland. The point is that it is sometimes necessary to 'push the envelope of the law', as lawyers say, in order to get perhaps a bit of what you want or achieve your ultimate goal by beginning in court but reaching your conclusion by another route. And that is what happened in this Canadian case. It got so bogged down in legal detail and procedure that it petered out, but not without a good deal of publicity for the cause the plaintiffs sought to bring to public attention. And so long as they don't go so far as to abuse the legal system, I say good luck to them.

So I bade farewell to Canada and turned my attention westwards, to Japan. The emotions of just thinking about what happened to the people of Hiroshima and Nagasaki were hard to dispel. I wasn't born until 1952 so I obviously have no memory of the war, but I vividly recall black-and-white television pictures of half-burnt bodies and the flattened cities. I also clearly remember being told at school about how the scientists who had developed nuclear energy had effectively been tricked into believing that their work was to be for peaceful purposes. I got out the law books with a sense of fear in my belly at what lawyers might have done to the truth. But I also had confidence that, unlike the child sitting in class being told about government trickery, if there was any stink to what I was about to read I would spot it a mile off. Looking at the matter from the opposite point of view, I was just as confident that if there was anything less in the cases than rigorous legal analysis, then I'd spot that too.

The biggest nuclear case the Japanese have handled is called the *Shimoda* case and centred on compensation for innocent victims rather than the breach of particular laws. In a way I was glad of that because the nuclear weapons system that The Trident Three disarmed was nothing like the scale of the bombs that were dropped by the *Enola Gay* bomber. Although the world will never erase the memory of what happened in Hiroshima and Nagasaki, it must be kept in mind that the nuclear bombs dropped there were relatively small by today's standards. Those were tiny by comparison with Trident and don't exist any more as a viable, supported technology. If they did, they would not be described as 'massive' any more. Also, I have not the slightest doubt that the US team would have been on that point like a shot when they were trying to get out of answering the World Court's point about whether nuclear weapons can discriminate between military targets and civilian life.

The day I read this case was the day we sorted out who was to represent whom in court. Angie was to appear for herself, I was to represent Ulla and John McLaughlin was to act for Ellen. At that point I had never seen Angie argue in court. We'd had a procedural hearing where it was agreed that I should help her out with Scottish legal procedure and we'd had a quick conversation afterwards along the lines that I would do the same at trial. I knew she had been to Japan and spoken on nuclear issues there so I wondered how she would take the news that I had decided to steer clear of using the Shimoda case when it came to defending Ulla Roder in Greenock Sheriff Court. I figured I'd leave it and find out nearer the trial.

My round-the-world trip ended nearer home, in Europe. At this preparatory stage I had not yet met Judge Ulf Panzer, a presiding judge in the city of Hamburg who would eventually give evidence in the trial of The Trident Three in Greenock. That was a pleasure awaited. Right now I was struck by the efforts of the Dutch people.

Perhaps when you are next asked to sign a petition in the street for or against this or that, you should enquire of the person standing, usually in all weathers, asking you to sign, 'Who are the people behind the petition and, furthermore, who approves of it?' I recommend this course to you because, I'm sure you will agree, it is usually impossible to grasp the whole substance of a matter that has led to such a petition whilst standing in the rain. So if you hear a name you trust then you are more likely to make a judgement on the limited information you have, and sign the thing. If you had been in the Netherlands in the mid-1980s the chances are that is just what would have happened.

The monumental Sean MacBride was right behind a legal action in the Netherlands that sought to get the popular support of the Dutch people for a court case against the state of the Netherlands. The petition was to 'ban cruise missiles', which were about to be deployed on Dutch soil. What was so surprising was that over 20,000 Dutch people were prepared to 'go public' and allow their names to be among the list of those suing their own government. In a small country like the Netherlands, almost everyone must have either been on that list or knew someone who was. It was an incredible achievement.

The task of building the case was assisted by, amongst others, academics from Amsterdam University, two clerks of the Supreme Court, a teacher of international law, a practising Dutch barrister and an officer in the Dutch air force. Up until this action, the Dutch peace movement had concentrated solely on the political issues and hadn't used the law at all. However, this new departure saw the beginnings of a new non-violent way to oppose the decision of the Dutch government to bring nuclear weapons to Dutch soil. The summons against the government was legally served on 21 November 1984. The date was deliberately chosen, as it marked exactly three years since the date of a massive demonstration in Amsterdam calling upon the Dutch government to vote against the proposal to bring US nuclear weapons to the Netherlands for targeting against the Soviet Union. A second large demonstration was held on 29 October 1983 but the powers that be remained deaf and blind to the pleas of a very large segment of the people. Those who felt strongly about the issue were appalled at that arrogance of power. So they sued.

The District Court of The Hague, home of the Peace Palace where the World Court sits, was the court in which the summons was served. The summons sought a number of orders of the court. These were:

1. To render a declaratory judgement that deployment of cruise missiles at Woensdrecht and/or in any other place within the Netherlands *and* the use of such missiles is a tort [legal wrong] towards the plaintiffs collectively and each plaintiff individually.

2. To forbid the defendants to proceed with deployment of cruise missiles at Woensdrecht and/or any other place in the Netherlands, or to cooperate in any way with such deployment.

3. To forbid the defendants to permit the future launching of cruise missiles from the Netherlands and/or to cooperate in any way with such a launching.

The plaintiffs also sought subordinate assurances that should the Dutch government be allowed to cooperate in any way with the US then a treaty ought to be signed setting limits upon what kind of cooperation could be given and the circumstances in which it could be given.

This was no ham-fisted attempt. The plaintiffs cited all the international law from the Declaration of St Petersburg in 1868 through the Treaty of Paris in 1928, the Treaty of London (with the Charter of Nuremberg attached) of 1945, the United Nations Genocide Convention of 1949, the European Convention on Human Rights (which by the mid-1980s had been in force in the Netherlands for many years) right up to an exchange of diplomatic notes between the Dutch and United States governments signed at Tractatenblad in 1981. These people obviously knew their onions, and just seeing that list of international law treaties lifted my spirits to a new height.

The body of the summons relied heavily upon both international law, some of which we've seen elsewhere in this book, and the European Convention on Human Rights. What was very impressive was that the arguments were put in ways I had not seen before. The arguments were so well laid out, one can only wonder at the look on the faces of those Dutch government ministers who would have the job of responding to them. Well, did they respond? Of course not. Not in any meaningful way. They did what we've seen before when confronted with an argument they can't win in open, independent court. They played for time.

In fact they played for so much time that both the technology of nuclear weapons and the whole political situation in northern Europe changed. On the technology front, cruise missiles were getting old anyway and were ripe for replacement. Trident 1 was built and, with its extremely long range, there was no need to place batteries of above-ground missiles in either the Netherlands or Germany, pointing so ominously at the Soviet Union, as it still was. So paradoxically, by the time the lawyers had lingered, the politicians procrastinated and the plaintiffs' frustration mounted, the world had moved on to larger and far more deadly nuclear weapons.

13

Sisters in Arms

One evening after a hard day at the Steamy I was walking through the Queen's Park (this one does actually belong to the Queen) when my instructing solicitor Matthew Berlow rang me on my mobile phone. There was nothing unusual about that. The man lives most of his life on the thing. But this time there was a special note of excitement in his voice.

'I'm sending you a press cutting about Angie. I think we can plan our defence around it,' he said glibly.

For a man who had just done a round-the-world trip (in research terms at least) I needed a quick-fix defence like a hole in the head. He tried to explain what was in this cutting and I tried to give his explanation due attention. But the truth was I let some flying swans on their way from Duddingston Loch in the village to Dunsapie Loch on top of Arthur's Seat take me with them – in the way that Einstein's children, for a bedtime story, used to hop aboard a tramcar called Relativity and be taken by their dad on an interstellar journey before falling asleep.

I was passing the 500-year-old Duddingston Kirk in the village when he said, 'So that's about it. What do you think?' The swans were just disappearing over the moss.

'Great,' I lied. 'But let me call you back when I've read it.'

The following morning it was waiting on my doormat. He always does that with things he's keen on. He knows perfectly well that he should send all case papers through the Parliament House clerks' system for acknowledgement and insurance purposes. But when Matthew gets excited he wants results yesterday. It's part of what makes him the right lawyer for cases needing the personal attention of the person in charge.

By now my wife and I were living this case. The days were counting down to trial and she'd heard innumerable versions of the legal argument. Now there were papers arriving at our house instead of Parliament House. She looked up Matthew's number whilst I retrieved the papers from the bin.

The article wasn't just about Angie. It involved three other women called Andrea Needham, Joanna Wilson and Lotta Kronlid. But Angie was the planner of the group. As soon as I saw the names I remembered the case. It was English and didn't make the law reports, but I remembered the publicity.

What had happened was that on 29 January 1996 the women (minus Angie) had got into the British Aerospace hanger at Warton near Preston in northern England and disarmed a Hawk jet 109 fighter aircraft that was about to be sold and sent to East Timor. How come? Well, in 1993 British Aerospace had agreed with the Indonesian government to supply 24 such fighters. They'd done exactly this kind of thing before, so they were old hands at the game. But of course you don't just stroll into a shop and order 24 Hawk jets for delivery next Wednesday, in the morning please, I'm going to visit my sister in the afternoon. You need an export licence for your jets. And where do you get one of those? Why, those nice people in Whitehall will give you one. Not too many questions asked. Just so long as your order is boosting export arms sales and that is helping to keep domestic interest rates down. It's a cosy little deal. Lots of people are doing it, so it must be all right. Mustn't it?

Well, not quite. In this case there was a little unrest in East Timor. The Indonesian government was using these UK-supplied Hawk jets in air attacks on its own people. Why? Well, the government didn't like the leader of the opposition, Megawati Sukarnoputri. Ever since East Timor was forcibly annexed from Portugal in 1975 the government, according to Amnesty International, had killed over 200,000 people, often by fire-bombing defenceless villages. Well, those elections. I mean, they are so tiresome to organise and so attractive to international observers. It's quicker and certainly more predictable just to dispense with them and get straight down to firebombing the villages. Particularly when the people start that nonsense of freedom of assembly and talking about legal rights for citizens. I mean, you just can't have that sort of thing. I mean. Next they'll be saying that the people in Government House are not superior to them. Really, this kind of thing has to be trampled on at an early stage, and genocide of that ethnic group should do the trick nicely.

The United Nations didn't like it. Not a bit of it. It got very upset and passed six resolutions. The Parliamentary Assembly of the Council of Europe twice called upon member states, including Britain, for an arms embargo to Indonesia. All the while the Indonesian government was receiving its Hawk jets and carrying on the business of government as usual.

After doing £1.4 million pounds' worth of damage to the Hawk jet the women did what The Trident Three later did. They waited to be arrested in order to get to court and put the case of the British government aiding and abetting a totalitarian regime committing genocide to stay in power.

The prosecution stated in its opening speech that the Hawk jets were 'trainers', so they couldn't be used to firebomb villages. There was one little difficulty with that. They forgot to tell the people from British Aerospace what to say. The British Aerospace people gave evidence that these jets had 'lethal capacity' because of their excellent characteristics of having 'the flexibility of a fighter with the payload of a bomber'. Great stuff; let me have half a dozen for delivery next Wednesday, but not in the morning... They also testified that they could not possibly do any sort of 'moral audit' on their clients. They were jet manufacturers, not international political scientists. They relied on the people in Whitehall to do all that. Surely only when they were satisfied that the British people would approve of the purpose for which the jets were being supplied would the minister sign the licence?

The jury were treated to a video left behind by the women to demonstrate their openness, honesty, non-violence and accountability. Large

bells were ringing in my head and I wondered why Angie had not men-
tioned this case when we had our joint consultation in Cornton Vale jail.
As you get to know Angie, one thing above all stands out – her modesty.
That was it, no more and no less.

After my reading into the background of Trident Ploughshares 2000
and the US cases it came as no surprise to read that there had been a vig-
orous campaign since 1992 attempting to get the British government to
see sense and, incidentally, meet their international law obligations and
stop sending these jets to Indonesia. It was all the usual stuff: letters to
MPs, petitions, vigils, lobbying the British Aerospace shareholders' meetings, getting a one-to-one meeting with a director of the company,
getting sympathetic MPs to put down early-day motions in Parliament,
trying to get the police to prosecute the real guilty people in Whitehall,
letters to the English Attorney General, etc, etc. It all came to nothing. In
other words they did everything they could have done when they could
have done it. Only then did the women take responsible action as global
citizens and put a stop to the firebombing themselves.

They were well informed. They knew that the delivery date for the
first batch of jets under the new contract was the end of January 1996.
They got in. They damaged a jet to the point where it could not be sold
as part of the contract and in so doing they got past the point of simple
gesture, like cutting a fence or standing in the way of busloads of
workers. Their action was taken at a time when the danger was imminent
and directly linked to the prevention of the firebombing. That was a
good start for a legal defence, but the women knew the legal problems
and had planned well for the opportunity to deal with them. What they
had done was truly an act of crime prevention. Bingo!

In England there is a criminal statute called the Criminal Law Act
1967. A bit of it, section 3, says that, 'A person may use such force as is reasonable in the circumstances in the prevention of crime.' Over the years
the English courts have had to decide what that legislation means. In
other words, they had to work out what Parliament meant when it
allowed the people of England to use force in public in the prevention of
crime. Everybody knows that it is the job of the police to deal with

crime fighting. That includes detection and the business of arrests and preparing the evidence gathered for use in court. So why do the public need this legal right? The answer lies in our old friend necessity. Remember that US judge who talked about having no time to call the police and the futility of complaining to the prison authorities? Well, here is the same principle laid out in English law.

Luckily the court in Preston allowed the women to lead evidence from people of East Timor to demonstrate that what they were trying to prevent was real. Genocide of the East Timorese really was being aided and abetted by John Major's British government. Over the years the English courts have said that, as in the United States, it is for the jury to decide whether the defendants have answered the prosecution case and, if so, then they are to be found not guilty. There is no doubt that all defendants raising such a defence face a heavy burden. You have to be 100 per cent correct. If the jets had really been 'trainers' or the Indonesian government had not been using British Aerospace Hawk jets to fire-bomb villages, then there is no question that the women should have been convicted under the criminal law. But they were not wrong. They were 100 per cent correct. The jury in Preston listened very carefully to a case that may well have stunned them. However, it did not take them long to find the three women who disarmed the jet, and Angie Zelter who planned it, not guilty on all charges.

FOUR

THE TRIAL OF
THE TRIDENT THREE

14

Much-Needed Inspiration

Ian Hamilton QC is a great inspiration. He was one of the small gang of patriots who on Christmas Eve 1950 reclaimed the Stone of Destiny from underneath the Coronation Chair in the Palace of Westminster. These days I suppose they would be called terrorists, and television reporters would say on the evening news that their gang was 'a cell operating secretly in London'. The stone is otherwise known to the world as 'the Stone of Scone', upon which Scottish kings had been crowned for centuries. Ian and the others returned it to Scotland where it has remained ever since. Don't believe what you hear from the British government about the stone being returned to Scotland, indeed Edinburgh Castle, in early 1997 as part of John Major's Conservative Party plan to bolster the Scottish Conservative vote in the upcoming elections. The stone has actually been in Scotland since Ian returned it to its rightful place over 50 years ago. During the uproar that followed reclamation of the stone, the newspapers reported that King George VI would be pleased to see Ian hang, along with the rest of the gang. Happily they never did. Ian is truly a father of the resurgence of Scottish nationalism and an inspiration to all who seek to question authority and think for themselves. He has been a sheriff court judge, though he didn't like it and returned to the Scottish Bar, where I met him. It was an unlikely meeting in the car park of Parliament House where there is no official place to park a motorcycle. However, that seemed to suit us both.

I ride a 1200cc V4 165 mph Honda Pan European, but then I am only 49 years old. Ian rides a 600cc 140 mph Suzuki Bandit, but then he is only 74. One bright morning in October 1999 we pulled off the Royal Mile into the car park at Parliament House, behind St Giles' Cathedral, almost simultaneously, delighted to cause 'the posh boys' to raise their eyebrows in disgust at the idea of counsel riding motorcycles. Little did they know that Lord Hope of Craighead, a House of Lords judge, had often engaged me in conversation about motorbikes in the same car park, before he reluctantly had to move to London.

Preparation for the defence in the trial of The Trident Three had gone well. Matthew wasn't far off the mark with the article he'd sent me about Angie and the other women. The law they used was English, certainly, but I considered that the principle they used was right 'on the money'. So I had my tail up as we counted down the last few days before trial. Virtually all I had left to do was get my hands on the original records of the United Nations resolutions from the British Library in London, but Andrea would take care of that. I knew I was in good hands.

I was in better hands when I met Ian Hamilton taking off his motorcycle helmet and bidding me good morning. Meeting a legend is always uplifting, especially when the legend's fires burn just as brightly as history records them. His hair is now silver-grey and his complexion is that of an elderly gentleman. But his voice, oh his voice – that deep, proud and completely Scottish timbre is unmistakable. It is also inspirational, especially if, in the next day or two, you are just off to Greenock Sheriff Court to try to have international humanitarian law upheld.

Sitting in the splendour of the Advocates' Library reading the United Nations original motions and resolutions saying that all races and ethnic groups of people in the world must be protected from annihilation, I wondered at the wisdom of presenting this case myself. I was dying to have Ian Hamilton instructed in the case but, regardless of my own views, the Scottish Legal Aid Board had dug its heels in and initially refused to pay for an advocate at all. Only when I had written a 'freebie' opinion and Matthew had got very heavy, threatening to have the Legal Aid Board's decision judicially reviewed, did they reluctantly agree to pay for an advocate. Even then, there was much disagreement about the rate they would pay. So against that background there was no way they were going to pay for two advocates to represent one client. To the authorities, this was a simple vandalism case in the sheriff and jury court. The idea of having a top QC instructed was out of the question. In terms of money, justice is simply not that highly valued in Scotland.

So I had to do the case 'solo'. I had my beloved big red flying machine (motorcycle) serviced and was confident it would glide me every day from Edinburgh to Greenock, some 120 miles round trip, without a hitch. I had my wig and gown in a pannier on one side of the bike and a lot of papers in the other side. I was also very aware that precious documents from the National Library in London were in a waterproof bag 'bungee-clipped' to the back parcel shelf as I slipped over to Greenock at precisely one mile per hour under the speed limit.

Greenock is now a town of faded glory. It was once a bustling trading port where ships from America on their way around the world, drawing too much keel for the silt in the upper Clyde, pulled in to take on coal and fresh water. These days it has social problems with drugs and unemployment. Well, where doesn't? Its sheriff court is in an out-of-the-way street, almost an aside to what is happening in the town amongst those who commute to the city of Glasgow for their honest living or those who do business of a kind that is best kept to the darker side of the town. Nevertheless, the court is like all other sheriff courts in Scotland: it has its rules and procedures. It is like some other Scottish courts in another respect too; its sheriffs are independent-minded judges.

Matthew had told me that Sheriff Margaret Gimblett was to preside at the trial. I hadn't appeared in her court before but she had recently presided over a few difficult high-profile cases and her reputation for being fair-minded was spreading.

The weather on the morning of 27 September 1999 was dreich, as we say (that is Scottish for when the freezing mist is down to the pavements and seeps through overcoats, vests and skin with the greatest of ease). It's very difficult motorcycling weather, especially when your mind is jumping from the correct gear for accelerating away from trouble to presenting a case that no one in Scotland has ever presented before. Riding 60 miles in these conditions fairly drains the energy. However, as I wound my way through the Greenock traffic and pulled up outside court my spirits were lifted. Indeed they soared. The Trident Ploughshares 2000 pledgers were virtually camped outside the court. Banners made of white bed-sheets with slogans denouncing Trident and the British government's nuclear death research in the United States were strung along the full length of the railings in front of the court. Someone inside an old van with its back doors wide open was dispensing hot tea and good cheer. Locals were wishing them well as they passed along the street and a tiny woman dressed in white from head to toe was sitting cross-legged on a small red rug at the entrance to court holding a burning candle and chanting a Buddhist prayer.

Japanese and Danish television crews raced across the road and filmed me getting off the bike and unloading the papers for the case. For professional reasons I asked them not to do that but none of them seemed to speak English. Dutch and German newspaper reporters wanted an interview but I had to decline. For reasons I don't agree with, solicitors can speak to the press about a case but advocates cannot. So that was that. I was missing Ian Hamilton but I knew he would be with me in spirit. Just then the prison van arrived and as it was pulling in to the side entrance a huge cheer went up from the Trident Ploughshares supporters. After nearly four months in jail, excited waves were exchanged and kisses blown. The Buddhist at the entrance never broke her prayer and the media pack charged over to get a glimpse of Angie, Ulla and Ellen as they were led in to the holding cells. As I went through the procedure of getting security code numbers and checking on the canteen for morning rolls I paused to absorb the atmosphere and figured it was a good start.

15

Delay, Worry and Expense

Like every other profession the law has a language all its own. I don't mean the Latin phrases or even the convoluted phraseology so much beloved by those who write the tax laws. I mean the everyday stuff of the knockabout world of the criminal courts. For instance, there is a very old and very good law firm in Edinburgh called Maclay Murray & Spens who are affectionately known as 'Delay, Worry and Expense'. Their name is often bandied between court lawyers when there is a need for an adjournment of any kind. In the Scottish criminal courts we also talk in football analogies, for example to be convicted by a majority is to 'go down 1-0' with the ball going 'in off the cross bar'. The most obvious one is to talk of a case 'kicking off on time'. On the morning of 27 September 1999 down in the agents' room at Greenock Sheriff Court amid the changing from 'civvies' into wigs and gowns there was an excited buzz during which all of the above phrases were bounced from solicitors to counsel and back again.

Scottish advocates look a lot like English barristers, the only outward difference being that we wear wing collars and white bow ties whereas they wear 'bands' at the collar. Otherwise the wigs and gowns, morning coats and Marlborough trousers are all the same. A curiosity in Scotland is that we can appear in brown shoes, but only when we are north of Perth. As you can imagine, it takes a bit of getting into, and one gets into the way of using reflections in windows to check all is well before stepping out into a public place.

Cases or 'diets', as they are known, 'call' at 10 am unless otherwise notified. However, experience tells one when there is not a snowball's chance in hell of that happening. And such was the case on the first morning of the trial of The Trident Three. In fact all was chaos. The clients were in the holding cells having endured a kind of mystery tour in a prison van around a number of sheriff courts in central Scotland, dropping off women who were appearing in courts here and there. We were told they were hungry and thirsty and asking if there were any lawyers present to represent them. We tried but couldn't get near them. Our instructing solicitors were bombarding John McLaughlin and myself with questions about how this or that point of law would be dealt with. Did we have copies of the latest version of Angie's typed speech? Did we have any idea when we might need this or that witness? Would we authorise certain people to be on the end of a phone instead of waiting needlessly in a witness waiting room? The regular solicitors were earwigging like mad because they knew as well as we did that this case was to be unique.

Welcome word came downstairs from the clerk of court that it was all right with Sheriff Gimblett if we needed a little time to organise ourselves. Breath was duly drawn and the last mouthful of tea slipped down. Court 2 had been dedicated for the trial and we thought it best at least to get the hefty bundles of papers up there and meet the procurator fiscal, Mr David L Webster. As we struggled to open the door to Court 2 we were met with the familiar scene of a silent, empty court, except for the lone figure of the prosecutor sitting in his position as 'Master of the Instance' in the well of the court just below the judge's bench, to her right.

David Webster is as nice a chap as you could hope to meet: a career prosecutor, with an area of jurisdiction known as the Sheriffdom of North Strathclyde, round about Dunoon in the Firth of Clyde and a bit on the mainland. His legal powers do not quite extend so far as those of his ancient predecessors, the Lords of the Isles, whose council met not far away at Finlaggan on the island of Islay, but they are not far short. In court he is simply referred to as 'the Crown' (or sometimes 'my friend the learned fiscal') because he traces his authority up to the Lord Advocate, who traditionally is the 'presence of the Crown in Scotland'. Handshakes were appropriate and were duly but warmly exchanged. We had been legally served with a copy of the Crown list of witnesses whose testimony David would take in court and whom we could cross-examine. Also, we had seen a list of the Crown productions (exhibits) that he sought to rely upon. So we pretty much knew his case. I only wish we had known our own case as well as we knew his.

The trouble was we had seen some of our expert witnesses, but not all. For instance, Professor Francis Boyle from Illinois wasn't even in the country, though Jane Tallents, our Trident Ploughshares 2000 liaison, had squeezed my aching shoulders and assured me he would be coming to London 'in the next few days'.

I shuddered to the skeleton at the news. 'London, Jane? He's no use in London!'

However, Jane and I were good at being Yin and Yang. 'Calmly, John. Call on your angels, man. He's coming up to Glasgow on the shuttle as soon as he gets in. Well, nearly as soon as he gets in. Don't worry, I'll get him here.'

I was worried. He was our international humanitarian law expert and we hadn't even met him. I'd read a whole lot of stuff about how he'd given evidence in US courts so I had confidence he knew what he was talking about. It would just have been reassuring, as the trial was about to begin, actually to clap eyes on the man. I was also concerned that we had never met our expert on international political relations, Professor Paul Rogers. Jane had been equally reassuring about his presence, so I was getting used to it. I don't mind telling you, this was well and truly 'winging it'.

We were in the course of discussion with David Webster when a police officer approached, wanting to know who was the advocate for Ulla Roder. I identified myself.

'She's asked me to give you this, sir,' he said politely, handing me something signed by David Webster.

I took a closer look, as I had never seen this sort of legal document before. It was a notice under the Immigration Act 1981 telling Ulla that if she was convicted of malicious damage and theft, then the court could make a deportation order against her. There was tons of it: four pages of close type setting out in complex legal detail exactly what the position was under an earlier Act, the 1971 Act, what happened to people under 17 and what else happened to people over 17. The notice defined a British citizen 'otherwise than by descent' and then a Commonwealth citizen, and discussed the situation for those who had acquired British citizenship and so on ad nauseam. I needed this like a hole in the head.

I (metaphorically) grabbed the clerk of court and asked how much time we had. Not much, apparently. I had to see Ulla. Luckily the same policeman who had handed me the notice was on guard at the door leading from the court to the holding cells. After a bit of persuasion, a consultation with Ulla was allowed. To say 'consultation' was putting a gloss on the situation. Matthew and I were allowed to stand in a 12-foot corridor between two heavy, locked jail doors. Ulla is tall, about 1.8 metres or thereabouts, but when she appeared she was even thinner than I remembered her; and her face was pale and very drawn. To say she looked like a worried woman would be putting it mildly. She looked to me to be close to tears, so it was time to think about human rights.

We tried to listen to Ulla's excited thoughts but we were getting nowhere fast. Then it came to me that the Lord Advocate's office in Edinburgh had previously introduced a nation-wide practice that was not yet enshrined in our law, but would soon be so when the Human Rights Act 1998 came fully into force. Article 6 of the European Convention on Human Rights says that everyone is entitled to a fair trial 'in a language (s)he can understand'. Bingo! I was sure there would be a Danish interpreter somewhere within the court precincts. I was walking a tightrope with an agitated Danish-speaking client on the one side and a sheriff sitting in her chambers drumming her fingers on the other. I tried to reassure Ulla that we were not abandoning her but would be back as soon as we had located the interpreter. Thankfully, I didn't have far to look.

Back in an empty court, sitting at the big table in front of the clerk of court, was a well-dressed Scandinavian-looking woman I had never seen before. She was chatting to the sheriff's 'macer' (the person who calls everyone to rise when the sheriff comes on the bench). It was obvious from her accent that her native language was not English so she was probably the interpreter. She was. I didn't really get her name at first but Matthew later slipped me a piece of paper saying it was Pia Walker. I don't think the poor woman had ever been among such madness, but as the weeks went by she became an indispensable part of the team, and we were all grateful to her. Now the thing was, court had not yet formally convened so she had not been formally sworn by Sheriff Gimblett to do anything, let alone 'well and truly discharge the duties of interpreter in this court', but I had no time for formalities like that.

The corridor to the holding cells was getting crowded and time was tight so we got straight down to it. I had to keep Ulla from trying to recite every international law point she had ever learnt and keep her to the notice about immigration. I didn't pretend to understand the whole thing but in the white heat of court practice one becomes used to focusing on the main point and quickly taking an overall view. I assured Ulla that the key words in this notice were 'in the event of your being [convicted]' so we should just forget about this piece of paper until the end of the trial. The Danish language seemed to me to have a whole lot more words for that proposition than the English language and Ulla gave me some resistance, but I gave her one of my 'one eyebrow up, one down' looks and she seemed to accept we had bigger fish to fry.

Just then, with the familiar sound of a big iron key into a bigger iron lock, Angie and Ellen were led by three police officers into the corridor from one end and John McLaughlin and his instructing solicitor joined us from the other end. The corridor was mobbed. Angie was flushed with excitement but also a little apprehensive. She is self-confessedly nervous in courts. She actually doesn't like them but, as a global citizen committed to ridding the world of nuclear weapons by use of the rule of law, she accepts appearing in courts as a necessary evil.

As the door to the court opened I was surprised to see that the court was packed – not a seat left in the press or public galleries. The layout of a Scottish criminal court is that the judge sits on the bench with the clerk directly below him or her in the well of the court. In front of the clerk is a big table at which sits the procurator fiscal plus any assistants, on the judge's right, and defence lawyers on the judge's left, in a line according to who represents whom in the dock, which is straight across the court directly in front of the judge.

I was not prepared for what happened next, but it was a sign of the whole tone of the trial ahead of us. As the three accused women entered the dock, every Trident Ploughshares pledger in the court stood up. I took my place as the first counsel in our line and told Matthew to straighten his tie. Only seconds later the call arose. 'Co-ou-rt,' cried the macer properly, that is in a strong rising voice without the need for extras like 'Please all stand' or the like. If it's done properly, everyone gets the idea.

This was the first I had seen of Sheriff Margaret Gimblett. She belied her 61 years, and looked tiny under her wig and gown. But her deep bow to the lawyers in her court together with her cheery demeanour immediately demonstrated something not common in our criminal courts – a touch of humanity. Her macer ensured her comfort in the big leather judicial chair. Pens were laid out neatly and the judge's personal notebook was opened in readiness for the next formal part of the process. I glanced over to the dock and looked each of the accused in the eye in turn. We were as ready as we'd ever be.

At precisely 11.22 am the clerk of court rose to his feet holding the indictment out in front of him and said the formal words required by law: 'Call the diet. Her Majesty's Advocate against Angela Christine Zelter, Bodil Ulla Roder and Ellen Moxley.' The police officers who sat in the dock alongside the accused nudged their three prisoners to stand. The clerk called their names in the order on the indictment. Usually the order is kept simple by using dates of birth, which would have meant Ellen, at a sprightly 64, would have been first. But somehow Angie had been cited as number one, Ulla was second and Ellen was third. The women nodded their acknowledgement of their names and Sheriff Gimblett, looking at me, asked, 'Who appears?'

At that moment all worries, nerves, jitters and hesitations have to be submerged because it is time to do what advocates train for years to do –

appear 'ad voca'. I rose, bowed to the judge and broke the ice with the formal words, 'My lady, I appear for the second pannel [as Ulla was formally known] and tender a plea of not guilty to the entire indictment.' I thought it best to acquaint Sheriff Gimblett with the way we had handled the procedural hearing before a different sheriff, that was to explain that Angie appeared for herself but that I would assist her with any procedural or criminal law that she didn't know. Against that background I explained that it also seemed sensible for me to lead, with John to follow and Angie coming in at the end to put any points that we had not raised and that she thought important. That was nodded into acceptance all around the table, and Sheriff Gimblett replied, 'I'm obliged, Mr Mayer, that's helpful. Miss Zelter, would you plead on your own behalf, please?'

Angie then drew a very deep breath and said proudly, 'I wish to plead not guilty to the… I mean to all charges.' John McLaughlin then stood and pleaded for Ellen, who gave him the biggest of her motherly smiles, as though to say, 'That's my advocate and I'm proud of him.' She was not to be disappointed.

With those formalities completed David Webster moved the court to swear in the interpreters, Pia and a man who seemed to have appeared out of nowhere. Sheriff Gimblett duly swore them in and asked if there were any preliminary points anyone wished to raise. I thought of delay, worry and expense, and rose to move that defence productions numbered 1 to 14 be allowed to be officially received by the court. Everyone around the table had seen these before so there was no unfairness to the Crown. I then raised the thorny issue of Professor Boyle who, Jane had since informed me in a note helpfully slipped to Matthew by a police officer, would only be in Scotland for one day on Friday 1 October. We would have to take the highly unusual step of hearing a defence witness during the prosecution case. It felt a bit bizarre, to say the least, but what else could I do?

Sheriff Gimblett then did something I had noticed once before and would see many times again in the course of the trial: she tilted her head down and to one side, looked at me and asked 'Now, Mr Mayer, where do we go from here?' I thought of saying, 'My lady, it's a case of more delay, worry and expense,' but thought I'd better keep it formal. I explained that before swearing in a jury we could actually save time by refraining from doing that and the Court allowing the rest of the day for the defence to agree anything it could with the Crown and then to write that up into a document we call a joint minute of admissions. That way there is no need for either side to lead witnesses on the points in the joint minute because there is agreement about the facts in that document, although there may still be disagreement about what those facts amount to in the eyes of the law. John and I had agreed that in advance and he had the extra bad news that his lists of witnesses and productions on Ellen's behalf didn't seem to have survived the journey from the office where they were lodged to the court. David Webster had some hesitation in sitting down around the table to agree anything with Angie, who was an unrepresented party, but Angie, who must have become a little bit more relaxed, just smiled at him implying, 'I won't bite you.' I did my first bit of assisting Angie, and directed the sheriff to a paragraph deep within our Criminal Procedure Act. Sheriff Gimblett took the point and the clerk was ordered formally to enter all of that into the minutes.

And with that the macer called, 'Co-ou-rt,' and we rose and bowed, and Sheriff Gimblett adjourned until 'tomorrow at 10 am, gentlemen and Miss Zelter'. We had a long day ahead of us of going through Crown and defence productions and typing up a joint minute, but we had made a start. We had pleaded not guilty in a solemn Scottish criminal court and that was what The Trident Three had in mind when they stepped from *Maytime* aboard the police launch that summer's night out on the waters of Loch Goil.

16

Call Your First Witness

Tuesday 28 September dawned damp and miserable, so I put on my waterproofs over my motorcycle leathers, thanked my wife for slipping an apple into my pocket and accelerated quietly away from Duddingston towards the Edinburgh city bypass. As I sped past the wet fields in the half-light of 6.55 am, Day 2 of the trial seemed a million miles from Edinburgh. Central Scotland is narrow, and travelling from the east to the west coast is an everyday commute for some people, though not me. The weather remained foul all the way but my big Pan European ate the miles with a throaty confidence that no other V4 can match.

When the traffic thinned out there came to mind an occasion when my son Sam and I had ridden into the remote Scottish Highlands, just like Professor Robert Pirsig and his boy in that essential book, *Zen and the Art of Motorcycle Maintenance*. It was just before the mobile phone era and we were parked up by a glistening mountain loch eating lunch when Sam asked me what would happen if the Pan didn't start. I looked him lovingly in the eyes and, as usual, gave him an answer he didn't expect. 'Son, if that motorcycle did not start, then a few days from now, on the other side of the world, a small team of Japanese designers would pass long, sharp blades through their own hearts. That's what would happen.' As a boy he always accepted my answers and tried to figure them out later; so he went quiet and we ate the rest of our lunch in silence. My point was that the technology was so well thought through, the engineering materials so well tested and the integration of human and machine so well calculated that it was a matter of vital personal honour that these bikes did everything they were designed and built to do, every time, for many years. Now as I sped towards Greenock I contrasted the exactitudes within my Pan European motorcycle with the early nuclear bombs and shattered the mental tranquillity of lunch with Sam in the Scottish Highlands. I couldn't get my mind off the name that Louis Slotin and the other scientists on the Manhattan Project gave to their first clumsy nuclear weapon. They called it 'the Gadget'.

An hour and a half later outside Greenock Sheriff Court the Buddhist was still there, as were the banners and the tea man in the old van. We hadn't had the first Crown witness sworn in but already there was an atmosphere of 'bedding in' for a long haul. Down in the agents' room a different kind of tension from the false dawn of yesterday was palpable. The trial was about to begin in earnest and, as we went upstairs in wigs and gowns to discuss the joint minutes prepared overnight by David Webster, there was a definite sense of 'bombs away'.

It was 9.30 am and we were about to hit the day's first problem – no Angie yet. The prison van was late. As she was a 'party pannel', we needed her up from the cells to read and sign the five joint minutes of admission. John McLaughlin and I used the time to read them over. Twenty minutes later there was much slamming of prison van doors, keys turning in those big locks and the image of immaculate prison officers marching Angie straight into our 'consultation corridor' outside court. Angie is always ready to switch into professional mode but, with the best will in the world, she was just out of a prison van after a two-hour run. I was satisfied that she should sign the joint minutes of admission and she had an added nod from John. As Angie signed her scrawl an air of trust crystallised between us and we were ready for the trial ahead.

David Webster had noticed overnight that the women were, amongst other things, only charged with throwing one of DERA's acoustic amplifiers into Loch Goil, whereas it should have been two. So we changed that and got to our seats in the well of the court. The place was again packed to the gunwales, this time even more so because all of the public who were cited for jury selection were sitting patiently in the public galleries alongside the Trident Ploughshares supporters and the press people who had underestimated how long it takes to get from Glasgow down to Greenock in the mornings.

Whilst awaiting Sheriff Gimblett's arrival on the bench, Jane Tallents passed me the first of that day's helpful notes. Someone had overheard a potential juror saying he had worked in the Trident submarine base at Coulport for nine years, though he had since left. I turned towards the public gallery where Jane had cleverly manoeuvred herself right behind the man and was pointing at the top of his head. I gave her one of my 'both eyebrows up' smiles and she gave me one of her 'index finger making the sign of a tick' signals. Not for the first time a potential disaster had been averted by the quick actions of a citizen intervener.

There was a moment or two's delay in the sheriff coming on to the bench and the court fell absolutely silent. The Trident Three were sitting stoically in the dock, Ulla and Ellen looking straight forward while Angie made final adjustments to her papers for the day. I glanced around and scanned the public benches. It's something most criminal court advocates do, just to see if you know anyone personally, because personal relationships, good or bad, mean that person should not sit as a juror in your case. As usual, I didn't know anyone but as I was looking around Jane again caught my eye. This time she was directing me to look at a man sitting in the back row who looked very out of place. He was middle-aged, tall, balding and dressed in a very good suit – Jermyn Street by the looks of it. However, it wasn't his suit but the laptop computer on his knee that gave me cause for concern. I couldn't deal with this right now, so I left it to Jane to explain later.

A smiling Sheriff Gimblett entered to the usual rising call, and the court filled with a sound like a sleepy herd of rhino getting quickly to its feet. Her usual smiling 'Good morning' was widely extended to one and all, followed by a good look around, checking that we had all the ingredients to begin the trial in earnest. The clerk of court then did the formal thing he did every morning of the trial – he called the diet, which formally begins the proceedings for that day. David Webster presented the joint minutes, which Sheriff Gimblett gratefully received, saying these

were very helpful. Judges like it when parties in their court can agree formalities so that time and money are not wasted on unnecessary proof of
these things and jurors don't fall asleep in boredom. These were kept for
the appropriate point in the trial where their contents would make sense
to the jury.

John McLaughlin then moved the court to receive again his list of
witnesses and list of productions, as investigations revealed that these had
been lost. We had agreed that whilst he was on his feet he should move
the court to allow John Ainslie, the chair of Scottish CND, who was on
our witness lists, to be allowed to sit in court during the prosecution case,
or, at the very least, during the evidence of the manager of *Maytime*, a Mr
Iain Christopher McPhee. But we had jumped the gun. David Webster
had not seen John Ainslie's CV so he could not say whether he wished to
object to Ainslie or not. You see, as with most systems of law, we have a
provision for experts to sit in on the other side's case so that the lawyers
don't get bamboozled with jargon or evidence we can't follow. (Oh yes,
we get bamboozled quite a lot.) We just reserved the question of John
Ainslie sitting in until David could decide on his position, and were
about to get on with the next bit when Angie raised her hand and
politely said, 'Excuse me.' Sheriff Gimblett was taken by surprise but
immediately stopped proceedings to see what the problem was. It was
Angie's middle name. It should be 'Christina'. That was duly noted and,
all three having formally pleaded not guilty to the indictment, at last the
precipice came. It was jury time.

Juries perform a vital function in society. If you have never served on
one, then, should the opportunity arise, I urge you to undertake that
civic service with due care and attention and with a sense of duty to
yourself and your community. Without juries, criminal courts could not
function. In Scotland we have 15 members on a criminal jury, chosen
from around 35 members of the public who get an official brown envelope from the Scottish Courts Service saying they have been selected to
sit in a particular court during a particular period. At that stage they
know nothing about which case they will be trying, if they are selected.
Only when the clerk of court calls the names at random do they come

forward and take a seat, in series, in the jury box. Because of the geography of the courts, defence counsel often have their back to the jury but we can see the jurors coming forward to take their places. We don't do any testing of jurors, let alone psychological testing, and we have no legal right of objection to a juror being selected unless we have a good reason why someone should not sit as a juror. With that in mind and with Jane's eye meeting mine, I listened carefully as the whole 15 names were read out. The man with nine years' service to Trident was not called. So no problem arose.

Everyone was nervous. As the jurors shuffled into place I noticed each of the accused women mentally sizing up each one. The solicitors noted their names and juror numbers, and worked out the balance of men to women. There were more women than men. We initially thought that was good, but then, you never know. One problem in a case like this was that the defence has no specific legal right to question the jurors, asking if any of them work or have worked at the nuclear submarine base at Coulport, or whether their husbands, wives or partners work there. God forbid we should be allowed to ask them their views about nuclear weapons or, regardless of their views, whether they are financially reliant on the base to put their kids through college. You only get that depth of legal rights in the United States.

Even the clerk of court was nervous. As he read out the indictment to the empanelled jury he fluffed an important part, the name of the place where the Crown says that crimes were committed by the accused. Lochgoilhead is easy enough for a Scotsman to say, but this was no ordinary day. So upon making his small but important mistake, the clerk, with true professionalism, simply went back to the beginning and this time flawlessly read through the whole indictment. His soft tones provided a welcome opportunity for everyone to draw breath and familiarise themselves with the new scene. For us at the defence side of the table there were now 15 more people breathing deeply and shuffling just behind us. And as for the jurors, they were as near to the criminal justice system as they would ever get. Indeed, whether they knew it or not, they were now a very important part of it.

Only Sheriff Gimblett remained perfectly cool. Her gentle confidence pervaded the well of the court and the jurors naturally focused upon her as their source of discovery about what was to happen next. Only now that they were sitting in the jury box and about to take an oath was it possible, within Scots law, to ask them anything about themselves. However, unlike in other systems, such as the United States for instance, they are still not quizzed individually. Leaning slightly towards them so as naturally to put them at ease, Sheriff Gimblett then did what all Scottish judges do at that point in a jury trial. She simply asked the jury as a whole if any of their number knew of any reason why they could not try this case impartially, that is to say, whether any of them knew the accused women personally, for instance. There was the usual general silence and looking at feet that our judges take as a 'no'. Sheriff Gimblett nodded to her clerk and with that the most important part of any trial ensued – the oath was administered.

The clerk rose to his feet, held up his right hand, inviting the jury to do the same, and said, 'Ladies and gentlemen, do you swear that you will well and truly try the accused and give a true verdict according to the evidence? Say "I do." Please sit down.' The jury therefore don't need to answer pesky questions from lawyers nor even answer out loud to the oath. I think it is a disgrace to our criminal law courts that that is the situation. But there it is. I always note those words, even though they are emblazoned on my mind, because I always begin my jury speeches by reminding the jury that they took that oath and now it is time to deliver upon it. However, we were a long way from there.

I was just writing a note to myself when John McLaughlin stood up. I was surprised because I couldn't think of what he might want to raise. John is a great man for pressing his client's case to the utmost and this was no exception. It turned out that his concerns about the impact of a 'mole' within the jury were greater than mine and he moved the court to hear him outside the presence of the jury. So without hearing a word in earnest, the jury were asked to retire while John made his point. Sheriff Gimblett was firm. She would ask if anyone had any particular reason why they thought they could not serve but she would go no

Ellen Moxley, Angie Zelter and Ulla Roder (The Trident Three) on their way
to disarm *Maytime*.

Left: The Trident Three on climbing manoeuvres in Loch Goil.

Below: The village of Lochgoilhead and the launching site for The Trident Three's little boat (bottom left-hand corner).

Maytime, the central control of Britain's Trident Nuclear Submarine Fleet, was disarmed by The Trident Three.

Maytime and its sister acoustic testing vessel, *Newt*.

About half of Faslane Nuclear Submarine Base.

The Gare Loch from which Trident sails out to sea. The Ministry of Defence owns the land as far as the eye can see. The Ministry also approves of the logging shown in the bottom right-hand corner.

Faslane Nuclear Submarine Base, where Trident rests before going on patrol in the oceans of the world.

Coulport Centre, where The Trident Three were held after being arrested aboard *Maytime*.

The beautiful West Highlands of Scotland and Faslane Nuclear Submarine Base.

John Mayer and John McAllion MSP in Greenock Sheriff Court at the
presentation of the Petition of Support from 26 Members of the Scottish
Parliament to The Trident Three.

The Trident Three outside court after being acquitted.

Angie Zelter, Ulla Roder and Ellen Moxley receiving the Right Livelihood Award in Sweden in December 2001. This 'alternative Nobel prize' is awarded to those who offer 'practical and exemplary answers to the crucial problems facing the world today'. (Photo: Karl Gabor, Sweden)

further. The jury came back but the sheriff's question was met with the same general silence and looking at feet. So we got on with it.

Sheriff Gimblett looked at David Webster and said, 'Now Mr Fiscal, call your first witness.' David rose to his feet and said, 'Number one on the Crown list, m'lady, Police Constable Thomas O'Brian.' This was another important moment in a Scottish criminal trial because our Supreme Court has ruled that the accused only actually begins to stand trial when the first bit (we say 'adminicle') of evidence is given, even if that is only the name and address of the first witness. Officer O'Brian was led into court and stood firm and upright in the witness box. With only one and a half years' police service, his right hand was raised so high in anticipation of taking the oath that it looked like a Nazi salute. I glanced at Angie, who was smiling all over her face at such youthful enthusiasm.

Officer O'Brian was the scenes of crime officer who provided the court with insight into a book of photographs he had taken. He is not a forensic scientist. We have others who are highly qualified to do that sort of work. The prosecution was trying to prove that the crimes were committed by the accused at a particular place. So the idea is that everyone in court first familiarises him- or herself with the general beauty of Loch Goil and the exact position of *Maytime*. Officer O'Brian's first photo was taken from Douglas Pier and looked down the loch. I was glad he had taken such care with the natural lighting and had captured the beauty of the place because his pictures seemed silently to scream that this beautiful place may as well have had a giant label slapped on it from the sky saying, 'Targeted by Russian Nuclear Missile Silo Number 78'.

He explained that he only got to *Maytime* the day following the disarmament, 9 June, at about 1.30 pm and made a point of saying that, during his eight and a half hours on board, he was at all times under the control of the *Maytime* manager, Mr McPhee. He went on to show us pictures of the details of *Maytime*'s gangways and winches and then the empty cages, tables and work benches where once there had been sophisticated computers, amplifiers and other acoustic research and testing equipment. Then he came to the upper deck. There was a close-up of a welder's mask and some rope, and a hacksawn padlock and the window through which the women had climbed.

Sniggers went around the jury when he reached photographs K and L in his book. There were the banners the women had brought in rucksacks and strung up for all the world to see. The poor man was in the land of the Keystone Cops as he explained how, when he was not present, McPhee had ordered that the deeply embarrassing banners be taken down. As O'Brian photographed one side of *Maytime*, McPhee's men were taking down banners on the other side. O'Brian of course is not an MoD policeman but a serving Strathclyde police officer. When he saw what was happening he nearly had a fit. He told us how he quickly explained that you can't just treat a crime scene any way you like in order to cover up embarrassment. There are laws about that sort of thing. You can just imagine how McPhee lost all authority as he ordered the banners to be put back up, even tied in the same way, so as to leave the defence advocates no room for criticism in court. John McLaughlin and I joined the jury in laughing about it all but, if the case had been of the usual type, it might well have been over, there and then, before the first witness had left the court. However, we knew very well that our clients had no wish to win on any sort of technicality.

I half swung round in my chair to check the jury as they came to the pictures of the inside of *Maytime*. These were crucial to our argument that the women were not common vandals and thieves. They were well informed, concerned, global citizens who had tried everything known to the law to get their government to comply with the World Court judgement, had been ignored and were now intervening on behalf of all of us. David Webster was as fair as fair could be. He went through each photograph and accepted how clean and tidy the place had been left, how the first aid box was untouched and the floor had even been swept by Ulla. He got his evidence that there were empty spaces where once there had been computers, anechoic testing equipment and sophisticated programming processors and left it at that. For now.

The jury were being very attentive. I knew what was coming next so I swung back around. Sheriff Gimblett also seemed to be ahead of the game. This witness was taking a very long time in explaining each photograph's angle and subject matter. That suited me because as the jury flicked page after page I was sure that, far from being an innocuous young officer with hardly anything of importance to say, he was introducing both the judge and the jury to the enormous scale and intricate details of what the MoD was doing in that beautiful part of the world. As you will have gathered, I like sharp contrasts, and another one was just around the corner.

'What does photograph O2 show, Officer O'Brian?' asked David Webster.

'Some peace-related materials, sir.'

'Where did you find these, officer?'

'By the security cage shown in the previous photograph, sir.'

'And what is that in the photograph, just beside those materials?'

'A picture of a Japanese woman on fire, sir.'

All 15 heads in the jury box lifted sharply and looked intently at the three middle-aged women in the dock. I thought of Ellen Moxley in Vietnam and then the 1968 world-wide sit-down to protest at the way in which the war was being unnecessarily prolonged. I'd seen the picture now being discussed in evidence before, and didn't particularly want to see it again. It was a poignant moment for the defence and this was just the first Crown witness. Then it got better.

'What does photograph L16 show?' asked David.

'It's an envelope, sir, with writing on it. Do you want me to read it out?'

'Yes, please.'

Officer O'Brian then read out the message on the envelope inviting the finder to open it and examine the contents. Inside there was the videotape that the three women had made before the raid and explanatory written materials saying who the three women were, what Trident Ploughshares 2000 was and why the women were aboard *Maytime* doing these things. Officer O'Brian went on to testify about the finger- and footprints that he had lifted, together with technical information about police procedure, but I don't think the minds of the jury were on the rest of his evidence at all. When I came to cross-examine him I wanted to maintain the air of gravity that had now descended upon the jury so I asked very little of this young man, whose voice had swung from its training-course clarity to emotional breaking point. Very quietly I asked if the jury had the full impression from the photographs of what it was like for him on board *Maytime*.

'Oh no, sir. You really can't imagine what that place is like until you actually get on board. It's huge, sir,' said young Officer O'Brian with a note in his voice that told the jury how edgy he had been while doing his duty that day. I knew I had made my point and left it to John McLaughlin to cover what the banners said and embarrass the hapless Mr McPhee once more.

But it had been a long, hard day and Sheriff Gimblett was alive to the fact that the jury had been flung in at the deep end, so to speak, having to look at some of these pictures and listen to a lot of technical stuff. So her ladyship then adjourned the court until 10 am the following morning.

The dock police allowed us a quick word with the clients but it didn't amount to any more than much shrugging of the shoulders and accepting that we were off to not a bad start. However, I could tell from their faces that the women were not in the least looking forward to several hours in the back of a prison wagon. For my own part I had been up since 5 am and ahead of me lay a long ride through heavy traffic that I knew would treat me as invisible; small saloon car drivers would suddenly change lanes, brake inappropriately and generally do anything in their collective power to kill me before I got home. Still, I knew that when I got halfway along the motorway the traffic would thin out and I could mentally return to that mountain loch where Sam and I could eat together again.

I was finally escaping downstairs when Jane tugged my gown.

'He's MoD and high up by the looks of things,' she said with some concern in her voice.

'Sorry, Jane. Who is?'

'The man in the back row. He's just got into an MoD car, plugged in his laptop and a wee dish thing on top moved around. I'm sure he's sampled all the voices and is transmitting the day's events to Whitehall. What do you think?'

'I think that's illegal without the sheriff's permission, is what I think. I could make a motion to have him found in contempt of court.'

'There's a problem with that. We're sworn to act safely, openly, honestly, etc. I mean, what's he going to hear that no one else hears?'

'Very true. OK, I'll leave it if you will.'

'Yeah, we'll just have fun with him in the back row then,' she chuckled.

'Jane! You're a married woman.'

'Tactical fun, you nincompoop. Get back to Edinburgh. Your brain's obviously had enough for today.'

'See you in the morning, Jane.'

'Bye, John.'

17

Voices from Within

I go right along with those who say that listening to Miles Davis's 'Kind of Blue' is taking a periodic visit to heaven on earth. I knew this trial was being watched from government departments and universities around the world. It was of monumental importance; but I couldn't get those breathy horn solos out of my head and so I was living a kind of split-life between East 30th Street in New York in 1959 and Greenock, Scotland in late 1999. Something had to be done. After all, I couldn't just say to Sheriff Gimblett, 'All you have to do is allow Miles Davis and John Coltrane to seep into your soul and you'll get the point.' My biggest problem was that the daily commute from Edinburgh to Greenock was punishing in the bad weather and it was time to start thinking about using a great British tradition, the B & B. This of course means moving into someone else's home in the local area where, for much less than hotels charge, they provide bed and breakfast. The regulation rates paid by the Scottish Legal Aid Board to advocates have not risen in over 12 years and therefore don't run to much more than a B & B, not if you want to take any money home from the case. I quietly mentioned the matter to the sheriff's macer, a local woman who knew most people in the town. By the end of the day she had fixed me up in a very comfortable house with a pleasant retired couple, where the breakfasts were bountiful and the company friendly. I was even provided with a writing desk and a spare bed on which to lay out my big bundles of papers. My landlady even said I could go home at the weekends and take my pick of coming back on the Sunday nights or the Monday after court. She would have clean bedding, towels and a supper ready for me either way. A bit of heaven on earth really.

Trials are tiring for everyone concerned. They are emotionally tiring for the accused, intellectually tiring for the lawyers, physically tiring for the witnesses and all of these for the judge. For the lawyers much anguish goes into things that never happen, or happen but are never seen by the public. I was glad it wasn't my turn to cross-examine and wondered how John would handle the recreation of last night's atmosphere.

With great eagerness he was on his feet immediately the diet had been called and Sheriff Gimblett had given him the appropriate nod. John never disappoints. He got straight into it.

'Look at photo L4, officer, and tell us what it shows.'

'A big banner, sir.'

'And please do the same for photos 5, 6 and 7.'

'I've got them, sir.'

'What do they show?'

'Stop nuclear death research, sir.'

'And the next one?'

'Trident equals mass slaughter of innocents, sir.'

'And the next?'

'It's partly obscured, sir.'

'It's all right, officer. I'm sure we have the point.'

John went on to take from his witness something that is often just as important as what we see in photographs, that is, of course, what we don't see in them. Officer O'Brian told us how he had been sent to this job and told that it was just a vandalism case – nothing much to bother about. He was careful to explain that he nevertheless photographed every area from every direction and every piece of 'foreign' material pointed out by McPhee. He was at first reluctant but soon came round to the idea that there was no point in trying to spar with John, saying he could only testify to what he saw, not what he didn't see. He was on to a loser there. So he just agreed that there were no graffiti on the walls, and no obvious malicious destruction of anything such as the first aid cabinet

— indeed nothing to suggest that the temporary occupiers, although they had obviously acted wilfully, had acted with the usual kind of intent that we expect of vandals and thieves.

'Can I use my own word for the situation, sir?'

'Please do,' replied John.

'Sanitised, sir.'

'What do you mean by that, officer?'

'I mean that the people who had got aboard *Maytime* and flung the computers in the water had otherwise been very careful, sir. To the point of being squeaky clean, if you follow me, sir.'

'Oh, I follow very well. No further questions, Officer O'Brian,' said John with a look to me that said we were getting off to a very good start.

It was now Angie's turn to cross-examine the young Officer O'Brian and he looked relieved that the advocates had finished with him. Angie is of course not a legal professional but she knows how to make her point and got straight to it. She directed her witness to the locker rooms and he again had to agree that essential personnel gear like oilskin overalls and wet-weather boots had been left intact. The kitchen area where staff ate their meals was tidied to the point of crumbs wiped from the table and the cloth left hanging over a tap to dry. I kept my head down but thought how anyone listening to this without seeing the pictures would be forgiven for thinking we were discussing a self-catering holiday, not DERA's most vital installation in the chain of maintaining the secrecy of the world's most devastating weapons of mass destruction. I made a note to use that comparison in my jury speech and turned my attention to the materials I had on the next witness.

'Who's next, Mr Fiscal?' asked Sheriff Gimblett.

'Number 14 on the Crown list, Detective Sergeant Peter Cassidy, m'lady.'

Witnesses are often called in a different order to that on the indictment. Today it suited the Crown to call DS Cassidy because he was a ministry man and David needed an early direct link between the three women in the dock and the events on *Maytime*. Indeed Cassidy was Ministry of Defence police, Criminal Investigation Department (CID), stationed at HM Naval Base Clyde, Faslane. I had noted from my copy of his statement to Matthew that he had 19 years' service, so he was going to be a completely different nut to crack from young Officer O'Brian.

By now the jurors had the general idea. The Crown would lead its witnesses, attempting to prove that the charges on the indictment would hold up; the defence side was not necessarily going to call those witnesses liars, mental defectives or question their parentage. The whole process would be conducted under the watchful eye of Sheriff Gimblett, and the defence might often want to take a Crown witness further than the Crown did. The jurors were getting the idea that this was no ordinary case.

Officer Cassidy explained how he had finished his shift and gone home for the night but his colleague, DC Hazel Brooks, recalled him to duty at half past midnight on the morning of 9 June. So far David's questions were innocuous but DS Cassidy was an old-timer and could see what was coming. When David asked if he was told the reason for being disturbed out of his bed at that time of the morning he flashed a look at John and me. We were poised, pens in hand, to take down a verbatim note of his answer. All he said was, 'Certain information was relayed to me, sir.' David squinted at me, left the matter to us and moved on. David then asked him if he went somewhere. 'Yes, sir,' was all he said. By this time he was playing right into our hands. It was a bonus we didn't expect and one that the jury were beginning to sense.

David needed a little more for his case so eventually DS Cassidy explained that, on information received, he had gone to the Royal Navy Arms Depot at Coulport. But no one there knew what he was talking about. He was looking for the arresting officers, Constables Blair and Byres, but they were nowhere to be seen. Nobody knew anything about three white-haired women and a major breach of security at *Maytime*. I turned and looked at the jury, wondering how many of them would be old enough to appreciate the story from the trenches of the First World War that goes like this. A rare opportunity is spotted for the British Tommies to advance, but they need help to achieve their objective. So a radio message is sent to HQ saying, 'Send reinforcements; we're going to advance.' However, when read by the commander at HQ the combination of poor equipment, haste and people writing down what they think they've heard rather than what they really heard brings out the message as 'Send three [shillings] and four pence. We're going to a dance.' This was precisely the situation in which DS Cassidy found himself in the early hours of that fateful night and there was very little he could do about it.

Eventually the confusion lifted when Blair and Byres walked in with their prisoners in tow – well, not exactly in manacles, you understand. A certain friendliness had formed between that unlikely group. Cassidy was at last on firm ground. His job was to debrief the officers, that is to hear what they had to say, and then interview the prisoners on tape for later use in court.

When David asked his next question, 'Do you see those women here in court today?' a big moment occurred. The women in the dock were formally identified as being the same women who had become his prisoners that night. It was a necessary legal step for David, who paused to let everyone note the details of the evidence. Such a true professional wasn't going to let an appeal point arise over such a fundamental procedural requirement at trial. Cassidy, using all his training and experience, straightened his right arm and with his right index finger pointed directly to each woman, describing for the record which position each occupied in the dock and what they were wearing. He'd done it in court a million times before but no doubt his pointing had never been met with the congenial smiles and thank-yous now befalling him from Angie, Ulla and Ellen.

David put Crown productions 2, 3 and 4 to DS Cassidy who confirmed that these were the completed 'Rights of accused' forms, showing that each woman had had certain legal rights explained to her and that in response each of them had made requests. Angie and Ulla had named Matthew as their solicitor and requested that he and the indefatigable Jane Tallents also be told where they were and why. Ellen asked that her dear friend Helen Steven be informed but didn't bother about naming a lawyer. I don't suppose Ellen cared two hoots about the legal process she was about to endure, but she was concerned that her friend should not worry about her a minute longer than she already had.

David then indicated to Sheriff Gimblett that he now proposed to play the tapes of these interviews. John and I nodded that there was no objection, the clerk of court plugged in a tape player and the jury sat back to listen to the sounds of what happens in a Ministry of Defence jail room in the early hours of the morning when you've just brought the British Trident thermonuclear submarine fleet to its knees. The tape player was only about 2 metres from the jury box and when the clerk pressed the 'play' button a few jurors jumped in fright. The volume was set at maximum and the test signal that always precedes the speaking pierced our quiet court atmosphere like... well, you know what like.

The recorded voice of DS Cassidy then filled the court whilst he got a chance to take a seat for the duration of the performance. Angie's interview came first:

DS CASSIDY: The time is 0312 hours on Wednesday 9 June 1999. I am DS Cassidy, Ministry of Defence police at Faslane, and we are in the interview room within the prisoner process centre at Royal Naval Arms Depot at Coulport. The following other persons are also present and will identify themselves.

'DC Hazel Brooks.'

'Angie Zelter.'

DS CASSIDY: Angie, I'm going to caution you first, so if you listen to this, please. You are going to be asked questions about being on board the vessel *Mayfair*, sorry *Maytime*, eh, on Tuesday 8 June 1999 and the, the damage that was caused on board that and the removal of two life-rafts from it. Em, you're not, you're not bound to answer but if you do your answers will be tape-recorded and may be used in evidence. Do you understand?

ANGIE: I do.

DS CASSIDY: OK, Angie, could you tell me your name in full, please?

ANGIE: Well, my name is Angie, Angela Christina Zelter.

DS CASSIDY: And your home address?

ANGIE: (Angie gives it.)

DS CASSIDY: OK. Now on Tuesday evening 8 June 1999 you were arrested by two MoD police officers on board the vessel *Maytime*, which is berthed in Loch Goil. Is that correct?

ANGIE: That's correct, yes.

DS CASSIDY: Now, you were arrested for malicious mischief caused on board to that particular vessel. Is that correct also?

ANGIE: Eh, it was correct, that's what I was told. In fact, I was doing a disarmament action for Trident Ploughshares 2000, trying to uphold international law when in fact it's your duty as a police officer to uphold international law. Britain is breaking the Geneva Conventions Act with their weapons of mass destruction which can destroy people and it's our duty to try to disarm every part of that nuclear chain and that's what we were doing there.

DS CASSIDY: OK. What did this disarmament consist of, Angie?

ANGIE: I think it is quite clear that what we were doing was stopping *Maytime* from contributing to the whole Trident programme and we have given in a statement and a video. It's all written down there. I'm not going to be saying any more in this interview except to say that it is your duty to be doing this work and it shouldn't be up to us to have to disarm weapons of mass destruction that are illegal in international law. I'm not being impolite. It is all written down.

DS CASSIDY: Who did you give that video and statement to?

ANGIE: To the two police officers outside there. It's a four-page statement.

DS CASSIDY: And the video?

ANGIE: It's a Trident Ploughshares 2000 video.

DS CASSIDY: OK. Now who were you with during this action, Angie?

ANGIE: I was with Ellen and Ulla. We're an international group.

DS CASSIDY: Can you give me their full names, please?

ANGIE: Ulla Roder and Ellen Moxley. Just the three of us. We were there for three hours and we were quite peaceful at all times.

DS CASSIDY: Can you tell me when you went on board?

ANGIE: Mm, 7 pm. We were there for three and a half hours, I think.

DS CASSIDY: And what were your intentions?

ANGIE: To disarm it.

DS CASSIDY: What does that mean?

ANGIE: Disarm means to make sure that any part of Trident, which is an illegal weapon of mass destruction, [pause] the complex parts of the chain become unable to do the harm that they can do. Our action is crime prevention. That's what it is basically.

DS CASSIDY: Would it be fair to say that you intended to damage it?

ANGIE: I don't call it damage. I call what Trident does damage. I call what we do 'disarmament' and I'd rather have this discussion in a court of law, please. I think your duty is to arrest the real criminals and to interview them. We should be allowed to live in peace rather than having to do this kind of work.

DS CASSIDY: Do you think you left the laboratory clean, as it says in your statement? Did you remove anything from it?

ANGIE: I'm not willing to go any further. I can answer these questions in a court.

The interview was stopped there and the jury heard no more other than DS Cassidy saying that he was terminating the interview and that the time was 0322 hours. In fact there was more but it would have been unfair for the jury to hear it because it was not directly about the events on board *Maytime* the previous night. What the jury did not hear was that DS Cassidy showed Angie a faxed document sent to the Whitehall Press Office announcing that the action on board *Maytime* was about to take place and inviting them to come and see for themselves. If such a fax was received today, after 11 September 2001, then one can only hope that someone would be at the other end to act upon it.

The clerk stopped the tape and all 15 members of the jury lifted their heads up from their typed transcripts and looked right at Angie. Apart from her personal reply of 'not guilty' to the indictment at the beginning of proceedings, when all of these 15 good people were sitting at the back of the court amongst a larger group of potential jurors, and a few questions to young Officer O'Brian, they had not heard her in full voice. Now quite suddenly, for them, the first pannel had come to life. Her snow-white hair, reddish face, white shirt and trim spangled waistcoat were nothing compared with what rose up from inside. They had heard her passion for her disarmament action, which was straining at the leash to tell the whole story there in the cold jail in the middle of the night.

But Angie had kept to her plan. She had made the main point that the women's actions were not common vandalism but rather 'crime prevention'. The crimes were against humanity and this well-informed, active and determined little group of humanity had done everything it could to waken up its political and legal leaders to that fact. They had been ignored and were now intervening to save us from the horrors of mass destruction. It was not lost on the jury that Angie had insisted on making her points in a court of law. That meant here and now, and it was obvious the trial had just moved up several gears.

'M'lady, the next interview is with the third panel, Ellen Moxley, and I now propose to play that tape,' said David, whose quiet professionalism was doing everything it could to keep the prosecution case on track for proving the basics: first, that the crimes set out on the indictment were actually committed; second, that they were committed at the place and times in the charges (and therefore not at any other place and time); and third, that those crimes were committed by the three women in the dock.

The jury's gaze switched to the other snow-white-haired rounded woman at the near end of the dock. Some jury members were less than 8 feet from her and I have no doubt their eagerness to hear her voice was heightened by Ellen's inviting, gentle smile to them as they flicked over the pages of their typed transcripts to find Crown production number 9.

The same interviewing officers were present and Ellen announced that she was the other person in the room. When DS Cassidy told Ellen that he was about to caution her she replied 'Yeah' in her American accent, which seemed to me to be more pronounced than usual. I put that down to her being under the stress of the situation. DS Cassidy went through the routine of explaining that he would be putting questions to her about the events on board *Maytime* and got down to details. When he asked for her address and got the simple reply, 'Garden Cottage', I heard short exclamations of breath tinged with the beginnings of laughter from some of the jurors behind me. They were telling us that they were now enjoying this case and would listen as carefully to these interviews as they would their favourite music or reading their favourite author. I smelt danger. We didn't want a sympathy vote. We wanted to establish that the accused were not involved in crime, but crime prevention. It was our turn to be strictly professional.

Ellen explained that she was with Angie and Ulla and was on board *Maytime*. When asked how she got aboard Ellen said, 'Climbed on board from a rigid inflatable boat.'

Some of the jury now actually sniggered. DS Cassidy was keen to get more from Ellen than he had from Angie and he wasn't to be disappointed. Ellen was keen to help. She was keeping to her beliefs of being open, accountable and safe at all times and we all got the strong impression that she would have talked all night to this nice man. Yes, we launched from the shore at the village of Lochgoilhead. Sure, we brought the boat on tow by car. Yeah, we tested the doors for a while. No, I'm sorry, I can't tell you the name of the driver, nor who owned the boat. I'm so sorry. Gosh, we stayed on board a long time. Hours. I don't recall how many. All that equipment was illegal. That's why we had to disarm it. When you consider what's happening in the Balkans right now and what happened in Iraq. We're really fed up with the number of innocent people being killed. You know? We are all Trident Ploughshares 2000 pledgers. We've tried writing to the government and protesting and all sorts of legal means to show that nuclear weapons are illegal. Did you know that 78 per cent of the British people don't want nuclear weapons? [All our efforts] made no difference and therefore we have to do something and this is what we have chosen to do.

DS Cassidy was silent for a second. The standard technique in police interviews is for the officers to keep control of the agenda. The pause on the tape told us that the standard techniques had just gone out the window. So he took the next step with some unease but made the fatal error of asking Ellen to explain their actions on board *Maytime*. Ellen let rip. She must have been physically exhausted but nevertheless she excitedly explained how they formed a chain gang and passed the computers along from one to another until they were flung into the sea-loch. DS

Cassidy then dug himself in deeper by asking how they managed to lift such things and throw them overboard.

'Oh, Ulla and Angie are very strong women. We first disconnected the electricity. We have to be completely safe, you understand. That's one of our first principles. Then we decided that the electricity cables were a necessary part of the work of assessing Trident for fitness to sail so we disconnected these and they went in the water. They may be recoverable, but I doubt it.'

DS Cassidy was now well behind the agenda. He was wholly in Ellen's slipstream when he asked, 'What about the stacking equipment?'

Ellen corrected him, saying, 'Those are stacking computers and...'

DS Cassidy had had enough and quickly jumped to the end, asking, 'What happened when you completed your action?'

Ellen was 64 years old at that time but her voice was now that of a strong young woman. She drew a deep breath and replied, 'We felt we had already completed a major disarmament action but we decided to go up on deck and cut the crane cables they use for winching essential equipment with our bolt cutters.'

DS Cassidy fell for it again, asking what other equipment they had with them.

'Oh I can give you a list. Let's see. The bolt cutters, the hammers, the superglue, the computer...'

DS Cassidy stopped her in mid-sentence but Ellen was on a roll. 'We were mainly interested in the control room and it was just as important to use liquid metal...'

DS Cassidy pulled hard on the reins and halted her in her tracks, taking Ellen to the end of the disarmament action.

'I think we had decided we were very hungry and so we had a picnic on the top deck. We had brown-bread sandwiches and grapes...'

'Mmh,' said DS Cassidy.

'We were waiting for the police but they didn't show. Yeah, we had a little trouble with the instructions for the lifeboats. That's right. But what you have to understand is that that vessel is a vital part of the support infrastructure for Trident and that is illegal under...'

DS Cassidy had the point and stopped Ellen by showing her the Trident Ploughshares 2000 press release to the Whitehall Press Office and asked her if she'd seen it before. Ellen said she hadn't but wouldn't have minded if she had seen it. What it said was true.

DS Cassidy formally concluded the interview with Ellen Moxley with the time recorded at 0345 hours within the prisoner process centre at Coulport. That should have been the end of it but there was one word left on the tape. It was the radiant voice of Ellen saying, 'Fine.' Angie Zelter is always a hard act to follow but in my opinion it had, purely inadvertently, just been done in style.

Sheriff Gimblett broke the spell by announcing that the heat in court had become intolerable and that court would rise for a break. Sheriff Gimblett left the bench rather hurriedly, leaving everyone else in a bit of a muddle. The police didn't know whether to take the prisoners down to the cells and the jury were left without their attendant for a minute or so. The result was that Trident Ploughshares pledgers had the chance to lean over the back of the dock and provide hugs for Angie and Ellen while Ulla chatted in Danish to the interpreter. The women police officers stood respectfully back as silver-haired men shook the three women's hands and women friends lavished kisses and good wishes on their friends in the dock. The police are only too aware that normally drugs or weapons can be passed in this way and would arrest anyone even trying to get close to dock prisoners. But with the jury whispering amongst themselves and pointing to the women in admiration there was an overall sense that certain members of the jury would have welcomed them into their homes, if only they were on bail.

When court reconvened it was late in the afternoon but Sheriff Gimblett was minded to sit late in order to make up for previous lost time. So the clerk set up Ulla's interview and we got down to it. DS Cassidy was our main man once more and he began by recording the time as being 0410 hours. Truly it was by now the middle of the night when the now-familiar routine began. From the formal legal caution it was obvious that Ulla spoke English with a strong, jerky Danish accent and, without the aid of an interpreter at that early stage, wasn't getting the full meaning of DS Cassidy's questions. On a wide interpretation of the European Convention on Human Rights such an interview would be illegal on the grounds that it is unfair to the suspect, but if anyone had mentioned that Ulla should get special treatment then she would have been the first to put a stop to that. And so the interview stumbled through words in the police questions like 'life-raft', 'vessel', 'obliged' and 'approximate' and in Ulla's answers like 'unfunctionable' until they got to the press release to Whitehall. The officers must have thought they had Ulla on the run when they showed it to her because she went silent. They pressed their point quite firmly until Ulla responded that there was no point in asking complicated questions about Whitehall because she didn't have her glasses on. The jury now actually broke into laughter and there was a lot of shuffling in seats and rearranging of bits of paper whilst DS Cassidy wound up the interview. It was now after 5 pm and it had been a long day. The women had been heard by the jury, albeit on tape, but I thought it had been a very good day's work. I was sure the jury had taken away for the night the right balance between the serious purpose behind the women's action and the humanity that inspired them to become such activists.

I was just talking to Jane about an important witness for the defence who was coming over from the United States when I noticed a fresh-faced young woman with long, dark hair hovering by the back of the dock talking to Angie. The police were in a hurry because the van was late due to court sitting on. There would be women prisoners in other courts waiting for the run back to the only women's jail in Scotland, and the whole schedule had been delayed. The girl rested her hand on Angie's and Angie did something I had never before seen her do. She seemed to melt into tears. Jane's explanation that this was Angie's daughter was just out of her mouth when I stopped the officer from opening the dock gate. 'Go on, hug her,' I said, pulling rank on the police I didn't have. Angie and the girl fell into each other's arms and both wept openly. It was one of those rare moments that happen in criminal cases. To the credit of the police officers they let mother and daughter alone in their tender moment until Angie dried her daughter's tears and gave her daughter a final kiss. I wondered what the finality was about as the case had a long way to run. Jane explained that the girl was off to university in England the following day and that it would, in any event, be months before they saw each other again. I have the tears of several clients on my court gown but none so precious as those of Angie's daughter as her mother was led away by police officers to the sound of slamming iron gates and the revving of a big blue van with caged windows.

18

All Merry Hell

The following morning I could tell when I got within 50 metres of court that we had a problem. Jane was waiting outside with that look on her face that says, 'I've done everything I can, John. Here are the options, so what do you suggest?' It was the old delay, worry and expense problem. This time it was the arrival and departure times of our US witness, the one we had discussed in court the previous day. His name is Francis Anthony Boyle, professor of law at the University of Illinois. He was flying into London today, Thursday 30 September, and had to be in talks with Greenpeace for most of the day. He could fly up to Scotland tonight but that gave us no time to speak to him before giving his evidence in the trial. Scots law demands that a jury trial be continuous unless there is good reason for adjourning it. In these days of video links and e-mail there was not a hope in hell of Sheriff Gimblett allowing us the luxury of even a few hours. We had the guy's written materials and I had read his work on nuclear weapons and the law. It was impressive, and I knew he had given evidence many times in courts in the United States, so I had every confidence that he would hold up. The only option was to get him out of his hotel in Glasgow early, get him down to the temporary office rented by TP 2000 round the corner from the court and do the whole of his expert opinion evidence in the two hours before court sat. Jane was on her phone before I had even finished thinking out loud, and the arrangements were made. Easy. Now all I had to do was persuade Sheriff Gimblett that the court should hear a defence witness in the middle of the prosecution case. Not easy.

The Scottish courts are generally sympathetic to the schedules of expert witnesses but this was taking the rule to the limit. I talked the matter over with John McLaughlin and he agreed. We should emphasise the status of this witness and the limits to his availability. If necessary we should appeal to the general fairness of taking him out of sequence. We had our approach; now all we had to do was persuade David Webster not to object and we would have ourselves an 'unopposed motion'. Again, not easy.

David's boat did not get him to court in the mornings until about half an hour before we sat, and an anxious time was spent trying to think of any case law on this point. Nothing suggested itself, and the Advocates' Library was two hours away in Edinburgh. As suspected, David was in a similar position. The Crown hadn't taken a statement from this witness, even though he had been on our formal list of witnesses for over a month. I was sure everyone was underestimating him. They hadn't read his CV, but I had. There was no doubt about it. This guy was a heavyweight.

David agreed not to object to our motion to call this witness out of sequence but reserved his position as to the relevance to the trial of what the witness had to say about the events on board *Maytime* on the date in question. Fair enough. That turned out to be good enough for Sheriff Gimblett who ruled that Professor Boyle's evidence could be taken tomorrow. Right now we had the return of DS Cassidy to deal with.

His evidence for the prosecution hadn't finished the day before but it may as well have. This morning he spent a while identifying things for other witnesses to speak about later. He told us that he had taken possession of various things found around Loch Goil, some of them handed in by the public and some recovered directly by the police. John and I indicated that we had no objection to him being 'led' on this part of his evidence so that he could speak freely without legal interruption. We figured it was best for us that the jury got the full impression of what occurred after the women were arrested.

DS Cassidy went through the items with great care, identifying his signature on labels, giving police reference numbers for the record and identifying equipment as being the items mentioned in the indictment. He got a bit stuck with the names of some of the microprocessor switches and chips but he sped through the instruction manuals for some very high-level computer programs. He ploughed through bags of diodes and resistors, and six trays of electronic parts that had been recovered intact from the sea – a testament to the technology of click-shut boxes. He got past the DIM plugs without difficulty and identified a label in lieu of the Gemini dinghy used by The Trident Three. Then he was shown a handset belonging to the Marine Unit HQ and asked to identify it. With obvious embarrassment he nodded slowly and told us that it was supposed to be used for security checks. The laughter around the public galleries was suppressed but the serious point was made. There just was no security that night.

David moved on to the heavy stuff occupying a large corner of the court. Mostly these were computer monitors that had floated away on the tide. There were boxes of shoes and boots, which bewildered all of us. When these were presented to DS Cassidy, John and I put our heads together but couldn't work out where these fitted in at all. Whispers to our clients and Angie gave up no further clues but in the big scheme of things we let it pass. A further anomaly was a big drum of cable. This was really heavy stuff and the label said it was found 1,500 metres from *Maytime*. Strong as they were, there was no way the women could have moved it that far. It couldn't have floated and the women left *Maytime* on a police launch so we figured someone must have had a go at stealing it but abandoned their efforts for reasons best known to themselves.

David's expression gave away that he was delighted to have finished with DS Cassidy and it was my turn to cross-examine. I kept to Ulla's interview knowing that John would pounce on him for an important answer near the end of his evidence. DS Cassidy was reluctant to answer me directly and seemed to think there was a hidden agenda in my questions. He was wrong. We had a hidden agenda but he was looking at the wrong advocate. Eventually he agreed with me that Ulla was as cooperative as could be expected in the circumstances. And yes, she seemed intelligent to him and very committed to what she was doing. I moved over to sit down but then said, 'Just one more question, DS Cassidy. What did you say to the learned fiscal about why you were recalled to duty that night?'

'I don't recall, sir.'

'Would it be fair to say that DC Hazel Brooks told you that all merry hell had broken out?'

'Oh, I wouldn't go that far, sir.'

'How far would you go?'

'Just all hell had broken out, I suppose, sir.'

'Thank you, DS Cassidy. I have no further questions.'

The poor man must have thought he was at last off the hook, but, as I said, he was looking at the wrong advocate. John began quietly by taking DS Cassidy through his client's responses to questions and then put to him the joint statement that the women had left on board for the police to find. DS Cassidy sighed a deep sigh of frustration. He could see what was coming. Or at least he thought he did. What John was doing was trying to establish a direct link between *Maytime* and the smaller barge downstream called *Newt*.

But for now John asked DS Cassidy to read the fourth paragraph of the joint statement. He was far from pleased. As a fairly senior MoD police officer he said it was not his duty to promote such things. 'Nevertheless,' said John, 'the prosecution have produced it for this court to hear and you are the witness who took possession of this document, so let's hear what it says. We can skip the introduction and read from paragraph 4, please.' DS Cassidy then read:

We were especially mindful of non-violence and safety ground rules endeavouring to make sure in all our planning that our actions would cause no harm to any living being. We were also careful to make sure that our actions would be accountable and open. TP 2000 as a whole has communicated with the Government, Military and Judiciary on numerous occasions, sending them copies of the Handbook, Video and full lists of all

Pledgers and saying we would welcome either that those responsible for planning Crimes Against Humanity and grave breaches of humanitarian law be put on trial or that all the Pledgers be put on trial. This pre-prepared Joint Statement is a part of that process. We are not trying to hide our actions or to evade the consequences of our actions. Apart from a very necessary secrecy *before* attempting this disarmament work in Loch Goil we will be very open and will stay with our action to explain why and how we have done it. Copies of this Statement, with its accompanying enclosures, will be left with our banners at the separate sites where we do this disarmament work. If we manage to complete our crime prevention task without interruption then we will go to the nearest police station to explain what we have done. We will do this, not because we feel we have committed any crime but because we understand that at first glance our act of disarmament and crime prevention may be misinterpreted as simply a matter of property damage or even of vandalism with a political motivation and we wish to explain what we have done and why.

'Thank you, DS Cassidy, please continue,' said John.

We wish to make it quite clear that our actions are not politically motivated (although we realise they have a political dimension). Our actions are based primarily on the legal and ethical premise that the UK's Trident nuclear weapons system is a system preparing for the mass murder of innocent civilians over untold generations and we believe that the Trident system is ethically unjustifiable as well as being unlawful under International Law. As loving, feeling, human beings we feel responsible for trying to do everything in our power to prevent the Trident system from being able to operate with the proviso that our actions are safe, non-violent, open and accountable.

'Please continue,' anticipated John.

All three of us have spent long years trying the many conventional ways our society has devised for the righting of great wrongs. After having educated ourselves and thought about the issues, hearing the different viewpoints, we concluded that nuclear weapons are terrible weapons of mass destruction that could never be used ethically or lawfully. We have demonstrated against them, written and published articles and educational materials, arranged public meetings, leafleted the general public and military personnel, signed petitions, held vigils, lobbied Parliament and spoken to our constituency Members of Parliament. When our attempts to get Parliamentary Representatives to act on our behalf have failed we have gone to the courts, the police and other official institutions in our societies and asked for their help to bring the Government to Court to hear our legal arguments on the lawfulness of British preparations to use nuclear weapons. On an international level we have supported similar initiatives including the successful NGO-led campaign to ask the International Court of Justice to advise on the legality of all nuclear weapons. Applying this general Advisory Opinion of the World Court to the specific UK nuclear weapons system it is quite clear that any use of even one of the UK's 100 Kiloton warheads would be unlawful. We have tried all manner of ways to stop this terrible threat to our lives, those of others and the environment but have failed. Each person or institution we encountered along our way has agreed that, in general, nuclear weapons are terrible and that the world would be a better and safer place without them; but each has denied their own personal responsibility, saying the responsibility lies with someone else. We do not agree. Each of us must take responsibility and not just pass it on to someone else. Therefore, we can see no alternative to taking direct disarmament action ourselves. We have thus, each in our separate ways, come to the point where we have decided to disarm equipment essential to the full deployment of the UK's Trident submarine-based nuclear weapons system.

We will attempt to disarm the floating laboratory complex in Loch Goil such that it will not be able to contribute to that active deployment of Trident with its weapons of mass destruction. We will try to: (a) board the floating laboratory barge *Maytime* and disarm the equipment which is used to collect active acoustic signatures, and then to, (b) board the separate satellite platform *Newt* and disarm the equipment there which is primarily used for data collection from operational submarines.

The recent revelations that the Chinese now have details of how to track Trident by satellite using sensors to detect minute changes in the earth's magnetic field means that Trident is no longer invisible. Thus this DERA facility is even more important to the Trident programme as better techniques to hide the magnetic noise will need to be researched and tried out. The reporting of the Chinese incident confirms us in our belief that this DERA facility plays a key role in the Trident threat and will be essential in keeping Trident deployed. Any disarmament action that we do here is therefore of prime importance for the prevention of nuclear crime.

We plan to disarm such items as:

• The Variable Depth Hydrophones and Vertical Line Arrays which provide close measurement of acoustic profiles.
• The Range VHF and UHF surface and underwater communications equipment that permit vessel-to-shore communication of the tracking information.
• The Trisponder tracking system.
• Radar and electronic warfare calibraters.
• Extra low frequency emission testing equipment.
• Equipment used for the mechanical testing of cables and towed arrays.
• The pull-down winch on *Maytime* that controls the model submarines.
• The long-baseline experimental set-ups.

Our disarmament work is done in a spirit of love and compassion. We understand that it may not be viewed sympathetically by the authorities but hope that it will help the nuclear disarmament process.
Signed: Angie Zelter, Ellen Moxley and Ulla Roder.
Dated: 6 June 1999.

John had done his work well. Yesterday DS Cassidy had introduced the case for the women by way of the taped interviews played in court. Today he had done it again, this time by giving their case the authority of his own voice. John next asked DS Cassidy what *Newt* did but he wasn't for answering. Having to perform for the jury had got to him and he flatly refused to answer on the grounds of national security. But he wasn't on. The Crown had not seen fit to introduce any ministerial certificate nor in any other way restrict the evidence that the jury would hear. So he was stuck. John gave him one of his quiet tilts of the head, as much as to say, 'Do you really want me to get legal with you?'

Sheriff Gimblett intervened and asked John if he wanted to rephrase his question. He did and got his answer. DS Cassidy had to accept the obvious: that *Newt* was owned by the MoD and that it was directly connected to *Maytime*. Bingo. We were out of the woods as far as the 'remoteness' argument was concerned. From now on in the trial there was no danger that we could be convicted of damage to *Newt* but not *Maytime*. It was a big legal point that I'm sure was not spotted by the jury but very important to us. This time DS Cassidy was off the hook and I have seldom seen a man so glad to leave a witness box.

Our next treat came from prosecution witness number 17, Robert Thomson, who is a Royal Navy diver. He had been instructed by high-ranking MoD officers to get out his submersible unmanned submarine and check that the video gear aboard it was in good working order. It was going to the bottom of Loch Goil. The idea was that he meet the vessel manager Iain McPhee, and DS Cassidy, who would brief him on the likely spots where his submarine video camera would see some very expensive computers and other gear used to analyse and modify the acoustic signatures of Trident thermonuclear submarines. It wasn't an everyday job by any means.

We had no problem with this witness just coming into court and showing us what he recorded. We had no agenda for him and we were just looking forward to the show. Mr Thomson began by describing his methodology, that is he got his colleagues into a police launch and went out into the loch where McPhee pointed to where he thought the computers lay. Thomson then dropped a 'shot line' down to the seabed in order to get a reference point. He then drove the police launch round in a circle whilst watching a video screen and controlling the submarine with a joystick, not unlike a computer game stick. Once he had described his procedure David showed him Crown label 46, which he identified as the video he took on Tuesday 15 June.

However, because he wasn't very adept with court procedures he very honestly said he couldn't be sure. There was panic in the ranks. David Webster needed this video to be shown. We wanted it to be shown. The only part missing was the legal authority to show it. If it had been the wrong videotape then our trial or another trial might have gone off the legal rails, leading to a serious miscarriage of justice. Sheriff Gimblett was perturbed so I got to my feet and suggested that, without prejudice to either the Crown case or the defence, the video be shown in order to establish its contents. The jury, having had the experience of listening to taped interviews, were obviously dying to see the big picture show so off we went.

The picture was very grainy and not assisted by the murkiness of the seabed. Whilst Mr Thomson was obviously trying to get his bearings with the thing from up on the police launch all we saw were fish swimming by and occasionally coming so near the ROV (as the witness called his little roving submarine) that they bumped into the screen. One elderly lady on the jury said out loud, 'Och, the poor wee things,' to which Sheriff Gimblett raised her eyebrows in what seemed to me to be agreement. Then Thomson got his aim right and we began to see luminous writing standing out through the silt and shoals of tiny fish. The objects were fancy-looking computer central processors stamped unmistakably with the legend 'Ministry of Defence Property – Do Not Remove'.

We were asked to bear with Mr Thomson because the strong tide kept pushing the ROV backwards and we could all see the same large fish coming into view several times. A wag in the front row of the jury remarked to his neighbour, 'That would do for my dinner.' At that moment I wondered how much this exercise had cost and realised that, however much it was, it wasn't worth it. The exercise had the hallmarks of orders given in haste and probably anger. Mr Thomson began to name the items in view but of course that was not his job. He was an expert in diving, not identifying MoD equipment. However, as usual in this extraordinary trial, the defence let the infraction go. Nevertheless, the experts of the facts of the case, that is the jury, could see for themselves that there were some items that were obviously computer-related and some that were of a technical nature such as voltmeters and shiny discs that could have contained vital MoD or NATO information. There again these could have been Bob Dylan's Greatest Hits Volume 1 and Madonna's new single. There was no way of telling. However, we had not yet heard from Mr McPhee, the vessel manager, and David knew he could overcome any such difficulties by taking from him what he had lost on the night in question, having him describe the equipment and letting the jury draw the appropriate inference. The biggest surprise was that it took his team a week to recover the property from the bottom of Loch Goil. I said earlier that it is the deepest sea-loch in the UK and that was the problem. The divers could not stay down for any more than 15 minutes at a time before they needed a break. So the recovery work was painfully slow. But another impression had been left in the minds of the jury – if you're going to deploy a nuclear weapons system of such unimaginable magnitude then you need two things: first, the physical depth to accommodate these monsters of the oceans, and second, some-where where they will be out of sight and therefore (mostly) out of mind of the public – in other words, Loch Goil.

No one cross-examined Mr Thomson. There was no point. So Sheriff Gimblett thanked him for his evidence and released him from his cita-tion to court, meaning he could go back to his diving duties, whatever they may have been. It was just after 4 pm anyway and a convenient moment to rise for the day. By this stage in the trial the jury were less intimidated by the court and its procedures and were chatting on the way in and out of the jury box. On their way out, whilst collecting my papers for Professor Boyle in the morning, I clearly heard the wag who had referred to the fish say to the man behind him, 'I don't know about you but it's definitely Loch Goil mackerel in our house tonight.'

It was therefore in cheery mood that John and I and our instructing solicitors found ourselves down in the agents' changing room. But unfortunately our good cheer didn't last long. Every organisation has its extremists and mine is no exception. During the trial a few advocates passed through Greenock Sheriff Court doing mundane one- or two-day cases. Some were very glad that, at last, someone was making this argument in court. But one guy, after a few moments listening to gossip about how the defence case was going, condescendingly called out that my argument was complete shite and that 'I'd have my sergeant major shoot the lot of them – haw haw haw.' The remark poisoned the otherwise good-humoured atmosphere and left a bad taste after a day of strong progress; but in my years as an advocate I have come to expect such crassness from certain of my learned friends. I'm glad to say the remark stopped with me and did not get the chance to affect The Trident Three who had quite enough to deal with as they trundled back across country to their jail cells for the night.

After dinner that evening I silently raised a glass to Angie, Ulla and Ellen before getting down to the work of figuring out what to say to the man from Illinois in the morning.

19

The Man from Illinois

The Greenock office rented by TP 2000 for the duration of the trial was a run-down, two-rooms, straight-off-the-street affair with cobwebs on the back windows, a couple of 1930s stout wooden tables and original door handles from the late 19th century. As I entered, the place smelt of tea and fresh scones laid out by volunteers who were now busy in one corner refreshing banners with paint whilst David McKenzie updated the Web site with the previous day's events in court in another. Somebody's dog lay bemused under one of the tables. Jane Tallents led me through to a small back room with bare plaster walls where John McLaughlin was drinking tea and tucking into his second scone. 'He's on his way,' said Jane with real excitement in her voice. John and I compared notes and agreed with Stephen Fox, John's instructing solicitor, that if this guy was as good in person as he looked on paper then we should not try to control him in the usual way. Rather we should learn from what he had to say. It was a plan.

The man from Illinois immediately looked like a real .90 calibre. He was very tall with silvery hair and a good tan. What struck me most about him was the thing I invariably use to gauge my first impressions. He had a deep, firm handshake.

'Francis Boyle. Good to meetcha. Call me Francis,' he said with what I thought sounded like a Southern drawl. It wasn't, as it happened.

'John Mayer, Advocate,' I replied.

'John McLaughlin, nervous Advocate,' said John with one of his deep raucous laughs.

It was just what was needed. With ice duly shattered all round, we sat around a rickety narrow table so that we were only a foot or so away from one another, and Francis did what he does best. He took over. I had his CV under the first sheet of paper in the folder in front of me and as he spoke I couldn't resist another peek. There was a juris doctorate from the University of Chicago in 1971, a master's degree in 1976 and a PhD from Harvard in 1983. He was admitted to the Bar in Boston in 1977. By 1987 he was a visiting professor to a university in Moscow. By 1989 he had become the legal adviser to the Palestinian delegation at the Middle East peace negotiations, and in 1993 he became the special adviser to the President of Bosnia and Herzegovina before the International Court of Justice in The Hague. His books contained the titles *Defending Civil Resistance under International Law* and *The Future of International Law and American Foreign Policy*. He sat on the UN committee on the exercise of inalienable rights for the Palestinian people and had been on the board of directors of Amnesty International (US). Oh, and he had one more publication that seemed appropriate, called *The Criminality of Nuclear Weapons*. This guy would do nicely.

I explained that the charges we were facing were not statutory but derived from common law. John explained that we had a similar statutory charge of vandalism and how the two differed. Francis skimmed them with an 'Uh huh' and his eyes lit up.

'There's two ways to go,' he announced.

'One, you can use the international law defence set out in my book, but that may not work here in Scotland as my arguments are based in the US Constitution. So secondly, you could go the risky road and get the jury to acquit on the ground that the women acted wilfully but not maliciously.'

'So how can you help?' I asked innocently.

'Well, the international law defence is pretty wide. I don't know if you guys know about the Nuremberg trials... where they...?'

I nodded that we were quite familiar with that area of law and said that was the way I thought we should go, as it seemed pretty clear to me that it was the starting point for the modern law on crimes against humanity. That was agreed and because time was speeding past us we got into a blizzard of questions about the techniques of getting his evidence out in court. David Webster had reserved his right to challenge the relevancy of this expert legal evidence and that remained a big problem. We broke up by clearing our own cups and crumbs and stepping over the dog, which had come to join us and didn't want to move. Court was sitting in 12 minutes.

The public gallery was packed with TP 2000 supporters for the appearance of someone whose reputation went before him but whom hardly anybody on this side of the Atlantic had actually seen. When Sheriff Gimblett took the bench I wanted, for reasons of expediency, to dispense with the interpreter for Ulla for the duration of Professor Boyle's evidence. I really did need to finish him in one day and let him get back to London. So I made the motion. Sheriff Gimblett was concerned about repercussions in the European Convention on Human Rights and so wanted a reassurance from Ulla personally that she would not use the absence of her interpreter as an appeal point at any later stage. I had explained the reasons for making this move and its consequences to Ulla so she was well prepared and gave her assurance in broken English.

The air was pregnant with expectation but the bubble burst pretty quickly. David took his objection at the first opportunity and Francis, having given only his name and professional address, had to leave the witness box and wait in a dull ante-room whilst we dealt with the legal relevancy of him giving evidence about international law. Sheriff Gimblett was no pushover, as she took me to task about why the court should listen to an essentially academic lawyer from the United States in a Scottish criminal trial.

I submitted that it was proper for the court fully to apprise itself of all applicable law to the case in front of it and that hearing the evidence of an expert in some system of law other than Scots law was done in many areas of the law, both civil and criminal. In the civil field of international private law we must bring experts in foreign law to enlighten our court as to what laws to apply from a foreign jurisdiction and what not to apply. This even applies in certain cross-border cases involving English or Northern Irish law. The case of the film star Errol Flynn was about which of his many children should inherit his vast fortune – some of which lay in England and other bits of which were all over the world – and which children shouldn't. The law of Jamaica was argued to apply because that was his legal domicile when he died.

Digging into my personal experience I told Sheriff Gimblett about the case of Glen v Glen in which we effectively brought South Africa into the fold of nations to which international child protection law applies. In that case I brought in a late witness who happened to be a Scottish advocate but who was also a South African advocate to explain the law of South Africa to our judge. (It worked and I won.) But here in Greenock, whilst I had to accept that criminal courts do not 'scout about' as much as the civil courts, there was a big point in my favour. Nowhere in the written laws of Scotland was there anything to say whether international public law (as opposed to private law) actually was the law of Scotland or not. This court was trying common law crimes. Common law is based on principles, not written law. We pride ourselves on the flexibility that our principle-based system affords us. So I submitted that Sheriff Gimblett was, in the absence of purely Scottish principles on the point, therefore free to explore international public law for any useful principles upon which to rely. However, my last shot really sealed the deal. I reminded Sheriff Gimblett that in any event, as her ladyship was the master of the law, that is all the law, in her own court, it was open to her to accept or reject what this or any other expert witness had to say about the law and, if she was wrong, then an appeal court could deal with the matter.

John McLaughlin adopted my speech and Angie did the same with a silently mouthed 'well done' in my direction. David Webster was unprepared to deal with such a submission because, in all fairness, he does not deal with such matters in the usual course of a regional prosecutor's work. It is pretty ethereal stuff after all. Sheriff Gimblett ruled that

Professor Boyle could, in the spirit of helping the court with his evidence, do just that. Francis was one very relieved-looking professor as he retook the witness stand and continued.

I wanted the jury to get the full details of the qualifications and experience of the man in front of them, so I took Francis through his full academic and professional history. I particularly wanted to bring out that this witness was not a 'hothouse flower', as we say in the law, in other words that he had the guts to put his theories into practice and pit them against the people at the very top of the military structures whose job it is to maintain Trident and be the top-line people in any Presidential decision to use it. So apart from the qualifications I mentioned above, I asked him if he had lectured on the legality of nuclear weapons to any soldiers.

'Yes, sir,' he replied in the formal way that Americans do. 'At West Point to 200 of the highest US government officials including the general in charge of legal operations in the Pentagon.'

Next I wanted to demonstrate his impartiality, so I asked him if he'd given similar lectures elsewhere. We got the full 'Yes, sir' treatment again before he explained that he had been invited to lecture on nuclear weapons and international law to a similar audience in Moscow. Then I figured we'd had enough of the big guys so I asked about his involvement with Bosnia and whether that had led to any special travel arrangements. I'm sure the question seemed a bit bizarre to most people in court but I had my reason. Francis looked a little embarrassed but reached into his inside jacket pocket and produced a Bosnian passport.

'President Izetbegovic of the republic of Bosnia and Herzegovina appointed me as their attorney and director at their law court. I filed the first genocide case at the World Court and won two orders of provisional measures of protection on behalf of the Bosnians from the World Court. So you could say their government was very grateful for the help I'd given them and the Vice-President honoured me with citizenship and a diplomatic passport. I like to keep it close to me.'

The jury now firmly had it. We truly were out of the presence of everyday military police folk and into the presence of those who breathe another air. Professor Boyle then treated us to a *tour de force* on the subjects of the legality, or rather illegality, of nuclear weapons, the political relationships that brought them into existence, the World Court advisory opinion and the reasons why the Nuremberg Principles were put in place to stop mass indiscriminate slaughter ever happening again.

He laid particular emphasis on the fact that it was ordinary citizens as well as those in positions of military command who had the legal right to act to save others from war crimes, even if no official announcement had been made that the aggressive country was at war with this or that other country. Citizens had the right to be informed about whether their government was planning to wipe out millions of innocent people or, indeed, was just about to do so. He took us to the words in the Nuremberg judgements that say that all of the world's citizens have these wide-ranging rights and against whom we have them, that is any states, organisations or individuals about whom there is reason to believe that they are planning such acts of pure terror – for that is what a nuclear strike would be.

I don't like it when my witnesses want to expand on good answers because they often go so far that they leave the way wide open for hanging themselves in cross-examination. However, Francis was a top man in full flow so I let him run. He went on to give the court an example of proper intervention from the war in Vietnam. An ordinary soldier called Hugh Thomson was amongst a platoon that had taken a village when his lieutenant lost the plot and gave orders to shoot the captured men, women and children on the spot. The order came as a complete surprise to everyone in the platoon and, although delivered in English, it was clear enough to the villagers, who were terrified. Nobody would carry out the order, which was in direct contravention of their own standing orders, and then there was the little matter of the Geneva Conventions. It was clear that the lieutenant was very serious and would, if not stopped, shoot the villagers himself. Hugh Thomson then took intervening action and shot the lieutenant. The villagers were taken prisoner and dealt with according to the laws of war. Francis let the story sink in for a second before delivering the punchline. Hugh Thomson was given a Distinguished Service Medal for keeping the honour of his platoon and the dignity of the US in the field of battle. He had intervened to save innocent lives, and the point was not lost on all who now sat in silence in Greenock Sheriff Court.

Francis went on to give chapter and verse about how such principles were incorporated into the highest laws in the world: the United Nations Charter, which was drafted by the UK and the USA after World War II and subsequently signed by every nation in the world, and the flow of international humanitarian law that succeeded it. He confidently reminded the court that those principles were not just collecting dust on a shelf in the UN building in New York. They were being forcefully used to deal with those who had planned and executed mass slaughter in Croatia, Kosovo and Bosnia, and of course they had very recently been specifically approved and used by the House of Lords in dealing with one General Pinochet. At this point Sheriff Gimblett looked at me as much as to say, 'I can see your closing speech forming before my very eyes, Mr Mayer.'

I needed to get away from the general (no pun intended) and get to the particulars of the British Trident thermonuclear fleet. So I paused to let the evidence he had just given so powerfully sink in and then asked the simple question, 'Can Trident ever be used legally under international law?'

'No, sir.'

'Why not?'

It's way too large. It is equipped with warheads each eight times larger than those used at Hiroshima and Nagasaki. Those were completely indiscriminate in effect but Trident's weapons are unimaginably more devastating and each Trident submarine can carry hundreds of these. There is just no way that sort of mass destruction can even come close to what is called 'allowable collateral [civilian] damage'. One submarine load of nuclear weapons could wipe out enormous parts of the planet, physically destabilising it in the process. Planning such action is not just illegal, it's criminal under international law and, in my opinion, completely mad.

I needed to focus on the details and quotes from the International Court of Justice so I homed in. Francis had done this before and was way ahead of me.

'Would you like me to quote you from what the World Court said?'

'Yes, please. You'll find defence production number...'

He didn't need the document in front of him. I knew his postgraduate students were in almost daily discussion with him about the World Court's advisory opinion of 8 July 1996 so it wasn't perhaps as much of a surprise to me as to the jury that he could quote from such a complex document without looking at it. But it was very impressive nonetheless.

He pointed to the parts where the court was dealing particularly with the submissions of the UK and the US on the argument that some sort of 'nuclear clean strike' would be lawful, and emphasised the gravity with which the World Court said they would not endorse such arguments; and that, in any event, there was a long-standing obligation on every nuclear state to negotiate the decommissioning of their nuclear weapons, not try to think of ways of getting round the treaties they had signed, ostensibly in good faith. The World Court commiserated that it could not, on this occasion, go further than that.

I next had to get to the subject of decision making. Here Francis had to explain the nature of the relationship between the UK and the US. He apologised for having to tell us that all targeting decisions were made in Omaha, Nebraska. The British did have a seat at the table but they behave like guests, not hosts. I asked if Britain could unilaterally 'de-nuclear' itself. Francis could talk about the subject of international relations all day long. I hadn't bothered to take from him that he also held a teaching fellowship from Harvard University's department of government in that subject.

He gave us the example of New Zealand and distinguished its decision to 'de-nuclear' from any possible similar decision by the UK. When New Zealand asked its people if it wanted to go non-nuclear and ban all nuclear armed ships and submarines from its territorial waters, the answer was an emphatic 'yes'. But that brought the wrath of the US, which tried every manoeuvre in the diplomatic and economic books to try to get the New Zealand government not to implement the decision. However, it was an important decision, reached democratically, so there was no way, even under enormous pressure, that the state of New Zealand would relent. He said the UK and the US were too close to disentangle the ultimate link that makes them the economic and military superpowers that they are. But the relationship was still that of superior and willing subordinate.

We got on to the old chestnut of nuclear weapons as a deterrent to global war but Francis was dismissive. He'd dealt with this in courts in the US and Canada and knew all the lame arguments put forward in textbooks. He would not be moved from his considered position that the civilised world should always use legal means to deter any aggressor long before the stage is reached whereby a nuclear strike is the only answer. In any event, such strikes by Trident would always be illegal for reasons we were all by now familiar with.

OK, what about deployment? Would it be legal to have Trident submarines but keep them in dock instead of patrolling the oceans of the world?

'No, sir. Trident is just as capable of firing its weapons of mass destruction from the dry dock as it is at sea.'

'So the British Prime Minister couldn't just tell the Americans in some time of crisis that he was sorry, our thermonuclear weapons were parked in a lay-by?'

'No, sir, he couldn't get away with that.'

It was a suitably light moment for cross-examination to begin. David began by asking Professor Boyle if he was against *all* nuclear or atomic weapons. Francis said of course not. It would depend on whether these were capable of discriminating between combatants and non-combatants. However, as far as he knew, no such weapon existed and, even if it did, there were the legal obligations emphasised by the World Court upon all nuclear nations to negotiate the decommissioning of nuclear weapons, not develop new ones.

David sparred with Professor Boyle for a while but he wasn't getting anywhere until he got to his last question. 'Would you agree with me that not one person has been injured, far less died, as a result of nuclear weapons since those dropped on Japan?'

'No, sir.'

Francis went straight into his well-rehearsed answer, quoting details from all the nuclear submarine accidents and the chilling numbers of submariners who were lost at sea with their deadly cargo. David was obliged by law to let him finish and, as Francis moved on to the subject of nuclear accidents and official complaints to the UN about Britain's nuclear weapons, he looked like he wanted the court floor to open up and swallow him.

As Francis stepped down from the witness box, Sheriff Gimblett thanked him warmly for coming to give his evidence and assured us all that it had been most helpful. And with that the first week of the trial came to a close. There was a public meeting in Edinburgh that night, chaired by Lord Murray, on the whole subject of the legality of nuclear weapons. Just about everyone was piling out of Court 2 into buses and cars to make the journey. Professor Boyle was a guest at the meeting, as his plane didn't leave until the following (Saturday) morning. As usual at the end of each trial day, Jane was buzzing around with six things going on at the same time. As I was going downstairs to change out of wig and gown she called after me to ask what time I would be arriving at the meeting. Her face turned to stone when I called back, 'I can't go. There's a law against it.'

20

History 1 Efficiency 0

The weekend provided welcome respite from the rigours of trial. Professor Boyle was back in the United States and we were left with the business of getting on with the rest of the case. David Webster had been kind enough to intimate which witnesses he would be calling on Monday, and John and I had breathed a sigh of relief when we heard it was to be a security guard and an arresting officer. This was going to be fun, fun, fun all day. And so it proved to be.

The weekend in Edinburgh was relatively quiet with Matthew only bothering me six times on the phone asking how we were dealing with Crown production this and line of cross-examination that. He worries. I prepare. We'd done it successfully before, and we've done it since. It seems to work. It was obvious even to my teenage son Sam that something drastic had happened to security at *Maytime* on the night in question. I figured the drastic deed had been conceived and executed in Whitehall. The security around *Maytime* had the stink of 'efficiency cuts' about it – a euphemism for job losses and wage cuts that make government claims look good in isolation but make no sense on the ground where real events happen to real people. It's not my job to get to the bottom of these things in court but I can get a good idea of what happened. So as I put my head on the pillow on Sunday night of 3 October I planned to do just that at about 10.30 am the following morning.

At exactly 10 am David Webster called 'Number 3 on the Crown list, m'lady, Ministry of Defence guard, Fraser McKenzie.'

Mr McKenzie is a foot soldier in the larger scheme of keeping the Trident system secure from interference, and it showed. A DERA employee, he looked jittery as he took the witness box. He didn't seem to know which way to look and when he caught sight of my wig he squared up as though to give his evidence to me. But when the rather diminutive Sheriff Gimblett stood with her right arm raised for the swearing of the oath, he was a little surprised but in no doubt about who was in charge.

The indictment cited him rather grandly as 'Ministry of Defence guard' but, with all due respect to the man, he was more of a nightwatch-man. Whereas DS Cassidy had been to briefings about TP 2000 and how to deal with mass protests, this witness hadn't. After all, who in their right mind would spend taxpayers' hard-earned money on briefing a guard on what to look out for? But for all that he was the most reliable kind of witness a court can hope to hear from, because he was honest and open.

Mr McKenzie told us how he had started work at 6.36 pm on the night of 8 June and had been on patrol at 9.45 pm when he noticed a small engine-powered inflatable dinghy floating in Loch Goil south of *Maytime*. David showed him Crown production number 1 and asked him to take a look at the first three photographs.

'Yes, that's it. That's the very dinghy all right,' he assured us.

He knew the loch well and explained that the dinghy was slipping along quickly on the outgoing tide towards the mouth of the loch. These tides can be very strong because the water is so deep that it has a huge momentum. He took a good look to see if anyone was aboard but thought the dinghy was empty. He was asked if it looked familiar and he was equivocal.

'Yes and no. You see that type of dinghy is quite popular both with the MoD and other larger boat users. But it's extremely unusual to see one half-deflated in the water. They are usually very reliable.'

He thought it must have belonged to a company that serviced boats but just in case that was wrong he began to make a phone call. But he didn't finish making the call. Something extraordinary caught his eye. At first he couldn't believe it; but yes, there was a person moving about on the south-east side of the upper deck on *Maytime*. He was so far away that he couldn't tell much more than that. He couldn't see if the person was male or female, just that it was a person, on board *Maytime* – and that should most definitely not be happening.

This was alarming. He wondered for a second how the person got there but immediately connected the person to the dinghy and thought there had been an incident at sea. He was right, of course; he just didn't know the magnitude of the incident that was occurring before his very eyes. It was time to phone the man in charge, barge master Iain McPhee and the MoD police.

McPhee was at home in Glasgow and was alarmed to get the call. The whole idea of putting *Maytime* in such a remote location in the West Highlands and in the deepest sea-loch in Britain was to protect against people clambering all over this vital installation. McPhee had trouble believing that what McKenzie had seen was right and ordered him to get a closer look. The MoD police would need details. All merry hell had begun to break out.

Mr McKenzie got a bit closer and phoned his site support manager, Ian McInnes, but whilst he was on the phone he had to stop speaking. McInnes was yelling at him to explain what was happening but McKenzie was dumbstruck for a moment. The person he had seen must have been Ulla and she was throwing the last of the computer monitors into the sea. McKenzie described how he could see the size of the splash it made. I was piecing this together and figured this would have been about a quarter of an hour before the women had their picnic. When McKenzie got his breath back he gabbled out to McInnes what he had just seen and the line went dead. Everybody was now calling the MoD police.

Whilst trying himself to get through to the police he saw another monitor floating by, which lodged near him on the south bank. He went down to the bank for a better look and noticed other small objects – 'computer stuff mostly' – floating south on the tide. He tried to keep a list of the items in his memory but excitement was getting the better of him and he tried calling the MoD police again. This time he got through and was told to keep watch with his binoculars and to report anyone on board trying to escape. How little they knew of their invaders.

Now in a static position about 500 metres from *Maytime*, McKenzie had the chance to keep to procedure. He logged the time of dispatch of the police launch at 10.10 pm and watched some more. These sea-lochs are enormous and, apart from the village of Lochgoilhead, only accessible by sea. That's the whole point. However, the distance meant that the powerful police launch did not arrive until 11 pm.

David asked him to identify some banners that were now neatly folded on a table in the corner of the court. It was their first outing and they were each about 20 metres long. As Sheriff Gimblett's court officer, the witness and David unfurled the banners, there was a general air of light humour coming from the jury just behind me because they by now knew from the interviews that the women's whole idea of course was to announce to the world as soon as they got on board that they were there. Being as honest as the day is long, McKenzie said these banners looked like the kind of thing he'd seen hanging from the rails on the top deck but he couldn't be sure. John and I were giving David the signal that he could lead his witness on this point because we didn't dispute for a second that these were the banners proudly displayed by the women.

David asked Mr McKenzie what happened next. 'Well, it is very quiet at night on the loch and I was trying to keep my radio and phone on as low as possible so that I wouldn't be spotted but that became unnecessary,' he said, leaving us hanging.

'Why was that?' asked David.

'Because after about 10.25 pm there was a lot of banging going on from *Maytime*. The noise was travelling all over the loch. You could hear it for miles. I was going to report it in but then it got louder. I thought they were demolishing the place. Ian McInnes was on the radio a lot asking for information and telling me that the police launch was on its way. If he told me that once, he must have told me a dozen times.'

After the arrival of the police launch at 11 pm Mr McKenzie was relieved of keeping watch and he made his way further up towards *Maytime*. His radio had gone quiet but the loch now resounded to the squawk of police frequencies, marine diesel engines and helicopter blades. A sort of dragnet fishing operation began to scoop up what items were bobbing about in the water but the tide had taken most of the stuff out for miles, meaning the boats in this operation were shooting about here, there and everywhere. He ended his evidence for the prosecution by informing us that he had gone off duty at 06.36 hours and, yes, it had been a night to remember, that was for sure.

Both John and I cross-examined Mr McKenzie but we were really just laying markers for later witnesses. What he did tell us was that from his hut he had 'no visual' of the east side of *Maytime*. He accepted that he might get a visual of a person if they had come round to the south-east side. He also accepted from us that the security of both *Maytime* and *Newt* was the main reason why he was there. We could have poked fun at the security operation for this hugely important nuclear facility but there was no point. The system wasn't devised by Mr McKenzie, nor was he responsible for its efficiency. He was just a foot soldier and probably not a very-well-paid one at that. So no one asked him what he had been doing between the hours of 6.36 pm and 9.45 pm. It was lunchtime and we had an interesting afternoon ahead of us.

I was quite glad the agents' room downstairs was quiet during lunchtime. It gave me a chance to think about the next witness, who was the first person to meet the women on *Maytime*. James Steven Byres was an ordinary police constable with more than 11 years' service, and I thought I had a good chance of getting the truth from him. He was a Highlander, and he seemed to have been straightforward when Matthew interviewed him.

Constable Byres was doing a night shift on duty aboard the MoD vessel *Agility* when a call came in at 10.25 pm to get straight up Loch Goil to *Maytime*. As it happened he had never been up Loch Goil that far. His usual territory was up Loch Long from the Firth of Clyde to Arrochar. When the call came in, the *Agility* happened to be two miles south of the mouth of Loch Goil, so Constable Byres and his colleague were first to attend at the scene. They saw the Gemini dinghy drifting out of the mouth of the sea-loch but didn't stop to do anything about it.

Also, although they were going at top speed, they could see red plastic boxes passing them on the tide. David showed him Crown labels 26 and 27 and, like McKenzie, Constable Byres was honest enough to say that he could not identify the boxes.

At that point I wrote a note in my jury speech, which it is good practice to start preparing as soon as the first witness is sworn in. The note was about another important event in history with a point well worth remembering. The event was the sending of a telegram to the Zionist leader Theodor Herzl by the two rabbis he'd sent to Palestine to look at the land that was under consideration as the new state of Israel. The telegram read, 'The bride is beautiful, but she is married.' The point was that this officer arrived to arrest The Trident Three but he felt in his heart that what they did was no crime in the first place.

Constable Byres explained that the first priority of the police was the safety of users of the loch, followed closely by the apprehension of the people aboard *Maytime*. So when they'd seen the life-raft floating half-inflated close by *Maytime* they recovered it and 'tethered it to the other MoD barge, the other one they use for testing Trident. I'm sure it's called *Newt*.'

Honesty is a wonderful thing. One link we had to make was get prosecution evidence that *Newt* was directly connected to *Maytime* for the purposes of testing the Trident fleet, and here it was. The source was unexpected but the way in which this police officer was giving his evidence had 'the ring of truth about it'. If necessary, we could now invite the jury to accept that evidence as both credible (they can believe it) and reliable (they can use it as a secure plank to link one group of facts with another).

Constable Byres confirmed that it was 11 pm when they pulled alongside *Maytime*. There was still some light in the sky but because of the height of the surrounding hills and mountains the loch was dark. They had their searchlights on, panning the vessel from east to west.

We saw three ladies on the top deck by the railings, waving to us. They had put lots of banners and things around the decks but just at that minute we weren't bothered about that. I would say the women greeted us very politely. They were awfully excited, calling down their names and trying to shout an explanation over the noise of our engines about who they were. We could see them in our searchlights. Quite clearly as I remember. I remember seeing their white hair and being quite surprised. I don't think I read the banners at that time, or if I did I just ignored them. I couldn't tell you what they said.

Constable Byres went on to tell us how, at the point of docking, Mistress Zelter (as he called Angie – that is polite usage in the Highlands of Scotland) ran down the metal stairs and took a line from their bow to the stair rail of *Maytime*, assisting Byres in tying up. Byres was concerned that she might fall in so he told her to sit down. The conversation was cordial and the police simply asked the women to come aboard their boat, which they did. Once they got down to 'answering a few questions', the women corrected one another along the way as they told the story of the last three and a half hours. When they got to the part about the lifeboats failing to inflate the police explained why they had got that wrong and pointed out from an instruction manual where they had fallen into error. Concerned for other users of the loch, the three women offered to try to recover the life-raft, which must have been well out to sea by now; but Constable Byres assured them there were 'plenty of other officers on this one who will attend to that'. Ulla and Angie then offered to help with casting off but the police told them that, if they didn't mind, they should take a seat below, as the police could manage to cast off by themselves.

Constable Byres referred to his notebook to confirm that the sail, even by the powerful Clyde Marine Unit One, to the naval jail at Coulport took nearly two hours at a speed somewhat reduced from that on the outward leg. Slotting the book back into his shirt pocket he recalled with ease how prisoners and crew sat close together as his colleague Constable Blair steered the dark but well-known course. He remembered the women explaining in detail why Trident was a weapon of mass destruction outlawed by international humanitarian law. He also remembered offering hot tea all round. Then, rather wistfully I thought, he recalled making the tea and scrambled eggs, which he gestured towards the prisoners. Acceptance was by way of polite thanks in at least two languages, and the conversation turned to organic farming, free-range chickens and Ellen's jokes about being a bit overweight for this sort of caper.

During the rest of his evidence to David Webster, Constable Byres was careful to identify every piece of MoD property that he could, together with the bags of tools the women had brought aboard *Maytime*. And once more there were broad smiles and thanks as he did his duty and for-mally identified Mistress Zelter, Mistress Roder and Mistress Moxley in the dock. However I got the sense that they were more like old friends meeting in trying circumstances than police officer and accused. I also sensed that it must have been with some regret that Byres and Blair pre-sented their prisoners to the charge bar down in Coulport MoD jail and the dull procedures of form filling and fingerprinting began their weary course before those middle-of-the-night interviews began.

If ever there was a witness I did not want to cross-examine, it was Constable Byres. The mood he'd set was just right for us. He'd men-tioned the women's motive, namely crime prevention under international law, he'd confirmed the whole place was left neat and tidy (except for the computers being in the sea instead of on their desks) thus supporting our position that the women had acted wilfully but not mali-ciously, but he hadn't done the very last bit that I really wanted. So I took a chance and rose slowly to my feet when Sheriff Gimblett invited me to 'cross, Mr Mayer?'

'Constable Byres, in the course of your 11 years' service, have you been on police training courses?'

'Many times, sir.'

'What do you understand to be the legal meaning of doing a "mali-cious" act or "acting with malice"?'

'Acting with evil intent in the mind, sir.'

'Well done, constable.'

'Thank you, sir.'

'Did these women seem evil to you?'

'There is nothing evil about these women, sir. They are peace-loving...'

Constable Byres stopped himself as he realised he was making a speech on behalf of the defence. I had taken my chance and it had worked out well. I was correct about my analogy with the rabbis, so I was delighted to shut my notes and say with real gratitude, 'Thank you very much, Constable Byres. No further questions.'

21

The Weakest Link

The next couple of days were taken up with witnesses who were essentially called to corroborate what others had said. We had Donald Cameron Blair, the officer with Byres on the *Agility*, who wasn't seriously cross-examined. He was followed by PC David Paton, an officer with 10 years' experience who did a lot of rounding up of pieces of evidence floating on the loch and responding to calls from the public informing the police that there was a computer screen washed up here and something else there. His testimony in chief for the prosecution was pretty mundane really and I wasn't very interested in evidence like how long he'd spent putting police labels on things for production in court, not until he mentioned that he'd spent a lot of time that night with the master of *Maytime*, Iain McPhee.

I got very interested when he started to tell us that he was the one who took McPhee out to *Maytime* from Douglas Pier and even went aboard with him. Never having been on board *Maytime* before, PC Paton wondered how the women had managed to do all the dismantling work they had done and leave the place so remarkably clean and tidy. He said that if he hadn't known what he did know, he wouldn't have suspected that a crime had been committed at all – well, except for the fact that a large pair of bolt cutters lay on a desk and a secure cage with thick steel mesh had been emptied and a letter left in the cage addressed to the police.

He straightforwardly said that McPhee had ordered the banners to come down and he had helped in that exercise. He then rather foolishly answered David's next question with shoulders straight back and in pure police-speak. All David wanted to know was who else came and went on *Maytime* whilst he was there but PC Paton misunderstood the question and took it as a slur on his policing abilities. 'I can assure you that no person got on board whilst I was in charge aboard *Maytime* until we left at 4 am on the night in question, sir,' he said indignantly. The jury were smirking behind their indictments at the idea of the proverbial horse bolting down the course whilst PC Paton stood guard over the stable door.

David assured him that no slur was intended and thanked him for his evidence. John McLaughlin got PC Paton on to ground where the officer felt more secure. By proper reference to Crown production numbers and giving his evidence in cross-examination to the judge rather than to the jury, he clarified that every lifebelt was intact in its proper place, as were the life jackets, fire extinguisher and medical cabinet. He particularly noticed the 'burns kit' for reasons best known to himself. John thanked him and PC Paton thought he was done. But he wasn't quite finished. I asked him just one question: 'How angry was McPhee when he saw parts of his laboratory floating about Loch Goil?'

'Oh, extremely angry, sir.'

David had the opportunity to re-examine him and took it. However, in my opinion it only made things worse for the anticipated arrival of McPhee. PC Paton got a bit lost for words when asked to describe McPhee's demeanour. He understood the word well enough. All police officers do. His trouble was that he didn't want to land McPhee in the sticky stuff but at the same time was doing his best to be true to his oath in court. So we got a demonstration instead, in which he showed bulging eyes and an unmistakable grimace. I thought it showed McPhee as being in a state of controlled rage and took a note to ask him about that.

Next on was MoD police constable Karen Gardner, who was a breath of fresh air. She gaily whizzed through her appearance in the witness box just to tell us that she had done the personal searches of the women on arrival at Coulport. She identified the rucksacks and told us about the tools she had found and how Angie was happy to help her with which tools went with which rucksack. She didn't go into why all of the women's clothing was removed from them, but as we had signed some joint minutes about that we didn't bother to enlighten the jury at that stage. She recalled that Ulla's feet were cold and how she had tried to explain to her that she had to take her boots away as evidence. She and Ulla then had a ridiculous discussion about how important these boots were. PC Gardner's evidence certainly lightened up the atmosphere in Court 2, not least with Sheriff Gimblett's broad smile. When we had all finished our chuckles the officer looked rather disappointed when no one in a wig cross-examined her.

Wednesday 6 October was a grey morning. However, I had a spring in my step as I walked to court because today we were having the master of *Maytime*. But before getting stuck in, we needed legal approval from Sheriff Gimblett to have John Ainslie, the chair of Scottish CND and our expert on everything to do with nuclear weapons, sit in court beside us during McPhee's evidence so that no fact beyond our meagre knowledge of the subject got past us.

Before calling his witness David Webster correctly thought it was now time to read to the jury the matters that we had agreed did not need to be proved with witnesses and so were contained in the written joint minutes. Only that way would the evidence of this witness make sense.

Sheriff Gimblett addressed the jury directly, explaining what these documents were, saying that it was important for these to be understood and, as there were six of them, some patience would be required whilst the clerk read them. The clerk distributed copies to each member of the jury and, no doubt recalling his stumbles when reading the indictment, he took it slowly and gingerly.

'Ladies and gentlemen, the following joint minutes of agreement have been entered into by Webster, procurator fiscal for the Crown, and Mayer, advocate for Miss Roder, the second pannel, McLaughlin, advocate for Miss Moxley, the third pannel and by Miss Zelter herself.'

The first dealt with logistics. It was agreed that, sometime between

4.30 pm when the staff left *Maytime* for the day and 11 pm when the *Agility* arrived, the property on the indictment was removed from *Maytime* without the permission of the Defence Evaluation Research Agency, which owned the said equipment, and also that property was damaged as specified in the charges and that the true value of the property lost was approximately £80,000. (This was one of these occasions when an enormous amount of work had been done behind the scenes establishing the correct figure, instead of the original figure, calculated by McPhee, which was nearly double our amount. It is always important in a criminal trial involving property damage or loss that, in the event of a conviction, the judge has as exact information as possible in order properly to impose sentence. Amongst other things we found out that the cost of the diving had been included whereas it shouldn't have been.)

Secondly it was agreed that the photos of the life-rafts were true and original and could be relied upon as accurately showing the correct life-rafts. Thirdly, it was agreed that a police constable named Stuart Chambers working from a police launch called *Millennium* had picked out of the loch a whole lot of things that were now produced in evidence by the prosecution, and also that more officers called Andrew Stewart and John Colman had been on patrol in Loch Goil in an inflatable dinghy and also picked things out of Loch Goil and brought them to court.

Items 14 and 15 of the third minute were the most remarkable. It was agreed that on Wednesday 7 July at approximately 10.45 pm Officer John Ingham was on patrol in Loch Long heading south near the west shore when he saw a computer screen lying on a beach at the high-water mark in the area of Port Dornage. He recovered it and brought it in for production in court. What is so remarkable about this find is that it happened a month after the night in question and took place miles upon miles from *Maytime*. This screen must have been swept down Loch Goil and out to sea but sometime, somehow, come back in on the tide and gone up Loch Long. In any other case we could have challenged this as having too remote a connection with the actions of the accused. But of course, this was no ordinary case.

Then we got to fingerprints. It was agreed that fingerprint officers from the Scottish Criminal Records Office had taken prints from inside and outside *Maytime* including the main laboratory area and inside the (not very) secure steel cage shown in the photographs. These prints were around the hatch where the accused women had entered the inner premises of *Maytime*, around the large searchlights and on the railings of the upper and lower decks. Of course, it was agreed that, as well as belonging to the staff, these prints belonged to Angie Zelter, Bodil Ulla Roder and Ellen Moxley.

Joint minute number 5 brought reminders of Constable Karen Gardner because it was all about Ulla's boots, which matched forensic lifts taken from the inside of *Maytime*, the clearest link between Ulla and the 'crime scene'. Last, in minute number 6, we got to fibre samples taken from around *Maytime* and matched to the clothing taken from the women at Coulport jail. I imagine the jury were bemused by this technicality because it was obvious from our cross-examination that we had not challenged the witnesses who identified our clients nor those who said that certain property was missing. Anyway, the clerk had read straight through without error and was congratulated by Sheriff Gimblett. One woman juror in the front row gave him a round of applause as he sat down. What with the legal bit at the start of the morning and the rest of the day's procedure, it was now 1.10 and time for lunch.

A few minutes into my lunch a messenger came down to tell me that a Miss Jane Tallents wanted a word with me upstairs. I had half a sandwich in my hand. Jane looked sombre.

'Something's up.'

'Like what?' I asked.

'You know the guy with the German suit at the back of the court?'

'It's not a German suit, Jane. It's a Jermyn Street suit. It's off the Haymarket in London. Very expensive, I should think, but equally well made. Bespoke probably.'

'Shut up about spokes in suits. Something's up. He's been tapping away furiously at his laptop and he's just got into his chauffeur-driven car outside, plugged the thing in and a wee dish thing spun round on top of the car. They drove off and the dish went about halfway round and when it settled on a bit of the sky it stopped for a second. Then he unplugged the laptop.'

'If he drove, sorry, if his chauffeur drove off, how do you know what happened to the wee dish?'

'One of our pledgers followed the car on his bicycle. He's very quick on it.'

'It's McPhee coming next. That's what it is. However, we can't prove anything. I don't want to stop the trial and I'm sure neither does John or Angie.'

'God, it's probably gone to the Echelon guys. You know they listen to all our phone calls and e-mails, don't you?'

'Yeah, it probably has. We'll just have to get on with it. If I get the chance I'll mention it to Angie in court after lunch, see what she says.'

I went back downstairs munching my sandwich thinking about the Echelon Programme. It is run by the US and the UK with varying degrees of access by other states. The programme is quite old now but the equipment is light years ahead of anything the public can buy in a shop. The idea was conceived during the Cold War, round about the same time as some people in the USA and Dr Chris Malcolm were thinking about ways of expanding a new-fangled gadget called 'the Internet'. Chris is a real 'greybeard', as we say in university circles. A top-drawer thinker, he worked on the first computer link to the UK from the US. He's now a bigwig in the world-leading department of artificial intelligence at Edinburgh University. He's a good pal of mine and has told me all about the Echelon Programme. The idea is a little hard to believe at first but it is true. The United States and Britain listen to every communication made other than by speech in the world. There, I told you it was hard to believe. But they are not interested in teenage romances conducted by mobile phone. They are only interested in communications containing certain key words, phrases or numbers. Then, once interested, they determine exactly how interested they want to remain in this communication. Those decisions go up in layers, hence the name

Echelon. This little flurry wasn't to be my last brush with the Echelon people – not by a long chalk.

The man from Jermyn Street, as I now thought of him, took his seat just before David called, 'Number 5 on the Crown list, m'lady, Iain Christopher McPhee.'

There was a good deal of anticipation in the ranks about this man. He'd been elusive when the solicitors' clerks had been trying to get a statement from him. We didn't know how high-ranking he was nor, now that we'd had the joint minutes read to the jury, what he would actually add to the Crown case of vandalism and theft. I'm sure with hindsight David would think twice about calling him again.

As Mr McPhee took the witness stand he looked around for something, or someone. He was very nervous and spoke so softly that he had to be told to keep his voice up, as some of the jury couldn't hear him. I flashed a glance at Jermyn Street man and thought of Anacharsis, a Scythian prince of the ancient world who was admired in his own time for having the rare combination of sharp wit and deep insight. He was a great cynic and summed up all the systems of man-made law known to him as being 'like cobwebs: strong enough to contain the weak but too weak to contain the strong'. I wondered if that would be apocryphal and slipped on my glasses for the big show.

It was a dud. He was the weakest link. David trudged through more photographs and labels identifying this and that as having been aboard *Maytime* when the staff left and not there when he was taken aboard later that night. He told us there was a secure cage but that nothing of any importance was ever kept in it. The computers were all just standard and the regular staff were all really just maintenance people.

'Gotcha!' I thought. I wondered if he really expected us to believe that or whether he was just going through someone else's motions (guess whose).

He kept looking at the women in the dock and it became obvious that there was something deeply personal about this trial for him. He was still in his job, so it probably wasn't that. He might be passed over for promotion but that would be unfair, I thought. If any aspect of the systems around *Maytime* were at fault then it was those 'efficiencies in the cost of security' decided in Whitehall. 'Yes,' I thought, 'that's more like it.' I sympathised with Mr McPhee having to stand there and wait for me to cross-examine him. And, just before I rose to do that, I felt the spirit of Anacharsis leave Court 2 with the time-honoured bow of his head towards Sheriff Gimblett, muttering, 'I told you so.'

I knew this was the last Crown witness so I had to go for broke on getting *Maytime*, *Newt* and the actions of my client entwined, like strands of a cable, into one homogeneous unit in the minds of the jury. We would be having a lot of defence evidence but there is nothing like building a defence from the mouths of one's accusers for impact on the minds of the jury.

'How long have you worked for the Defence Evaluation Research Agency?' I asked. It's the old 'When did you stop beating your wife?' question. To give any sort of answer in years, months or weeks is to accept that you did beat your wife. Mr McPhee dutifully told us how long. So that meant he must have had a boss in DERA somewhere. The next line was designed to establish the link between *Maytime*'s operational function and the secret operations of Trident.

'You work for the Executive of the Ministry of Defence, don't you?'

'Yes.'

'And the Executive "executes" MoD policy, right?'

'Yes.'

'Exactly how do you keep a Trident submarine secret at sea?'

'I don't.'

'Really?'

'Really.'

His monosyllabic answers were having the desired effect on the jury. They looked, to the last one of them, like they were dying to know the answer to my question and thought that he was bound to know the answer but wasn't for telling us.

'Please have the latest annual report from DERA in front of you. Now, you deal in systems, don't you?'

'Yes.'

'Please read out the first paragraph.'

'Me?'

'Yes, you.'

He looked increasingly anxious and flashed a look at the back of the court, but he had no choice. It was the truth, the whole truth and nothing but the truth or be found in contempt. So he cleared his throat and began:

> Specialist experimental and test facilities attract high fixed costs and can rarely be used to their full capacity. But if demand for them falls, the cost to individual users increases with the result that they can rapidly cease to be viable economically. The capabilities that depend on them are then at risk. One of the major challenges is to ensure the resilience of our facility-based capabilities against short term changes in requirements, a task made all the more difficult by the reduced demand for physical trials flowing from the reduction in the number of [weapons] procurement pro-grammes, the impact of more extensive modelling and simulation, and the increased cost and complexity of modern weapons systems.

'Is that longhand for saying that DERA is under financial pressure but it would be all right if real-life nuclear bomb testing was allowed in the atmosphere?'

'I suppose so.'

'What has DERA done about these financial pressures?'

'I don't know.'

'Please read the next sentence.'

'Our response has been to pursue every opportunity to drive down costs by rationalising activities, particularly in the support area.'

'Does that mean cut the jobs and wages of support staff, like security guards?'

'I don't know.'

I needed to get to the direct link with Trident so I moved him on to page 2. 'Do you consider what you do for DERA to be one of the high-lights, so to speak, of its work?'

'I don't know.'

'What do you know about DERA?'

There was no answer.

'Please read the bit starting with the word "Other…".'

'Other, more specifically programmatic, highlights of the year included… the magnetic treatment of the 3rd Trident SSBN (HMS Vigilant).'

'What is "the magnetic treatment of the 3rd Trident SSBN"?'

'Getting it ready for going to sea.'

'What does "getting it ready" mean?'

'Giving it magnetic treatment.'

These circularities were not lost on the packed public galleries whose occupants were doing the laughing that the jury would have done had they not been too polite. I moved on to his areas of expertise and asked if he considered that *Maytime* was an essential part of the infrastructure of the Trident nuclear weapons system.

'I don't know.'

I dropped my head. 'Please turn to the part of that report headed "Sea Systems". Got it? Now please read from the submarine-heading "Expertise and Experience".'

DERA possesses a wide breadth of skills that are appropriate to all aspects of Maritime Warfare and the understanding of relevant aspects of the marine environment. These skills have been developed over a great many years of research for the Royal Navy and have benefited greatly from a very close liaison with the Naval Staff, including those involved in developing operational concepts, through to the 'end users' on ships and submarines at sea. These encompass… Hydrodynamics signatures and systems.

'Do the skills mentioned in that passage refer in part at least to you and your staff?'

'Yes, I would say so.'

'What is a hydrodynamics signature?'

'They're not all my staff.'

'What?'

'People come and go all the time. They sign in at Douglas Pier and are brought out by armed guards. I don't know all of them. I'm sure some are MoD scientists. I'm responsible for them whilst they're on board, but I don't know them all.'

'Do they bring their own laptops?'

'Oh, yes.'

Now we were getting somewhere. The ghost of Anacharsis had returned to help the poor guy. My sympathies also returned and I just asked him in broad terms, 'Do these scientists and others check that the systems which keep Trident secret at sea both collect and deliver information to the computers on *Maytime*?'

'I think so. Yes.'

I forgave him for his anger and interfering with the 'crime scene' and left it at that. We had the picture. John worked on him for a bit, getting a few details about the relationship between *Maytime* and *Newt*, the fact that Loch Goil was a key facility and that as a result of the action by the three accused women the work of *Maytime* and *Newt* was 'knocked out'. McPhee had done his best to serve two masters but with that hypothetical knockout blow landing in the dying questions of the prosecution case, Mr Jermyn Street got up and left Court 2, taking his laptop with him.

FIVE

HUMANITARIAN LAW
WINS THE DAY

22

The Strongest Link

I am fortunate enough to have a number of friends who are old hippies and they often send me 'light', 'love' or 'empowerment' across the universe when they know I'll need it. I couldn't sleep on the night of 11 October, not because I had a big part the following day but because Angie did. I hadn't tried the 'across the universe' trick myself but as I lay in my B & B with the minutes and hours slowly passing I tried to picture Angie in her jail cell. She may have been sleeping soundly for all I knew but I imagined her pacing its four steps up and down, moonlight coming through the bars and her speech in her hand. Angie is self-confessedly nervous in courts so she always has a prepared script. I knew she wouldn't need legal help; in any case I could clear up that kind of thing with her before she left the witness box. What I sent was all my courage and whatever it is that makes me unafraid to advocate my client's case regardless of the charges, the judges or the public opinion that may be for or against it. And I sent it in wagonloads.

After breakfast the 500-metre walk to court gave me time to field three calls from Matthew and think about when to fit another foreign witness into the schedule. His name was Judge Ulf Panzer, a presiding judge in the city of Hamburg, who would testify to the German experience of 'citizen intervention' cases, his understanding of international humanitarian law and the application of the European Convention on Human Rights. I was almost at court when Matthew rang again. I was fed up with this but took the call anyway.

'The Scottish Legal Aid Board is playing silly buggers. They've refused to pay for Judge Panzer's flight.'

'What? They can't do that. He was good enough to fly over last week at his own expense and sit around while we tried to get to him. It's not his fault he couldn't stay. He does have to preside in the criminal court in Hamburg. Have you appealed?'

'It's a waste of time. I was told to phone the appeal guy at 4.45 pm yesterday. I did, but he had already left the office. Now this morning they say they won't entertain me. You know what they're like. You don't get reasons. They just do what they like.'

'Not in this case they don't.' And I hung up.

I was furious. When I reached the court precinct my mood was out of sync with the crowd of TP 2000 people who had gathered around the vehicle entrance where they knew the prison van would soon be arriving. They knew that this morning would see Angie take the witness box. It would not be overstating the matter to say that a life's work in the peace movement had been leading up to this day. I nodded good morning to them as I passed in and could feel that their mood was all about people. They were upbeat, concerned, committed people giving their time and energies for others. They are good people. There was the quiet man with the flat brown briefcase who seemed to have been present for every day of evidence, the silver-haired ladies who were fond of straightening my wig for me and the big man who made the tea and distributed it from the van. I didn't want them to be disappointed so I kept my peace and went downstairs to talk to John about what to do with the Scottish Legal Aid Board.

He agreed. We'd have to postpone Angie's evidence and sort this out. Sheriff Gimblett did not seem impressed with the way the board had handled our request so I pushed it. I made the submission that this trial was of such importance to both the Crown and the defence that, in the public interest, the board's chief executive should answer for his minions' recalcitrance. I know the chief executive. He's a nice man who is into classic cars. But I nevertheless moved the court to 'ordain' him to appear and explain why the board was refusing this request; it was worthy of being granted on its own merits and, in the big scheme of the trial, would cost very little. David Webster was not in this squabble, and the others on the defence side adopted what I had said. Sheriff Gimblett agreed with us and pronounced her order for the chief executive to be brought from Edinburgh the following day to approve this request or give his reasons for refusal – not quite across the universe, but an important 100 kilometres nonetheless.

We were about to get started when Jane whispered into my ear that Ulla was unwell. We saw her and she obviously needed a doctor. Unbeknown to me she was taking painkillers and had run out. The police were quick to arrange for the local police surgeon to see her and after lunch all seemed to be well, or as near well as one can get in those circumstances.

The legal submissions, the doctor and the further attempts to contact the appropriate civil servant took so long that Sheriff Gimblett asked Angie if she wanted to begin after lunch. Angie stood in the dock clutching her speech and said firmly that she would rather make a start. Once Angie was in the witness box, Sheriff Gimblett and Angie looked each other in the eye and there was a real sense of tension between the two women. It was plain that Sheriff Gimblett saw this as a key part of the trial. Our High Court had recently ruled that a personal 'sincere belief' that nuclear weapons were a bad thing was no defence to a criminal charge and I had not taken exception to that ruling at an earlier stage in this trial. Sheriff Gimblett was polite, telling Angie to take her time and get her papers organised. However, she was plainly expecting to hear about Angie's many years of work leading to the point where there arose a legal necessity to 'do what one can, when one can' to avert the constant danger of civilian annihilation by nuclear weapons. Angie was standing directly opposite me and I beamed her a bit more for luck, but needn't have worried. Her evidence was a *tour de force*.

Trident Ploughshares 2000 don't have leaders but if they did it would certainly be a form of 'cabinet government' and Angie Zelter would be one of them. Those who needed to cough and fidget got that out of the way and the court fell absolutely silent.

Angie began very strongly by stating her name, that she was 48 years old and a widow with two adult children. She then continued:

After completing my degree at Reading University when I was 21, I married and went to Africa. Three years working with my husband for the British government in Cameroon, West Africa, taught me directly how poverty in the Third World was caused by transnational corporations, backed up by the financial institutions and military might of the powerful nations of the world. This system works to provide profits that ended up in the UK and many other parts of the Western world. Whilst there I was kindly told that if I really wanted to help the people and forests of Cameroon, then I should go home and put my own country in order. I returned to England determined to take responsibility for what my country was doing in my name and to withdraw my support from policies and actions that were destroying the livelihoods and environment in other parts of the planet.

I have been working in a voluntary capacity ever since: in the peace and environment movements, mainly for nuclear disarmament but also for the protection of old-growth forests and the rights of indigenous peoples. I have taken part in many different campaigns over the years and worked with organisations such as Friends of the Earth, Greenpeace, Campaign against Arms Trade and the Campaign for Nuclear Disarmament. Although working mostly in England, I have also supported campaigns which try to prevent crimes from taking place in other countries like Malaysia, Canada, Poland and Finland as well as here in Scotland. I have also been imprisoned in some of these countries.

My experience has been that often a strong and purposeful international and public non-violent direct action campaign is needed before change can occur. This is an important point because many people may question how our disarmament of just one research laboratory connected to the Trident system can actually prevent nuclear crime. The answer is that when it is part of a sustained, publicly supported, non-violent and accountable campaign it *can* do just that. Our action is part of such a sustained and publicly supported campaign – called Trident Ploughshares 2000.

Now I want to give you some background to my work in the peace movement because today I need to present evidence to you to show that I have tried every other reasonable method to prevent nuclear catastrophe over the last 25 years before disarming *Maytime*. I did not disarm the nuclear research laboratory on a whim or in anger. Mine was not the act of a vandal or terrorist. I had tried everything else and in the circumstances there was no other reasonable legal alternative.

Although aware of the dangers of nuclear weapons for many years, it was not until the early 80s that I first realised there was a world-wide movement for nuclear disarmament which had begun in 1945 after the terrible US nuclear devastation of Hiroshima and Nagasaki. In fact, the very first resolution of the newly formed United Nations, unanimously called for '*the elimination of nuclear weapons and all other weapons of mass destruction*'. In 1978, at the height of the Cold War, millions of signatures were being collected for presentation at the United Nations special session on nuclear disarmament. I read the background documents very carefully, signed the petition and then joined a local group to help get more signatures, thus beginning my active involvement in the peace movement.

I helped form a local CND group and organised numerous discussions, debates and public meetings in my own area, which was surrounded by US nuclear air bases. In the course of doing this I was able to speak face to face with some of the direct victims of the nuclear weapons cycle – those who have suffered and continue to suffer from the effects of the uranium mining, production, testing and deployment of nuclear weapons. I heard directly from some of the survivors of the Hiroshima and Nagasaki bombings, saw records and photos of the devastation and heard of their suffering first-hand. I would also like to remind you of the photos we left in the DERA laboratory after we had disarmed it.

The reason these were placed in the laboratory was to show the technicians what we were trying to prevent from ever happening again. It is so easy for all of us in our everyday lives to forget the bigger picture, just to think of our own lives and jobs, and to forget the implications and consequences for the wider world. To forget to question ourselves. Is this a moral, justifiable and responsible piece of work I am doing here? Should I do it? We wanted to bring the ultimate consequences of the work on making Trident invisible out into the open.

I have also had the sad honour of introducing Darlene Keju-Johnson from the Marshall Islands and Lijon Eknilang from Rongelap to the mayor of Norwich at a public debate. I say sad because unfortunately Darlene has now died from the many cancers from which she suffered as a result of the testing of nuclear weapons. Their stories were heart-rending and I have never been able to forget them.

Lijon told us: 'I was eight years old at the time of the Bravo test on Bikini in 1954. It was very early in the morning that I woke up with a bright light in my eyes. Soon after we heard a big loud noise, just like a big thunder and the earth started to move. A little later we saw a big cloud moving towards our island. It covered the sky. Then it began to snow in Rongelap.

'For many hours poison from the bomb kept falling on our islands. Late in the afternoon I became very sick. Big burns began spreading all over our legs, arms and feet and they hurt very much. Many of us lost our hair. We remained on Rongelap for two and a half days after the fallout came. Then Americans came to evacuate my people to the American base on Kwajalein Atoll. We did not take our belongings or animals.

'After that we moved to Majuro and we stayed there for three years. In June 1957, when we did return, we saw changes on our island. Some of our food crops had completely disappeared and others stopped bearing fruit. What we ate gave us blisters on our lips and in our mouths and we suffered terrible stomach problems and nausea. In the early 60s we began to experience all of the illnesses we are having now. Many people suffer from thyroid tumours, stillbirths, eye problems, liver and stomach cancers and leukaemia.

'The most common birth defects on Rongelap and other atolls in the Marshall Islands have been "jellyfish babies". These babies are born with no bones in their bodies and with transparent skin. We can see their brains and their hearts beating. There are no legs, no arms, no head, no nothing. Some of these things we carry for eight months, nine months. The babies usually live for a day or two before they stop breathing. Many women die from abnormal pregnancies and those who survive give birth to what looks like strands of purple grapes which we quickly hide away and bury.'

In 1985, with the help of Greenpeace, the people of Rongelap evacuated themselves from their contaminated atoll to another island and have lived in exile ever since. They have never been compensated for the damage done to their island and livelihoods and in any case the genetic damage carried in their genes could never be adequately compensated for. The Marshall Islanders were told by the Americans that '*We're testing these bombs for the good of mankind, and to end all wars*'. The navy official did not tell them that the Bikinians would never see their home again. Bikini is off limits for 30,000 years. On June 8th I acted with them in mind.

I updated my information only just last year with information gleaned from Bradford University's renowned department of peace studies. I knew it was necessary for me to be able to prove that I am in imminent danger. This is a factual rather than a legal matter. However, the defences that I will be using will be:

1. A common law defence of necessity. That basically states that having tried all other means to prevent a very great wrong I had no other choice open to me but to join a campaign committed to practical and safe disarmament and to do my part in disarming a part of the Trident system by disarming *Maytime*.

2. A statutory defence that authorises me to act if I have a 'reasonable excuse' and where I shall be arguing that trying to help prevent mass murder is such a reasonable excuse.

3. An international law defence that authorises me to act in order to prevent the commission of crimes recognised under international law; and finally

4. A moral defence that is mine of right as a human being and essentially says that whatever the state of the law, it would be right and proper to try to prevent the mass murder of innocent people.

I need to make it quite clear from the outset that I will not be disputing any of the obvious facts of the case. I will admit that I disarmed the DERA laboratory with Ulla and Ellen. This dispute is not over whether we did, or did not, throw into Loch Goil valuable research equipment but whether these items would have been used for the unlawful and unethical purposes of aiding and abetting grave breaches of the Geneva Conventions Act, which is UK law, as well as breaching other international humanitarian laws which apply in Scotland, just as they do in all countries of the world. I hope by going through these that you will see we had a lawful justification for our acts of disarmament.

It is important to note both the political and legal aspects of the case. In keeping these in mind I can do no better than to refer you to the words of the International Court of Justice where the World Court said: 'The fact that this question also has political aspects, as, in the nature of things, is the case with so many questions which arise in international life, does not suffice to deprive it of its character as a *legal question*.'

Angie then went on to weave her work into that of organisations such as Pax Legalis saying:

[This organisation] was formed in 1984 and tried for more than 10 years to have the substantive questions of law on nuclear weapons addressed by the courts. After 10 years of cases having been laid in court and refused, summonses for the arrest of those responsible for decision taking were refused, and other legal attempts were postponed or withdrawn, Pax Legalis concluded that the judicial system was unwilling to hear the substantive case. Many such approaches have been made by Scottish people to the Lord Advocate in Edinburgh on similar lines. All have been met with the same official brick wall.

In the midst of these activities, I was invited by other concerned people to join with them to form a national charity called INLAP – the Institute for Law and Peace. We began to produce educational materials about international humanitarian laws and explored how we could persuade the authorities to uphold and respect these laws.

This was around 12 years ago. As part of an INLAP delegation, I went to the first gathering of international lawyers and non-government organisations in The Hague to join others to press for an approach to be made to the International Court of Justice to ask for an advisory opinion on the legality of nuclear weapons. This initiative started with an open letter by a judge in New Zealand and developed into the World Court Project. After many problems, including a great deal of pressure from the nuclear weapon states who tried to stop the process, the UN General Assembly finally asked for and received the advisory opinion of the World Court.

This advisory opinion clarified the international laws relevant to nuclear weapons, and stated that nuclear weapons are generally illegal. It highlighted the two principles of international law that can never be broken even in an extreme case of self-defence. These two cardinal principles are first that: 1) 'States must never make civilians the object of attack and must consequently never use weapons that are incapable of distinguishing between civilian and military targets'; and 2) 'It is prohibited to cause unnecessary suffering to combatants. It is accordingly prohibited to use weapons causing them such harm or uselessly aggravating their suffering.' No British Trident nuclear warhead of 100 kilotons can possibly conform to these requirements and are thus illegal.

After the publication of the advisory opinion, in response to letters from many concerned citizens, the government made it quite clear that it would still not disarm its illegal nuclear weapons. I considered this irresponsible, undemocratic and shameful as well as deeply undermining of the international legal order. Basically the eight nuclear weapons states (NWS) are holding the other 180 non-nuclear countries to ransom and are undermining the rule of law in the international community. They are abusing their power. This was one of the main reasons why I worked with others to start a project based upon directly upholding international law – the Trident Ploughshares 2000 campaign of people's disarmament.

On 18 March 1998, we wrote to the Prime Minister with copies sent to the major Cabinet ministers, heads of the armed forces and the heads of the Scottish and English judiciary. The letter outlined the need for immediate nuclear disarmament by the UK in compliance with international law and the advisory opinion of the International Court of Justice. I was subsequently phoned up at home by Commander Harbour of Faslane base to ask if I would mind sending him a copy of the book and our video directly. TP 2000 received a cheque for £25 from him in payment!

We did not *publicly* launch TP 2000 until 2 May 1998. We hoped this might make it easier for the government to talk quietly with us, and perhaps inform us that they were in the process of giving effect to their international obligations, and that therefore we would not need to start our campaign. However, we did warn them in our first letter that if we found they were not seriously engaged in a process of disarming all weapons of mass destruction, that could never be used in accordance with international law, then we would launch TP 2000.

We have continued informing the authorities at least every three months of our concerns, and asking pertinent questions which they refuse to answer. I have here a batch of letters that either I personally or TP 2000 as a whole has sent to the government from 1996 to the present. I have of course written hundreds of letters over the years but thought these more recent ones the most relevant to this trial.

These letters show a marked reluctance to answer important questions as to how Trident can be legal. I have here a copy for everyone of the most recent open letter sent on 23 March of this year which summarises the questions to which we have still not been given satisfactory answers. Every three months TP 2000 holds well-publicised opportunities for open disarmament by TP 2000 pledgers. The government is given the names of all pledgers, which is updated every three months. At present we have 143 pledgers from 10 different countries.

Angie then took the court through the international humanitarian laws, which she said were on her side. These included the Nuremberg Principles of 1946 and the Universal Declaration of Human Rights of 1948. She argued that these would be breached by a nuclear strike, not least because the long-lasting radioactive contamination would interfere with innocent people's right to life and health. She reminded us of what

Professor Boyle said in evidence – 'such a strike is not just illegal, it's criminal'.

Angie was in full flow. She held aloft papers from the European Court of Human Rights recognising the priority of humanitarian considerations over national security, and pointed to the World Court ruling, which said that the 'fundamental rules of humanitarian law are to be observed by all States whether or not they have ratified the conventions that contain them, because they constitute intransgressible principles of international customary law'. Angie now assumed the jury knew enough about Trident to follow her in thinking that its weapons were so massive, and thus completely indiscriminate, as to be illegal, indeed criminal, in all circumstances.

She concluded, 'A trial such as this gives the people, in the role of the jury, a chance to set the record straight and, by finding us not guilty, to send a clear message to everyone to take responsibility for the wrongs around us and to urge the government to finish the disarmament themselves. Thank you for your patience.'

As I said above, it was a *tour de force*. Like me, Sheriff Gimblett had a copy of the whole speech and so could relax during the evidence. I allowed myself the occasional glance up to the bench to see if Sheriff Gimblett was noting anything in particular. She wasn't. She was perfectly still, watching and listening to this performance with her chin cupped in her right hand, her index finger tapping at appropriate moments. It is not always the case that judges listen to what is being said in court. But on this occasion the judge was not alone in her concentration. I have no doubt that each person in Greenock Sheriff Court 2 that day will remember what they saw and heard for the rest of their lives.

I wondered how on earth David Webster was going to cross-examine her. I wouldn't have. Angie had been comprehensive in her treatment of the facts and the law about Trident nuclear weapons, but she had fallen into legal error once or twice. That is wholly forgivable for someone who is not, after all, legally trained. However, such errors are just the kind of basis one needs for an attacking speech at the end of the day. I wouldn't have given her the chance to do any better from the witness box, but

David decided he wanted to cross-examine and that was his legal right.

'When you're ready, Mr Fiscal,' said Sheriff Gimblett, using David's proper legal title.

David rose with his line of 'cross' well prepared.

'You are bypassing the democratic process. Why don't you write to your MP?' he asked curtly.

'What? I'm not bypassing the democratic process. The successive governments who keep ignoring the World Court and threatening the people of the world with weapons of mass destruction are the ones who are bypassing.'

David drew breath but Angie wasn't finished:

> I stood as a Green Party candidate in a general election. We've written to the heads of state of all the nuclear powers including India and Pakistan, MPs, Scottish and English law officers – a million times. What do you mean, I'm bypassing the democratic process? I can tell you that the government, Geoff Hoon *et al*, is listening very carefully to us. They're not acting yet but they are listening. Tony Blair was once in CND.

'You claim to be acting for all of us. But you haven't asked all of us whether we want nuclear weapons, have you?'

> I haven't, no. I don't have the resources. But STV conducted a poll in which 85 per cent of Scots wanted rid of nuclear weapons. In any case, you are talking politics, Mr Webster. On 8 June we were taking legal action to prevent ongoing plans, preparations and actual deployment of weapons of mass destruction at a time when there was an ongoing danger. The danger is still there today. I am very well informed about the situation and know my rights under international law to put a stop to that crime against humanity. We especially chose a very safe time to disarm *Maytime*. If Trident had been docked there it would not have been safe. We are very well briefed.

'But you didn't prevent Trident from doing or not doing anything?'

'You don't know that. Control of the Trident programme world-wide is very accurately timed. We know that. Our disarmament action must have acted like a spanner in the works – the same as when a jumbo jet crashes at an airport or a plane breaks down on the runway of a major airport. The whole system is disrupted because the system is world-wide and very closely timed.'

Angie had him on the ropes and the exchange deteriorated still further.

'You are just trying to get a not guilty verdict for the publicity. Aren't you?'

'That's nonsense. My action on 8 June is the most important disarmament action of my life. This is not a game, Mr Webster.'

'But nuclear weapons have kept the peace for 50 years,' said David, generalising and going over the legal line where he was actually giving evidence instead of taking it.

'More nonsense. There are more wars than ever now.'

The exchange then ran out of steam and they left it there. My own opinion is that Angie kept her cool throughout. She did not know what questions might be asked in cross-examination but if there is one person ready and able to answer any question about Trident on the hoof, then it is Angie. And she did it with dignity.

I was glad to hear that Judge Ulf Panzer would be joining us from Hamburg in the morning. We would be hearing from him right after we got the explanation about why a civil servant refused his modest expenses. As it happened the chief executive was, as expected, very reasonable and he promised to 'keep an eye on these things in the future'. Well, he does work for the government so I don't suppose we could have expected more than that.

I lay in bed knowing that Judge Panzer was flying out of Hamburg that night, and thought there might be something in this 'sending stuff across the universe' after all.

23

Sometimes the Mountain Does Move

Down in the agents' room we were so caught up in getting our experts' schedules arranged and checking last-minute details for their testimonies that we didn't notice the commotion upstairs. For once, the prison van was early and court was about to start when Jane wanted five minutes.

'There's a deputation from the Scottish Parliament coming in with a signed document. Any chance of asking Sheriff Gimblett for five minutes whilst they present it?'

The ever-dutiful macer had spotted the well-known faces of John McAllion and Dorothy Grace Elder, both Members of the Scottish Parliament (MSPs), and had delayed bringing the sheriff on to the bench. In fact they were two of a crowd who had come from Edinburgh to Greenock to pay tribute to the women on trial. The three accused were actually sitting in the dock when the deputation came into Court 2. The accused stood, still flanked by their police guards, as a letter of support was presented to them. What was encouraging was that it was cross-party support and 26 MSPs had signed the letter. Anyone who knows about the way these things work would agree that many more MSPs were back in Edinburgh privately wishing their names were being read by those who had the tenacity and courage to do what others only dream about. We were on the downhill run towards the legal speeches but it was nevertheless a great boost to all concerned to know that the trial was interesting to the government of Scotland as well as the many academics and practitioners around the world whose support came in by e-mail.

Five minutes had turned into 25 but Sheriff Gimblett didn't seem to mind. Sheriffs always have plenty to do. As the jury took their seats the names of the deputation were clearly audible to me, so they had obviously been told the reason for the delay. Sheriff Gimblett was businesslike, simply smiling her usual morning greetings and asking, 'Now, Mr Mayer, whom do we have?'

'Judge Ulf Panzer, my lady.'

We advocates are used to seeing important people in and around Parliament House but Judge Panzer was a truly impressive figure. He spoke fluent English but, I thought, with more of a Dutch than German accent. His collar-length white hair was thick and well groomed with a centre parting, and from the moment he took the witness box he held the court spellbound.

He accepted he was not an expert in international law in the usual sense although he had been a member of various groups dealing with such matters for many years. After explaining his legal qualifications and powers as a judge in Germany, he went on to assist the court with contextual evidence designed to demonstrate that the three accused women were not alone in their interpretation of international law. It soon became clear that Judge Panzer was a master of at least two things: first, the facts about nuclear weapons, and second, what rights in international law ordinary citizens had when their governments broke those laws and placed, or kept, them in danger from such weapons.

I asked him if he had any experience of 'citizen intervention cases' where nuclear weapons were concerned. We of course already knew his answer. It was Sheriff Gimblett and the jury who got the surprise. Judge Panzer directed his testimony to Sheriff Gimblett and, as they were similar in judicial status, there was an obvious mutual respect between them. He began his reply with a simple, 'Oh, yes,' and I let him run.

What surprised everyone was that, as a judge, he had not tried citizens for taking legal action against nuclear weapons; he'd personally taken such action. In fact he was one of several hundred judges in Germany who had written to the heads of their government protesting that the (Pershing) nuclear weapons openly sited on German soil and obviously pointing at Russia were in breach of international law. In particular, they argued, Germany was in breach of the United Nations Charter (which was built verbatim on the Nuremberg Principles) in that the German government was 'planning, preparing or initiating the mass destruction of villages, towns and cities'. They pointed out in the strongest terms that this kind of extermination ought never to be repeated by anyone, least of all Germans, and, to say the least, they were dismayed when their government ignored them.

I am sure his evidence was a revelation to many on the jury, whose shipyard town had been so heavily struck by the Luftwaffe in the Blitz. Judge Panzer realised he had stunned nearly everyone in the court and took a momentary interlude. He recaptured our attention by mentioning his daughter. He did not want her to ask her influential father what he did to rid Germany of these weapons of mass destruction and for him to give the answer that so many judges of the previous generation gave about upholding Nazi law – 'I did nothing.'

Eventually, he explained, the large body of judges, as very well-informed but nevertheless ordinary citizens, intervened by blockading the bases where the missiles were kept. They were all arrested by the police and charged with various crimes not unlike the charges now facing Angie, Ulla and Ellen. It was a gentle moment, as though we now had four accused in the dock. I thought of Bob Dylan's 'Blowin' in the Wind' and wondered how many people would have to face such charges before international law was applied to these weapons of ultimate terror.

Judge Panzer and his fellow judges defended themselves by claiming the government was acting beyond its legal powers in placing these nuclear weapons on German soil as a strategic favour to the United States. The case of course raised constitutional issues and unfortunately dragged through the German courts with no court official taking overall responsibility for its progress. Eventually the case went on so long that the supreme court ruled that each individual judge's human rights under Article 6 of the European Convention on Human Rights (which applied in Germany decades before it applied directly in the UK) were being breached, because the case had not 'been determined' within a reasonable time. In any case, by that time the German government had taken action to send the outdated Pershing missiles back to the USA.

Judge Panzer could not help but raise a wry smile when he assured us that the coincidence between these events had nothing to do with the fact that the German government knew they had hundreds of serving judges who would have been unlikely to convict other citizens who came before the courts on such charges. His evidence concluded, he bowed first to Sheriff Gimblett and then to the jury, who responded in a way none of us had ever seen before – they spontaneously and resoundingly applauded as Judge Ulf Panzer stepped down from the witness box.

I was just as touched as the next man, but it was difficult for me to revel in the moment as I had something else on my mind.

'I call the second pannel, Ulla Roder, my lady.'

Time was beginning to run quickly so Ulla and I had agreed that it would be best if she gave her evidence in English and resorted to her interpreter when required. Sheriff Gimblett thought that sensible and Ulla took the oath.

Ulla was a complete contrast to Judge Panzer in giving evidence. She is naturally shy and very quietly spoken, and a gentler soul it would be difficult to meet. I had to be very careful to allow her to give her own evidence in her own way and not to diminish her time directly before the jury with any ideas of my own. As it happened, we thought it worked very well.

The faces of the jury belied that they thought it heartbreaking to see her stretch for the English words and hear her tell of her first awakenings in Denmark to the plight of those who had suffered under the perennial plague of nuclear cancers. Ulla's job in a bank led her to think first about the plight of the poor, in the light of the mountains of money spent on nuclear weapons. After much local CND work she began to approach those who she thought might be able directly to influence global awareness of how the nuclear superpowers used their military might to gain massive economic advantage. She tried talking to ambassadors in Copenhagen and was surprised how well some of them received her. She wrote to the British Embassy there and then went personally to NATO headquarters, trying to raise awareness of international law and the advisory opinion of the World Court of 1996. She was largely ignored, and that finally sent her into the welcoming arms of Trident Ploughshares 2000.

She was cross-examined forcefully on the point that there was no urgency about what she had done aboard *Maytime* on 9 June, as no one was in immediate danger, but Ulla was indignant. She had committed herself, as all in Trident Ploughshares 2000 had done, to do what she could, when she could, to avert the dangers that Trident presented. She had moved out of her house, leaving her two (only just) adult children, moved to the UK and learnt the language. She had learnt about legal issues and knew the difference between what was allowable under the Geneva Conventions Act and the horrible truth of what a massive breach of the Genocide Act would look like on the evening news.

It had been another big day for the defence. However there was no rest. Tomorrow we had the man from Bradford coming.

24

They Breathe Another Air

The defence was going well. We had demonstrated through Angie and Ulla, with Ellen still to testify, that these women were very far from common vandals and thieves. We had set out our defence for the judge at an early stage and thus avoided the judicial frustration of Sheriff Gimblett having continually to ask where the defence was going with this or that witness. We had provided a wider European context for the women's actions and we had the jury applauding one of our experts. No lawyer could have asked for more at that stage. However, we still had to demonstrate that our defence of acting necessarily was, in the legal sense, correct; and for that we had to show, at the very least, that the accused women were in imminent or constant danger from a Trident strike or accident at the time of committing the acts set out in the charges. To do this we had to reach into the realms of those who work at the very highest levels of the British government and the United Nations. Fortunately we had them on our witness list.

On the morning of 15 October I called 'Professor Paul Rogers, my lady'. I had initial reservations about this witness but the fault was all mine. I hadn't heard of the department of peace studies at Bradford University, of which he was head – probably due to Edinburgh insularity. So I investigated and found the largest such university department in the world with 300 students from 25 countries offering excellence that was recognised by state departments, other universities and non-government organisations around the world. Professor Rogers himself had, amongst many other books, written four editions of his *Guide to Nuclear Weapons* and advised all over the world on the subject of nuclear strike policies and the political dangers arising from nuclear accidents. When I asked him if the supreme commander of Allied Forces NATO had only one civilian adviser, he replied, 'Yes.' You've guessed it: when I asked, 'Who is that?' I got the reply, 'Me.'

Sheriff Gimblett then ruled that his evidence must be kept to whether, on 8 June 1999, the accused (and thus all of us) were in imminent or constant danger of a strike or accident involving Trident, and off we went. Professor Rogers would have made a great doctor. His 'bedside manner' was impeccable as he calmly sketched out the type and scale of Britain's Trident nuclear weapons system on the date on the indictment. The proximity of the risk became crystal clear when he compared the speed of these weapons to the high-speed train that had brought him to Scotland. He linked *Maytime* very closely with Trident and set its work in the context of British defence policy documents. It was chilling to hear that, despite the World Court advisory opinion of 1996, neither the UK nor the USA had a policy of reversing the scale of their nuclear weapons, let alone decommissioning them.

When pressed on that point he quietly told us that for over 10 years now he had given evidence to the (Westminster) parliamentary select committee on defence. He had seen the documents that said the UK would be prepared to use nuclear weapons in a first strike, and that policy had not changed. He was taken on to the subject of sub-strategic warheads, that is the smaller 'clean-strike' weapons that the World Court heard would be legal. Professor Rogers first reminded us that no such weapons existed and, even if they did, they would be of the order of 5 to 10 kilotons each. That is close to what was used in Hiroshima, which, by any standards, was a weapon of mass destruction incapable of discriminating between combatants and civilians and thereby outlawed under international law.

It was time for us to strike, so Professor Rogers was taken on to the subject of deployment. A large part of our case was that Trident thermonuclear submarines do not go out on pleasure cruises. When they are in the water, they are at war. He explained the shuttle system of rotating the duties of the four British Trident submarines so that Trident was in constant use, and, obviously, that was the case on the date on the charge sheet. As to the dangers of strike or accident, we were all surprised to hear that Britain does not operate a 'safety link' between going 'active' and the 'permission code' being given to the commander of the particular submarine that will fire the weapons. Indeed the captain and one other officer can decide to fire and that can be done within 10 to 15 minutes. It ran through my mind to ask for the names of these faceless unelected supremos but I figured everyone had the point.

As to whether we were in imminent or constant danger, Professor Rogers lifted a dossier from his bag and dropped it with a thud in front of him. It wasn't theatrical. He's not like that. It was purely accidental but it was all the more poignant for that. He took us on a round-the-world trip through incident after incident and reminded us that the main danger from a policy of nuclear weapons deterrence was that either the decision making or the technical control system need fail only once for the consequences to be absolutely cataclysmic.

I'm sure most of the people in Court 2 leapt for the safety of the presumption that these control systems must be the very latest high-tech, well-tried, multi-safe systems imaginable. Professor Rogers dispelled such naivety with detailed evidence about the outdated, underfunded, inaccurate technology used in such systems by many of the nuclear weapons states. He reminded us that, whilst we sat in court in Greenock, US and British jets were bombing northern Iraq twice a week and that it would be foolhardy to assume that the retaliation that the Saddam Hussein regime was planning was not as massive as they could make it – not now, but 10 years from now.

Professor Rogers then went on to the subject of escalation, explaining that any nuclear attack would certainly be met with another, and another. He began his examples with the well-known 1980s incident where a Korean jet was shot down, leading to Operation Able Archer. The Russians immediately thought NATO was attacking and set in motion their 'three briefcases' nuclear key system. Only the swift reactions of NATO counter-intelligence saved everyone living near the Faslane base and many other strategic sites in Britain from certain death, fast or slow. And, just in case anyone argued that no such threats currently existed, Professor Rogers told us about a nuclear crisis that very week involving India, which perceived a nuclear threat from Pakistan. It was all becoming a bit too gory, and Sheriff Gimblett called a halt, asking if we were moving on to the subject of accident. Her ladyship's drift was well and truly caught and we got down to the written materials that Professor Rogers had supplied on that subject.

It was difficult to keep away from the gory details. The Russians had badly contaminated the Arctic with nuclear waste. No one knew for certain how long it would take for that to filter into the oceans. Neither did anyone know how much live nuclear material lay at the bottom of the Atlantic and the Pacific oceans. If all that seemed a bit remote then we were told about the Windscale weapons-grade plutonium production plant in England, which caught fire and could easily have been a Europe-wide tragedy. There were also plenty of recorded incidents involving B-47 bombers that seem to have been particularly close to causing massive death and destruction. With a glance at Sheriff Gimblett, Professor Rogers mentioned one where the bomber, whilst carrying nuclear weapons, had failed to rendezvous with its fuel supply plane and crashed relatively safely, whilst another actually crashed into a nuclear power plant. Amazingly the bombs did not explode.

By this point the court was as silent as a country church in the middle of the night and there was a definite feeling that all that had kept us from nuclear death was either divine intervention or plain good luck. The faces of the jury asked my next question for me: how long will those hold out, Professor Rogers? His own face gave the answer without any need for a written court record on the point.

However, Professor Rogers was used to dealing with this scary material and ended on a positive note. It was, he said, only by the power of civilian intervention that countries were beginning to go non-nuclear. New Zealand and South Africa had turned their faces away from such madness. Many leading figures in the Western alliance military were now openly speaking against nuclear proliferation. The power of civilian demand for change had worked near-miracles in Poland, and in the then East Germany and Czechoslovakia. If that was a high note then Professor Rogers went one higher and stated wisely that it was only through a sea change in civilian attitudes that the abhorrent practice of slavery had been abolished. It was a point well made and an appropriately high moment to end a week of defending The Trident Three.

On Monday 18 October as we arrived at court the sense of achievement amongst the TP 2000 supporters was palpable. Getting all of the evidence we had taken from the witnesses out in a court was the highest peak they had so far reached in their quest to have the rule of law applied to Trident. Some openly said they thought we'd never manage it but were hearty in their congratulations for our work so far. However, everyone knew that the moment was coming when strenuous objection would be taken to our next witness and we would need all our skills to argue that her evidence was of the highest importance to us. With Sheriff Gimblett's rulings fresh in our minds we were only too aware that we were still one very important step away from proving that the accused women acted in a situation of imminent or constant danger from Trident and its support mechanism, including *Maytime*. We still required to narrow down the international situation on 8 June 1999, and one other thing: we needed to prove that Britain's Trident nuclear weapons actually were a real threat in the world and not just a theoretical one.

It was time to call the woman whose physical presence had been missing as The Trident Three left the Glasgow office of Scottish CND to go disarming up Loch Goil, but whose influence was all-pervasive. It was time to call Rebecca Johnson.

As Rebecca took the witness box she had the air about her of a woman who led a fast-track life. She wore smart but comfortable clothes, wore no make-up but had the confidence that working in important places doing important things brings in abundance. What was not obvious was just how highly she moved in international circles. With the Crown objections to her dealt with and the limits of her evidence set by Sheriff Gimblett, I set about establishing her qualifications and credentials, which included bachelor's and master's degrees. When I asked her where she worked, she was a little embarrassed to tell us that she mainly worked in three places – the UN building in New York, the offices of the Geneva Conventions in Geneva and the offices where international treaties were drafted in Vienna. Oh, and of course, her other office in London where she was the head of a 'think tank', which published the periodical titled *Disarmament Diplomacy*, the subscription list for which included the White House, the Kremlin, most embassies, foreign ministries and university departments of politics. I needed to get to her reputation so I embarrassed her a little more by asking whether during the latest nuclear incident she had been quoted on the front pages of the *Washington Post*, the *International Herald Tribune*, the *New York Times* and *Le Monde*. Rebecca nodded a little shyly and had to be told to answer for the record. It was heady stuff so I asked if we could just refer to her as a United Nations permanent observer, which she liked better.

Rebecca developed the background to the political culture of having nuclear weapons, and then began to explain how the important part of her work involved being a go-between at the UN in New York and in Geneva. The idea is that certain nations, which are officially not speaking to each other, do what great generals of opposing armies have done for centuries – they communicate through a neutral third party who is above reproach. She explained how ambassadors and foreign ministers would often come to her with ideas and 'wonder' how other nations would respond if that idea made it beyond the walls of their particular embassy. It is Rebecca's job to find out and liaise between the nations until something worthwhile can be publicly announced.

I put the advisory opinion in front of her and pointed to the part where the World Court had reiterated the legal obligation upon all nuclear states to negotiate in good faith to decommission their nuclear weapons and asked whether she was a recognised expert in such negotiations, to which she simply replied, 'Yes, I am.' I then asked when she first read the World Court's judgement and was told 'within 24 hours of it being published'. Rebecca was keen to tell us that she had also discussed it during plenary session of the UN and advised many nations upon its contents from outside the closed sessions. How she managed that I wasn't sure but I was keen to get on. I then wanted to know what Britain's position had been about taking the legal advice of the World Court on nuclear weapons.

'When the resolution went to United Nations General Assembly, there were over 115 votes in favour of the whole resolution on that occasion, and on that occasion the British government voted against. But that was the previous [Conservative] government. The present government has abstained and moved into a more neutral position.'

I wanted to know if Britain is actually obeying the World Court and entering into these negotiations in good faith.

'In fact, it's not, no. But one of the reasons why it's not is not its own fault,' she added very fairly.

I went on to ask whether the British government had taken any steps of its own accord to go any way towards what the World Court was demanding.

'Yes, it has,' she said to my surprise. 'It has said that from now on it will not deploy any more than 200 warheads at any one time but these are Trident Delta 5 warheads and are each 100 kilotons of thermonuclear explosive.'

'That's very decent of them,' I quipped, moving on.

I asked her rather coyly whether any official complaints had ever been laid at the UN by other nations about Britain's nuclear weapons.

'In plenary session? Oh yes, tons. I could go back to just after the war...'

'What about unofficial complaints?'

That's where it really matters. The main reason so many states now have nuclear weapons is that they see America and Britain as deriving their economic power from their ability to exert a form of totalitarianism on the rest of the world. In my daily work I hear complaints all the time from many nations who feel under threat from Trident. For instance the Pakistani ambassador has clearly said that they have nuclear weapons because their former colonial masters have them and they will not be dic-

tated to any longer. It is simply the weapon of last resort and, when negotiations take place, everybody in my line of work knows that. For
example, Japan very often starts statements on issues by reminding the
delegations to conferences that Japan is the only country to have suffered
nuclear bombing by intention in time of war, and that it wants to ensure
that this can never happen again to anyone else.

Rebecca went on to list other countries such as South Africa, Egypt,
Sweden, Algeria and Ireland that regularly complain about being threatened by nuclear weapons. The most worrying name to her seemed to be
one she mentioned when she drew breath and said, 'and most definitely
China. Their concern is that the non-proliferation treaty is being
flouted. You see the Americans and the British don't build new warheads.
That's too obvious; they use the National Ignition Facility in Nevada to
blast off tiny mushroom-sized nuclear weapons and use computers to
simulate the global effects. Some of their scientists come to our conferences so we meet them.'

I then picked up a point made by David Webster about Angie side-
stepping the democratic process and asked Rebecca what influence one
MP at Westminster would have if elected on an anti-nuclear weapons
ticket.

'None at all,' she said emphatically and went on to explain that she had
lunched with a British foreign minister just two weeks previously who
had said he personally wished he could do more about nuclear weapons
decommissioning but his hands were tied.

I was nearing the end of my questions but had one big dambuster to
use. It was crucial that we got credible and reliable evidence about the
need for disarmament action on the actual date in question so I asked,
'Where were you on 8 June 1999?'

'I was at a meeting in Yvonne, which is next to Geneva, organised by
the Monterey Institute who have a programme for promoting non-proliferation which is part of the centre at the University of Southampton,
and we were basically trying to rescue the non-proliferation treaty.'

'Who attended that meeting?'

'Britain, France, China, the US State Department and the Russian Foreign Ministry.'

'What was wrong with the treaty?'

'The non-proliferation machinery was falling apart.'

'What was the problem?'

South Africa, Canada, Australia, Germany, Japan and the Chilean ambassador were complaining about the nuclear weapons states having a cavalier attitude towards their obligations to negotiate disarmament. There was a terrible deterioration between the US and China and between the US and Russia chiefly over the bombing of Yugoslavia. There was a general air of crisis at that meeting. People were taking their gloves off and speaking very openly behind closed doors, which is why I have to be a bit careful about how much of it I can state here, but I can talk in general terms without quoting anyone.

With the lesson from Professor Rogers fresh in my mind about the collapse of decision making only having to happen once, I wanted to know if Rebecca had known other such crises. She had.

'In 1995, there had been a similar air of crisis – just before and after the big conference on the non-proliferation treaty – when France resumed nuclear testing and then China tested. There was an air of crisis then, I would say.'

I had everything I needed so, pointing to Angie, I asked, 'Do you know this woman?'

'Oh, yes,' was all she said. Smiles were exchanged and the jury were clearly looking forward to the exchange between these two very powerful women.

As with the other witnesses, Angie had a number of prepared questions, which she read for Rebecca to answer. Each question was carefully worded to demonstrate that Angie was very well aware of both the international law position and the state of political tension over nuclear weapons when she took her action against *Maytime*. Rebecca pointed out that quite contrary to the World Court's demand there was considerable anxiety in the diplomatic community about nuclear weapons research going on under the guise of taking care of existing stockpiles when in fact the nuclear weapons states were retaining such weapons for the foreseeable future and even modernising for the longer term.

Next Angie raised the stakes and asked whether that included research into using nuclear weapons in space. Rebecca was certain there were very big concerns about that, particularly in view of the fact that there is an outer space treaty banning that. Angie moved in and asked if that added to the ever-present dangers from Trident that already existed on earth. Rebecca was erudite in her explanation of exactly how the danger of launching an intercontinental ballistic missile that is incapable of recall once fired – perhaps by a submarine captain – had escalated. Angie focused on 8 June 1999 and asked if, on that day, the diplomatic community perceived Britain's deployment of Trident as a threat. Rebecca was very clear in saying that in her mind there was no doubt about that. However, she did point out that, of course, on that date or the following morning, it was reported that the sound signature testing laboratory for the UK's Trident system had been disarmed by three women. The jury went into polite laughter but one man punched his right hand into his left and said out loud, 'Ya beauty.'

As one lawyer to another I really felt for David Webster. He was now being seen as the man who was spoiling the jury from retiring there and then to consider their verdict. It didn't help when he attacked Rebecca's objectivity by asking where she worked before her current job.

'I was an international coordinator,' replied Rebecca.

'Where was that?' asked David.

'Greenpeace.'

David had had enough and sparred with her for a while on who voted for what at which sittings of the UN and got her to accept that it wasn't just the UK that had voted against the motion to send the question of the legality of nuclear weapons to the World Court, but essentially it was all over.

We had all glimpsed inside the lives and workings of those who, so to speak, breathe another air in New York, Geneva and London. However, the rain clouds that soaked into the banners outside court as we left that night reminded us that there was a real purpose to things like the non-proliferation and outer space treaties – to allow us all to breathe the same air and to live without fear of annihilation. As the prison van pulled away for the long haul back to Cornton Vale jail I could just see Ellen at a window smiling and giving me a wave goodnight. I asked God to bless her and give her strength, for her big day was coming in the morning. She was to be the last witness in the trial.

25

Less Is More

On the Sunday night before Ellen took the witness box I got a call from an old pal whom I hardly ever see, arranging to have a few pints of real ale in Edinburgh's old town. He is, or was, a career policeman who is now in the SSS – that is the 'secrets, spooks and spies' – section of MI5. After about an hour of catching up with the price of school fees and rugby scores he said he wanted to tell me something. I knew the look and he began to recite a conversation my wife and I had in our bedroom. It happened to be only about how long the new curtains were taking to be altered, but his point was he knew it verbatim. The Echelon guys had done their stuff well. I explained that they were wasting their time because there was no point in bugging my house or screening my e-mail and phone calls. I had agreed with Angie and Ulla at the first consultation in Cornton Vale prison that everything done in the name of the accused women would be done openly and be freely available to anyone who wanted to know what our legal arguments would be in court. However, I took to whistling 'You'll Never Walk Alone' about the house and when friends called on the phone I would assure them they had come through to the tent of Colonel Gaddafi or the hotline to the Kremlin, just for fun.

When I got to court the following morning I mentioned the SSS. Some were taken aback but Stephen Fox, John's instructing solicitor, who has acted in some very heavy-duty cases, wasn't the least bit surprised. With that in mind we were all a bit sombre as we trudged upstairs to court for the last day of evidence. However, the women were in ebullient mood and picked us up for the last lap. Indeed the atmosphere was more like that of a group of friends gathered together for a potluck lunch in a church hall than the final day of evidence in a trial of such enormous political magnitude.

Ellen is a Quaker and as such had a special timbre in her voice as she took the oath to Almighty God to tell the truth, the whole truth and nothing but the truth. At the time of trial she was 64 years old and had settled in Scotland from California nearly 20 years before. Her lifelong love of animals had inspired her to graduate with a degree in zoology. She pointed out that she had actually been born in China but had 'been around a bit' since then. Ellen was the quietest, one would also say the gentlest, of the three on trial, and her soft grandmotherly American tones seemed immediately to capture the hearts of the jury.

But they got a surprise when Ellen said she had worked for the US government in the field of dynamics and other jobs in the General Atomic Division. Their next surprise was to hear about her humanitarian work in Vietnam during the war, ranging from orphanages in Saigon to other more dangerous work in the bombed-out villages. A lump rose in my throat when she told the court about adopting a Vietnamese baby who was now a thriving 27-year-old living in Perth, Scotland. Nearly all of the jury would have remembered the Vietnam War and I'm fairly sure the sniffles I heard behind me were not from colds. She was answering John's questions in a motherly way, stopping him here and there to include something that had previously slipped her mind, such as, 'We chose to live in Scotland because independence of mind is cherished here, you know.'

After outlining her history in Amnesty International and CND, Ellen said she objected to having to pray for peace whilst paying taxes in preparation for nuclear war. She had been at Faslane on 25 November 1993 to oppose the introduction of HMS Vanguard and left with a feeling of futility when the massed protest went entirely unheeded. Ellen spoke in erudite terms about the DERA Web site and the acoustic invisibility of Trident, and it was obvious that, if challenged, her understanding of dynamics would have left us all at the starting post. John took her through the joint statement left on board *Maytime*, the tools in her rucksack and the point of including the satellite vessel, *Newt*, in her disarmament action. She chided John in her motherly way when he read from the DERA Web site materials we had put to the master of *Maytime*, Mr McPhee, and asked her to enlighten us. Her answer was an incisive lecture on target echo strengths and the critical need for the equipment aboard *Maytime* to be kept properly calibrated.

Ellen then got away entirely from her subjective point of view and on to her objective understanding of the strategy used for deployment of Trident, the exact page numbers of MoD documents where the first-strike policy is set out and Britain's relationship with the USA at the National Ignition Facility. Her recall of exactly at which point of Rebecca Johnson's evidence the scientific testing had been mentioned was impressive. John then picked up the point David Webster had put to Angie about using the democratic process. Ellen delighted in proudly telling the jury that 26 Members of the Scottish Parliament had pledged their political support for the disarmament action aboard *Maytime* and 'the presentation letter is lying right in front of John Mayer there on the table'. Every head in the jury craned so I pushed my chair out of the way so that the royal blue presentation pack with the words 'Scottish Parliament' emblazoned in white across the top stared out at them.

In cross-examination Ellen said very pointedly that she had not delayed at all in taking 'such action as she could, when she could'. She, like her co-accused, had obligations to family and had to make preparations in case she was sentenced to a long jail term. I knew very well that if they were convicted then the sheriff could easily have used her discretion in deciding that the appropriate sentence was one beyond her powers and remitted the accused to the High Court of Justiciary in Edinburgh for sentence. I closed my eyes and pictured the women standing in front of a High Court judge being sternly lectured about the seriousness of their wholly irresponsible actions, how they had taken on the core policy of the MoD so that the very fabric of NATO's strategic defence policy had been placed in jeopardy. For that there could be no leniency and, just as I mentally saw the judge tighten his eyebrows and fix his stare on the accused, I shivered at the thought of the words '10 years' imprisonment' and broke the spell by picking up my plastic cup and sipping my water. I nervously fingered the tall bundle of legal books and papers that towered beside me on the floor and which no doubt had the jury wondering what was going to happen when the evidence finished.

As Ellen retook her seat in the dock and John closed the case for the third accused, Sheriff Gimblett let out a deep sigh that suggested she was glad to have reached the end of the evidence from witnesses. But of course, in the law, when one stage is over it just signals the beginning of another and so it was in this case.

I rose to my feet, paused and instinctively did something I had never done before. I of course bowed low to the sheriff but then I turned and bowed to the accused. Sheriff Gimblett let it go as I said:

My lady, a matter of law arises at this stage of the trial. My lady, no one has ever presented the submission I am about to make in a Scottish court before. Indeed, because my submission involves international humanitarian law and principles of Roman law which have come down into the criminal law of Scotland, I doubt whether any lawyer anywhere in the world has ever argued in the way I am about to submit to your ladyship. It is a fearful prospect and I think, from previous rehearsal, it will take me the rest of today and perhaps some of tomorrow.

Sheriff Gimblett placed her left hand on one of the books in front of her, smiled at me and then turned to the jury, saying:

Ladies and gentlemen, with your now long experience of these things it will come as no surprise to you to hear that Mr Mayer is about to address me on a matter of law. As you have heard Mr Mayer say, this is likely to take him the whole day. I agree with that estimate and accordingly I am now able to tell you that you can leave for the day. So please, enjoy the rest of today and I will see you in your places tomorrow morning at 10 o'clock.

As the jury was leaving I heard a man in the front row say to another, 'Too bad. I'd love to hear this bit.' The other, knowing I was only about 4 feet away and thus well within earshot, responded with an old Glaswegian saying 'Gawn yersel', big man.' The phrase literally translates as 'Go on yourself, big man' and is an expression of will, usually used on the terraces of Scottish football grounds. The underlying idea is that someone has got round his opponents, has the ball at his feet and is on course to score, though, that not being certain, the player is willed on by the supporter. There was no way of my acknowledging that expression of support and even if there had been it would have been wholly improper for me to do so. However, privately it gave me just what I needed at that crucial moment, a hint that the jury had seen what I had been driving at for the past month, and, I thought, if they had seen it then I was assured that Sheriff Gimblett had been there well before them.

As I waited I was transported back to my classroom and the occasion when my teacher told me that if I could tell him the meaning of CND then I could continue to wear my new badge. Now it was a case of 'If I can get this right, these women won't go to jail and we just might take the campaign for nuclear disarmament forward a bit.' A big bit. I tried to remember my teacher's face but Ellen was looking at me with the smile of an angel; and that captivated me. She seemed to be sending me the message that 'less is more'.

26

Badge of Office

Sheriff Gimblett took a short break. She is a sprightly award-winning gardener who always carries her own books and papers. When she emerged from her chambers I was glad to see she was carrying a larger-than-usual bundle fronted by the colourful cover of the Scotland Act. I took this as a sign that overnight the Sheriff had been reading the materials on the list I had passed to her the previous week through the clerk of court. I could feel my heart beating in my chest as I squared up my bundles of papers, keeping one eye on the bench. I breathed very deeply as I watched my judge arrange her bundle upright into a long line, each passage carefully bookmarked, and then announce in the soft tones I had become so used to over the past weeks, 'In your own time, Mr Mayer.'

At that moment I vividly recalled my teacher's face as I told him what CND meant and the pride with which I wore my home-made button badge to school every day. I was now wearing a very different badge of office and with it an acute awareness of my Faculty duties when presenting this legal argument. But I just couldn't help also feeling a deep sense of personal responsibility as I floated to my feet, bowed again and began:

My lady, in my submission, as a matter of the law of Scotland, these charges should not be allowed to go to the jury for their consideration because what has been demonstrated this past month is that the accused are not guilty of any crime known to the law of Scotland. What is clear in my submission is that, when they boarded *Maytime* on 8 June 1999, not only were these women not intending to commit a crime, but rather they were intent on crime prevention.

Rather extraordinarily, one might think, the crime they sought to prevent was, and remains, one being committed by the British government and, broadly speaking for the moment, the name of that crime is crime against humanity. That enormous crime is being committed, not periodically, but constantly, by the ever-present deployment of the Trident 2 thermonuclear submarine fleet patrolling the waters of the world for the purposes of threatening other nations with annihilation.

My lady, I trust I will demonstrate that the actions of the British government in deploying Trident are outlawed by at least two sources of the very highest law. In that regard I will turn in due course to examine the judgement of the International Court of Justice in The Hague, that is the so-called World Court of the United Nations, on the legality of nuclear weapons. Then, quite separately, I will examine what amounts to a crime against humanity and demonstrate how these awful crimes are, quite rightly in my submission, outlawed by Article 6 of the Nuremberg Principles. Because the latter were brought into international law some 50 years before the former, it follows that, regardless of whether the World Court's advisory opinion existed or not, and, being in existence, whatever it means, there is a much older body of binding law of the highest authority allowing citizens to intervene in the way done by all three accused when their governments either fail to keep them safe, or indeed put them in a state of constant danger. My lady, I need hardly say that the Nuremberg Principles were promulgated to prevent mass annihilation of civilians ever happening again.

I then cited the Scotland Act 1998 and pointed to the part where control over nuclear weapons was kept within Westminster and were chillingly called 'weapons of mass destruction'. History is full of examples of ordinary people rising up against massive oppression, and I was tempted to quote from the Declaration of Arbroath in Scotland on 6 April 1320 where Scottish freedom from English oppression was the heart of the matter. But, as none of the accused women was a born Scot, and there were the requirements of legal reasoning to be respected, I thought better of it. My argument had to form an unbroken line of international humanitarian law from my starting point to the actions aboard *Maytime*. It was time to turn to Lord Murray.

His article sets out the treaties applicable to nuclear weapons and summarises two very important points decided by the World Court. First, the court unanimously said that a threat or use of nuclear force that did not comply with Articles 2 and 51 of the United Nations Charter would certainly be unlawful. In Professor Boyle's expert opinion, such threat or use would be criminal. What these two articles do is basically outlaw such aggression but reserve to all states the legal right to self-defence or collective defence against attack. However, such action in self-defence would always be subject to full United Nations Security Council supervision. Second, the court unanimously said that, to avoid breaking the large body of international humanitarian law that has developed over a hundred years, nuclear threat or use would have to comply with those laws. Murray points out that, by themselves, these propositions severely restrict the way in which nuclear weapons can be deployed.

I paused to let Sheriff Gimblett make a full note but, as we were now reading from the same page, I could speed on. I pointed out that the World Court made its judgement on the basis that threat is equivalent to use, and respectfully said that one could most easily understand that by thinking of it the other way round, namely that these weapons were being 'used to threaten' a particular state or states. I then said that the World Court had taken care to explain that a general display of military might, like sailing a Trident submarine out to sea or 'merely possessing' one, was not of itself illegal. There had to be something more that ele-vated the sail into a threat.

To begin with, however, I submitted that there is no such thing as 'mere possession' of a Trident thermonuclear submarine. It is not an item, like say an ornamental sword, that one could argue was not intended to be used for aggressive purposes. There is only one purpose for having such a thing and that purpose was obvious from the evidence we had heard from our experts. But to prove 'threat' I required specifics, like a verbal warning to a particular state or the targeting of a city. These would be hard to prove on a changing daily basis so the court would be entitled to draw the inference of a general pattern from the evidence of Professors Boyle and Rogers, and Rebecca Johnson, who all spoke about the UK's various threatening postures on specific occasions and allied those to the wording in the strategic defence reviews and specific speeches by ministers. I invited Sheriff Gimblett to find that: 1) such a threat by the UK was in place on the day the women disarmed *Maytime*; 2) it was ongoing; 3) given that Trident is on constant patrol, those patrols amounted to a constant threat against the targeted states; and 4) that amounted to the people of Britain being in constant danger from reprisal strike or accident. Finally, I asked Sheriff Gimblett to accept the mountains of evidence spoken to by each of the three women on their decades of attempts to use democratic means to have their respective governments obey international law only to have their efforts ignored.

However, I had to accept that in this analysis the UK had one last-gasp loophole left. The World Court said that 'if the very survival of a State was at stake' then that state or its allies had the legal right to defend the state under threat, but always under the rules of international humanitarian law. I then remarked upon the obvious, that we had not heard a word of evidence about the very survival of the state of the United Kingdom being 'at stake' and accordingly the prosecution had not done what our law required it to do – rebut our defence that the women had acted 'of necessity'. Whilst Sheriff Gimblett was nodding her agreement to the obvious I glanced round to see what Mr Jermyn Street was up to. His stony face said it all.

So far as the Nuremberg Principles were concerned, I was careful to demonstrate how the UN had debated these and decided under Resolution 95 (1) to send these high principles to the department that drafts or approves the actual wording of international law, which is aptly named the International Law Commission. Our librarian, Andrea Longson, had done her work well and I was privileged to be able to pass up to Sheriff Gimblett the actual volume of that Resolution together with the response: the document that contained the final wording of the law on crimes against humanity. It is one thing to reason and to argue the law. It is quite another to hold in one's hand the legal volumes that declared to the world that preparation or initiation of wars of aggression or the indiscriminate mass murder of civilians would henceforth be a crime against humanity punishable in a criminal court. Not surprisingly, these were unanimously adopted by the UN and are binding upon every nation in the world.

I was in full flow and allowed myself the luxury of repeating Lord Murray where he says:

> International law, despite any appearance to the contrary, is real law, not just international morality or international expediency. It may be less developed than domestic law, but it has a genuine and growing force of its own. To ignore [it] is to ignore a factor which is significant, if less than conclusive, in the conduct of international affairs. Under international law slavery has been outlawed, world-wide post is regulated, navigation at sea and in the air controlled and, under very special circumstances, even war criminals brought to trial and executed. All law consists of organised, structured principles with an institutional base. What international law lacks is the state's power to legislate and to enforce the law. But, in contrast with morality's want of agreed institutions, international law has a court of law whose authority is almost universally accepted.

Against the background of a principle that allowed self-defence at international level, I said it was legal for citizens to defend themselves when their government would not do so, or indeed when it continued with policies that went so far as to put the citizens in danger. After all, international humanitarian law is there to protect humanity, not to be a mere plaything for politicians, judges or lawyers. Therefore it was necessary to be able to point to the specific rule of law that gave citizens that legal right. I confess to going a little cold when I informed her ladyship that in order to do that I had to remind the court of the judgement in the trial of the Nazi high command at Nuremberg.

The Nuremberg trials were of course first concerned with the specific acts and orders of the particular people facing charges. But in order to have the authority to try high officials of the German state and, if they were convicted, sentence them to death, the International Military Tribunal (IMT) had to have all the authority of an international court. It could not risk being seen as just part of a 'victors' celebration' paying lip-service to the rule of law. A glance at the legal reputation and high authority of the judges and prosecutors informs any interested person that the objective was well achieved. Neither my purpose in court nor the scope of this book allows me to reproduce anything but the conclusions of the IMT. However, I do recommend these as the starting point for all newcomers to the subject of what humanity has done to protect itself from minorities who would seek to impose their might over our rights.

The Nuremberg judgement, having dealt with the individuals standing trial, then moved on to deal with the type of defences they had raised. These are just the kind of arguments one hears every day in ill-informed discussion about nuclear weapons. There is first the defence of 'superior orders', which is basically, 'I was told by my superior to murder civilians so what could I do but obey?' The answer to that one is, 'You could disobey. You might get a medal for doing so.' Then there is the defence of 'inferiority', that is saying in court that no one individual had power to do anything because the state had decreed certain courses of action, like annihilation of an ethnic group.

Towards the end of its judgement the IMT issued one of the most important decrees ever pronounced by a court of law. The IMT said 'individuals have *international duties* which transcend the national obligations of obedience imposed by the State. He who violates the laws of war cannot obtain immunity while acting in pursuance of the authority of the State if the State in authorising action moves outside its competence under international law'.

Being such an important part of the argument I needed to tease out the important parts of those powerful few lines and put them into the present context. As I put my copy of the judgement back into its place I was acutely aware that there was absolute silence, broken only by the thud of the heavy tome as it slid in between the United Nations Resolutions and a book of Scottish criminal case law, marked at one case in particular called *Moss v Howdle*. I submitted to the court that it was the adjective 'international' that made all the difference. I restated the passage as a proposition, beginning with the word 'if' in order to create a syllogism, because for me the passage makes more sense that way. I read the passage again, beginning with 'if the State in authorising action moves outside its competence under international law, (then) individuals have *international duties* which transcend the national obligations of obedience imposed by the State'.

Now, without fear of contradiction, the judgement clearly applied to the threat or use of nuclear weapons. It is obvious that if a state did something outside its legal competence, like deploying Trident over a long period of time resulting in all the objections based on real feelings of threat that Rebecca had testified to, then individuals could do something about that. What could they do? The natural reaction for the uninformed about international law is to say, 'Well, write to your MP. He or she is the one who can do something about your concern at government level.' But what happens when the government is not part of the solution but the whole problem? The answer is to look outside one's own domestic government for the solution. That is where the word 'international' comes into play.

The IMT said ordinary people have legal 'duties' and the scope of these duties was 'international'. Therefore the same ordinary people must have legal rights in order to perform their legal duty. It is important to note that the imperative of 'duty' to the rest of humanity comes first, followed by the right to act. If it were the other way around, then people would have legal 'powers', which would carry the usual attendant discretion whether to use the power or not. That is clearly not what the IMT had in mind. If it were, then all that it had done to bring the Nazi high command to trial could be deprived of force in the future.

I had read that passage a thousand times and tried it out by e-mail on professors of international law, members of British and European parliaments and in pubs on pals of all political persuasions. No one disagreed that the reason for issuing such a judgement was to protect humanity. Neither was there any dissent that in times of imminent or constant danger ordinary people ought to have such duties. But for the purposes of this trial, the crucial question was, 'Is that passage part of the law of Scotland?'

Sheriff Gimblett was holding up well. I had been several hours in making my legal submission but there had been little or no interruption from the bench and I felt like I could see the end in sight. However, there was a problem. Nowhere in any law book that I (or Andrea) could find did any Scottish court actually say that international public law, such as treaties or the judgement of the IMT, was part of the law of Scotland. The university lecturers taught that it was. Other countries with different sorts of constitutions said it was part of their law. But was it part of the law of the place where I was standing making this submission to a criminal court?

Fortunately help was at hand from on high. The very same Lord Rodger of Earlsferry as had been Lord Advocate years before when Scottish CND were in correspondence with the Crown Office about building the submarine base at Faslane had become the Lord Justice General of Scotland, the highest judge in the land. I know Lord Rodger to be an approachable man who has been a great credit to all the high offices he has held over the years, and very good company at a dinner table. However, he is fiercely intelligent on the bench and few advocates could say he has been a comfort to them in court. Now, albeit in print, that is just what he was to me. I referred Sheriff Gimblett to *Moss* v *Howdle*, where Lord Rodger said:

> The law [of Scotland] recognises that 'danger invites rescue' in Scotland just as surely as in New York. So Scots law has never been so mean spirited as to confine the defence of self-defence to situations where the accused acts to save himself. It has always recognised that the defence may be available in situations where the accused acts in an altruistic fashion to save a companion. In the same way, if a defence of duress would be open to

someone who committed a crime to try to escape immediate danger to his own life or health, it should be open to someone who does the same to try to ensure that his companion escapes such danger. We can see no distinction in principle between various threats of death; it matters not whether the risk of death is by murder or by suicide or, indeed, by accident.

I then argued that if such a legal principle applied to an elderly couple about to be 'mugged', and to a classroom full of schoolchildren threatened by a gunman (as in Dunblane in central Scotland, where a crazed gunman walked into an elementary school, randomly shooting down children and teachers), and to a packed theatre at risk from an arsonist, and to a football stadium full of people at risk from a bomber, and to a town full of people at risk from a terrorist on an aircraft (I wasn't being crass, as this was almost two years before 11 September 2001 – I was actually thinking of the Lockerbie disaster), then it follows that it must also extend to a wider geographical area full of people at risk from a reckless indifference by their government to the consequences of a nuclear weapons strike or accident.

I then took Sheriff Gimblett through the other cases mentioned in Moss where our High Court had paid tribute to the supreme courts of Canada and England when dealing with the idea of ordinary people acting in times of imminent or constant mortal danger. I also referred to a passage from David Hume where he discusses with legal approval '[heroic] acts done in times of great civil commotion'. To bring my submission to an end I reminded Sheriff Gimblett of Rebecca Johnson's evidence about where she was on the day in question and her experience of the sense of heightened crisis there was over the threat or use of nuclear weapons, before formally moving her to find the women, as a matter of law, not guilty.

It had all gone very well. John and Angie adopted my arguments and David Webster did his best but he realised during my arguments that he had not done something required as an essential by the prosecution: that is to rebut our defence of necessity with his own witnesses. The person who had guided this prosecution at a much earlier stage had not realised that this line of defence would be taken and consequently left David with an almost impossible task. However, as I pointed out to the faithful after court, no judge anywhere in the world had ever been asked to put these three pieces of international humanitarian law (the World Court judgement, the Nuremberg Principles and the Scottish law of defending others) together in the context of constant danger from nuclear weapons. Sheriff Gimblett and I were within 10 feet of each other but her face gave no hint of which way she would judge the point. Instead she would consider the arguments overnight. I felt I had done my job for the day but it could hardly be called just another day at the office.

As we were leaving Court 2, I paused by the dock where Angie and I hugged. I don't normally hug accused people in the dock though they have occasionally hugged me. I had kept the legal arguments as tight and professional as possible and for that all three women were grateful. They and others in the public galleries, who were inadvertently blocking Mr Jermyn Street, had planned this action in order to put the arguments for the illegality of the massive Trident nuclear weapons before a court with a professional judge who was capable of making a reasoned decision on the matter: and that had now been done. Today's work was in every sense already a new height for Trident Ploughshares 2000 and everyone who had ever worn the button badge supporting the Campaign for Nuclear Disarmament.

27

Judgement Day

The all-encompassing air of excitement at the outset of the trial had turned to seriousness during the evidence and tense, tingling nervousness during the legal submissions that the women should be acquitted because they had acted wilfully but not maliciously when disarming *Maytime*. Now the press were back in Court 2 in droves. The daily TP 2000 press briefings had so far satisfied the media but their interest lay in the day of judgement and, now it was here, there wasn't a seat to be had. Microphones were stuck with gum to the wooden dock and the police obliged by shifting along so as not to block the sound. We knew if Sheriff Gimblett's judgement went against us that we still had the possibility of being acquitted by the jury, but that was not the objective. A jury acquittal in a trailblazing trial like this would almost certainly be trumpeted as a mere sympathy vote for three dear ladies who were very eccentric but also very misguided. As we sat waiting in a packed courthouse, it went without saying that every sinew of effort was now dependent upon the legal opinion of the judge, Sheriff Gimblett.

As we waited I fingered the statute of the International Court of Justice, which says in section 38 that, amongst other ways, international law is applied, and therefore made, by judicial decisions. This was the first case anywhere in the world that had amongst its ingredients the advisory opinion of the World Court, the Nuremberg Principles, the expert evidence we had been allowed to present and, of course, the personal testimony of how well the accused objectively understood the interna-

tional legal and political position of Trident on the day of their disarmament action. I could see the long months of prison regime now taking its
toll on the faces of all three accused; and so, in the seconds before Sheriff
Gimblett took the bench, I looked at them, put my index finger under
my chin and lifted it. All three raised their heads in unison and laughter
was breaking out when the door to chambers opened and the macer
called, 'Co-ou-rt.'

Sheriff Gimblett was sombre and kept away from her usual eye
contact with those in the well of the court. She was without her usual
stack of books, carrying instead a prepared speech on several sheets of
paper. After setting out that the defence was based both in international
law and the necessity to take such action as the accused could in all the
circumstances of their respective positions, Sheriff Gimblett went on to
say she was grateful for the careful way in which all the materials had
been placed before the court and had found that helpful. Lord Murray's
incisive article had been especially so.

She then hit us with a surprise saying:

> I am a relatively junior and inexperienced sheriff, but when I took my
> judicial oath it was to decide legal issues without fear or favour and that is
> what I am about to do. I have reached my own view of the law in this case
> with great diffidence and I take comfort from knowing that what I am
> about to do can be reviewed in the High Court.

At that stage it could have gone either way, which, when one is trying a
new line of argument with adverse consequences for the future of
nuclear weapons, is not encouraging. Then the sheriff had another surprise for us.

She used the failure of the prosecution to provide its own experts as a
stick with which to beat them. All Scottish sheriffs know very well that
the lawyer who presents the case in court will not usually have been the
one who prepared the case. Sheriff Gimblett knew well that this case was
probably subject to a calculated risk that it should not be tried in the
High Court because that is what the accused wanted in the first place.

Rather, it should be tried well out of the way. That risk was about to backfire seriously, as Sheriff Gimblett continued:

> In the absence of experts for the Crown, I have concluded that the three accused ladies, and many others who support them, were on the date on the indictment justified in thinking that the UK was illegally deploying Trident at a time of great international unrest about Britain's first-strike nuclear policy. Also, despite having the opportunity to do so, there was not a word of Crown evidence that the 'very survival of the State', that is the United Kingdom, was 'at stake'. If that had been the case then the Crown may have been able to bring themselves within the only situation in which the International Court of Justice ruled that nuclear weapons might be used. I say 'may' because of course these would have to be used in ways which accorded with international humanitarian law and, as we have heard, that would be impossible with the type of Trident weapons which the UK has.

At that moment Angie and I looked at each other in a significant way. We knew the day was ours and all we had to do was relax and enjoy the legal reasons why. Sheriff Gimblett went through the details of international law and at one stage lost her reference. It was about the developing law against deliberately targeting civilians or causing their indiscriminate destruction and I thought I knew exactly which one she needed. So I coughed and said, 'Lord Murray at page 133, my lady?'

'Thank you, Mr Mayer. That is indeed what I was searching for.'

Whilst Sheriff Gimblett was reading the law against indiscriminate mass destruction, the jury was in its room celebrating the 60th birthday of one of its women members, well out of earshot of the legal ruling being given in court; but right on cue there was a cheer that carried down the corridor and was audible in court. It only caused Sheriff Gimblett to blink for a second before continuing:

> In the absence of evidence from any such government official, then the threat or use of Trident is to be construed as a breach of international law.

That being the case the accused women had, not only morally, but a legal obligation in terms of international law to do the little they could to alleviate the threats which were perceived as real at international level. I therefore uphold the submissions made to me by the defence that the women were acting wilfully but not maliciously. Particularly I agree with the part where I was moved to accept that the women did not have malice in mind when doing their action. Indeed one of the arresting officers said that in evidence. I will accordingly instruct the jury to find them not guilty.

The elation was palpable. The faces of the women in the dock threw off all the cares and wearisome tiredness of five months in jail. Advocates don't shake hands, but, if we did, then John and I would have done so. The solicitors were scribbling down the procedural details that now required to be attended to. One of the smart young policewomen sitting on guard in the dock put her arm around Ellen who was crying and I could see Ulla holding hands with her interpreter. Angie beamed all over her face and didn't know what to do with her piles of papers, which she had trailed back and forth to court so assiduously. The women in the public gallery who were so fond of straightening my wig motioned to me to move it properly over the top of my head and John Ainslie, our silent expert who happens also to be an ordained minister of the church, said words of prayer out loud. For some unknown reason I thought of my favourite poet, Philip Larkin, and a phrase from his best work, The *Whitsun Weddings*, where he describes life's journey as a 'frail travelling coincidence'. Now, assembled there in Court 2 of Greenock Sheriff Court, somehow we all seemed less frail and life contained substantially more reason than it had the night before. If history has a taste, then we tasted it that afternoon.

SIX

THE FUTURE
IS IN YOUR HANDS

28

Boom

In most law the devil is in the detail. Late the previous afternoon The Trident Three had been found not guilty of maliciously damaging *Maytime* but David was insisting on every last line of the indictment. So the following morning we still had to disentangle the theft charge. My focus wasn't on it, but John McLaughlin rose to his feet and swept it aside with a powerful argument based on the analogy of taking the firing pin from a raging gunman's gun and throwing it into Loch Goil. From a legal point of view there is obviously intention to put the firing pin permanently beyond the owner's control. But that simple act, which alone would be theft, is justified in the circumstances where it is reasonable to take such disarmament action. Sheriff Gimblett gave his argument her usual depth of consideration and agreed. She then ordered the jury to be brought into court.

Ladies and gentlemen, you have been extremely patient whilst Mr Mayer and the others made their legal submissions and I can tell you that a good deal more has happened since you last left court. I also understand that one of you has turned 60 whilst on jury service. I speak from personal experience and can tell you that it's not so bad. In fact, it's rather good. Now, ladies and gentlemen, I must tell you that I have decided to uphold the legal submissions for the defence and for legal reasons the charges which you have been hearing about for some weeks will not now require your verdict. That is because the case has been decided upon legal grounds. I therefore direct you to return verdicts of not guilty for each accused on all charges. The clerk of court will now read your verdict, as directed, back to you.

There was then an unholy scramble from the press gallery as they crushed through the single door with mobile phones in hand and laptop computers dangling by the wires. The clerk of court flawlessly read the verdict back, and, in the time it had taken him to write it up, the jury and the women in the dock, now acquitted, shared much raising of eyebrows, teeth tight clenched and shoulders hunched in silent signals of approval. I thought Sheriff Gimblett now revealed the tiniest indications that she was feeling the immensity of what she had just done in upholding the rule of international humanitarian law. The white-haired macer who had led her on and off the bench throughout the trial pretended to pick something up from the floor and discreetly dabbed her eyes. David Webster with a genuine smile of congratulation mouthed a 'well done' to John and me, to which we each mouthed our thanks.

With order reigning once more Sheriff Gimblett then invited the three women in the dock to stand. With the same solidarity as they had shown throughout the long weeks they had kept vigil in the public galleries, every Trident Ploughshares 2000 pledger also stood in respectful silence as Sheriff Gimblett said firmly, 'Ladies, you have been found not guilty and are discharged from the dock.' The sound of tears now burst through from behind me in the jury box and beside me in the dock. Sheriff Gimblett then hurried from the bench into the care of her sympathetic macer as they left Court 2 for the last time in the case of The Trident Three.

The pledgers ran down to the dock and hugged their friends, who would not be going back to jail that night. The police and the clerk of court courteously stood aside. As the jury left the court, some turned to witness a sight the likes of which they would never see again. Some leant forward and offered their warmest congratulations, for which I was proud and grateful. But all credit truly went to the three women who had risked perhaps the rest of their lives in jail to carry through the promise they had made to the Prime Minister and the law officers of Britain that, in the event of them ignoring the World Court, then TP 2000 would take disarmament action.

Down in the agents' room we were barraged by the local solicitors wanting to know the defence case in a nutshell. Needless to say they were disappointed. A press conference had been arranged in the grimy TP office round the corner to which the lawyers were invited, so we changed and left court thinking it was all over for us. We were of course in joyous mood as I opened the large front door of Greenock Sheriff Court, pulling my load of books and boxes of papers on a trolley behind me, hoping the car didn't have a ticket. It was a shock to see what lay outside.

The Trident Three stood at the end of a guard of honour who threw rose petals over us as we passed along. At the end, out on the street, flash cameras blinded me. Each of The Trident Three shook us by the hand and hugged us carelessly. Ellen pinched John's cheeks and Ulla threw her arms around me, saying something in Danish. John Ainslie stepped forward and shook my hand vigorously saying, 'You don't know what this means to us all.' Bashfully, I said, 'Och, John, I am only a servant of the law,' to which he replied, 'Oh, no, John Mayer, from this day onwards you are a servant of all humanity.' I was prouder of my boyhood CND inclinations than I had ever been and I'm happy to say that none of the front-page pictures showed the tear rolling down my face.

When we got round to the office The Trident Three were sitting behind two old tables and some crates covered with white linen sheets to provide a surface on which to put microphones. The large front room was heaving with people. The journalists and photographers crouched around the table as David McKenzie, the TP press officer, thanked everyone for coming, handed out press packs and opened the conference up to questions. As I squeezed in at the back I noticed the same dog as I had seen before in this office lying bemused under a window, and squeezed down to give it a reassuring rub around the ears. My eye level was just above the window ledge and as I began to stand I saw a man sitting in a car across the road. He obviously didn't expect to see me peeking over a window ledge and we made eye contact. He was familiar but I couldn't place him. It was only later, when I was driving home, that I remembered him. He had been in the pub when my pal had recited the conversation I'd had with my wife. He was SSS.

The broadsheets were asking sensible penetrating questions about the history of Trident Ploughshares 2000, the personal histories of each woman and how they came together to do their disarmament. They were desperate to know about the UN involvement and about the network of legal and political support available to them. As The Trident Three vied to answer it was good to see each of them with laughing, carefree faces, washed and brushed up for the waiting world. They were doing now what they had done with us at that first joint consultation in Cornton Vale jail: cutting across one another to correct details and take the answers off on tangents hitherto unknown, even (or occasionally especially) to the lawyers. David McKenzie was directing the order of questions and eventually gave way to Scotland's best-selling tabloid. Looking at Angie and poking his tape machine within a foot of her face, their top journalist asked, in all seriousness, 'Do you dye your hair white?'

The roar of laughter from the whole room must have sent his machine into overload and he backed down like a dog rebuked for being too boisterous. Angie was consumed with laughter but spluttered out that no, she didn't. The incident lightened the mood in the room and an air of celebration took over. Now questions designed to throw light on the illegality of Trident in the USA came from the middle and back of the room. Arc lights from television cameras were blinding The Trident Three and had to be adjusted. In that vulnerable moment a man no one knew asked where he could reach them afterwards. It was an odd question, asked with no sign of sincerity or reason in it. Matthew was quick to catch Ulla's eye and he shook his head by way of instruction not to answer that. David McKenzie said firmly that it was he who should be contacted and quickly passed on. A few seconds later, with questions still being fired from all angles, I looked out of the window and wasn't wholly surprised to see the car I'd seen before drive the unknown man off. The car had to give way at the corner and I got my chance to wave them goodbye. They didn't wave back.

The story was of course top of the evening television news and stayed on the front pages of the papers through the weekend. Special colour sections on the story came with the Saturday and Sunday papers. But that was just the first wave of interest. The politicians had not yet had their say. I was driving home when I got a call from Alex Salmond, then the leader of the Scottish National Party, which has always had an anti-nuclear policy, asking if I could come into the offices of the Scottish Parliament and brief him. As I arrived home there was a foreign television news truck outside the house but the rules of the Faculty of Advocates didn't allow me to say anything. I hadn't kissed my wife before she told me that the editor of BBC's *Newsnight* in London had been on the phone asking if I could fly down that night to be on with the spokesman for the Pentagon, but again I couldn't because of the rules.

As reports were coming in about how many news agencies in Washington, California, New York, Asia and Europe were running the story I paused to read an e-mail from Jane Tallents saying that Angie was spending her first night at home by sleeping out under the stars. I was deeply touched by a US peace campaigner who wrote to me from California saying, 'As a result of this legal decision, all over the world the babies are sleeping more peacefully in their mothers' arms tonight and tomorrow morning the petals of each flower shall turn towards the sun for longer than they did today.'

By contrast the statement issued by the Pentagon was less romantic. It was simply to the effect that they were studying the judgement and would respond more fully in due course. I wondered how they already had access to a copy. I didn't have anything but my manuscript notes. Then I remembered our old friend Mr Jermyn Street and the mystery was solved.

In Westminster the reaction was one of rage that a Scottish judge had done the unthinkable and ruled on a matter that was specifically reserved to London by the Scotland Act. But they were off the point. It was operational control over the weapons that was reserved to them, not control over the international law on those weapons. The Greens, the Scottish Nationalists, the Irish and other like-minded Members of the European Parliament got busy tabling motions to bring the issue of nuclear weapons to the top of the European agenda. I am reliably informed that at NATO HQ there was a general feeling of being stunned. Whilst they were busy breaking treaty after treaty, no one dreamt that some women, some lawyers and some 50-year-old laws could strike at the core of Western alliance defence policy. I suppose that kind of complacency must easily set in when unelected officials and military personnel run the most powerful weapons system humankind has ever built.

A few days later I got an e-mail, sent from a tepee in the Trident Ploughshares 2000 peace camp at Loch Goil, asking if Matthew and I could give some advice on suing the MoD for continuing to act illegally by rebuilding *Maytime*. It is ironic, but not wholly surprising, that the peace camp sits cheek by jowl with the MoD, on land bought from them by a seasoned anti-nuclear campaigner whom the MoD lawyers failed to recognise. We soon met at the CND office in Glasgow where the legal teams were presented with framed photographs of *Maytime*, taken by the mystery man who stood on the vantage point as the women got aboard *Maytime* on 8 June 1999. As we thanked our clients for the gifts, the photographer's smile was broad and genuine.

In the months following the Gimblett judgement the popular protests at the Faslane Trident base continued with greater zest than ever before. The Moderator of the Church of Scotland was there giving vocal support on television whilst prayers were said in the background. High-profile MPs and my old friend and inspiration, Ian Hamilton QC, were carted off by the police to jail to the cheers of thousands. In particular, Tommy Sheridan MSP, a vocal supporter of The Trident Three, went to jail in Glasgow for refusing to accept that he 'breached the peace' when he stopped supplies going into the Trident base. At his trial the local lay magistrate ignored his plea based upon the Gimblett judgement. It is inspiring to have parliamentarians who actually live their beliefs and understandings instead of merely pontificating in a suit. The world-wide effect of seeing Angie, who had peacefully protested, and Tommy

Sheridan being carried very proudly and publicly to jail alongside hundreds of others was immeasurable.

As we were advising on further legal strategy we heard that the Westminster Cabinet was meeting in Downing Street to decide whether the Scottish Lord Advocate should petition the High Court in Edinburgh for its opinion on whether government nuclear defence policies were legal or not. There was no way of appealing Sheriff Gimblett's ruling in the normal way because she had directed the people of Scotland, in the form of the jury, to acquit the accused. That meant they had 'tholed their assize', as we say, and they could not be retried or found guilty by any back-door procedure. With some hesitation Lord Hardie of Blackford, then Lord Advocate of Scotland, referred several wide-ranging matters of Scottish criminal procedure and the nuclear policies of the British government to the Scottish High Court.

29

Sleep Well

A year after the trial The Trident Three and I stood in the regal silence of Court 3 within Parliament House in Edinburgh, letting them soak in the atmosphere of the place where three judges of the High Court would consider four questions posed by the Lord Advocate (drafted by an official in the Crown Office). Three of the questions were about technical aspects of Scottish criminal procedure and the other, which arose from the facts of the Greenock case, was: does any rule of customary international law justify a private individual in Scotland in damaging or destroying property in pursuit of his or her objection to the United Kingdom's 1) possession of nuclear weapons, 2) action in placing such weapons at locations within Scotland or 3) policies in relation to such weapons?

From a legal point of view, the three-part question was badly drafted. It was too wide for proper legal attention. But from the global citizens' point of view it was everything they had hoped for: to get the widest possible question on the legality of Trident before the highest criminal court in the land from which Trident was deployed – Scotland. I have long and varied experience of our High Court and had my apprehensions. But my three guests were, as ever, open to whatever challenges came their way. Their only concern was that the question was extremely politically charged and they wondered how deeply the hearing would penetrate into the deployment and policies of, for instance, Britain's first-strike policy. As we stood in the well of Court 3 a week before that hearing, there was no way of telling.

The hearing would be technically inquisitorial with counsel making submissions designed not to uphold anybody's particular plea but to assist the court in understanding the subject matter and issuing a ruling for guidance in future cases with similar facts. The accused from the particular trial that gives rise to such a hearing are statutorily entitled to appear at the hearing and put arguments.

I tried to put down some 'anchor points' around which there could be a meaningful debate but at a preliminary hearing the court decided to refuse my motion to send a novel question of European environmental law to the European Court of Justice in Luxembourg for a direction on whether deployment of Trident posed a threat to the environment of the European Union. It was a disappointment but there was worse to come. Despite the fact that such a legal hearing has a completely different focus from a criminal trial, where the objective is conviction or acquittal on specific charges, the court later refused to hear a word of evidence from expert witnesses about Trident. That left a dispute between the Crown and the defence about the facts of such things as deployment and policies. Nevertheless, the court decided it would proceed on certain hypotheses. Angie was again appearing for herself, so the court also decided that her position should not be compromised in any way and, against Angie's protestation, appointed Mr Gerry Moynihan QC to act as amicus curiae (friend of the court) to clear up any points that caused her difficulty.

At the hearing Crown counsel's central proposition was that 'Threat or use of nuclear weapons is not prohibited by international law. Quite the contrary in fact. There are circumstances where nuclear weapons could be threatened or used.' They relied upon the part of the World Court's advisory opinion where, by the chairman's casting vote, it had left open the possibility of nuclear weapons being used where the very survival of a state was at stake. In reply the High Court was directed to the chairman of the World Court's qualification of that ruling where he says that the narrow margin of that ruling was not to be seen as a half-open door. The door is to be seen as half-closed.

Mr Moynihan was seen by TP 2000 as an establishment man but the crowd who packed the court for the hearing need not have worried. He is one of the most able and well-respected seniors at the Scottish Bar, who applied his mind keenly and independently to the three-part question. They got something of a shock when he stood up to address the court and immediately said that Trident was illegal. The judges, obviously somewhat taken aback, had to ask if he had said legal or illegal. When he dealt with the massive indiscriminate effect from a Trident strike and pointed to the part where the World Court said that certain rules of international humanitarian law were 'intransgressible' and could thus 'never' be legally broken, the submission was clear. Never meant never.

I followed by adopting what had been said about the intransgressible rules of international humanitarian law and then developed my arguments based on the Nuremberg Principles, saying that these had been recently approved by the House of Lords in the case of General Pinochet. I also said there was no legal difference between outlawing the practice of terrorising a nation by use of tens of thousands of indiscriminate individual tortures and one indiscriminate nuclear strike. The amount of violence used and the effect were the same. The US cases decided before the World Court's advisory opinion were argued but the Scottish High Court did not find these persuasive.

Angie surpassed herself and, going without sleep for two nights, read her prepared script, which was both passionate and so well reasoned that the judges congratulated her for the way she had assisted the court. John McLaughlin's senior, Aiden O'Neil QC, one of our top advocates on human rights, developed arguments along those lines but he accepted that, for good legal reasons, these faded as the hearing developed. The Advocate General of Scotland had sent along a QC to protect any interests she may have in her position as the bridge between the government in Edinburgh and that in Westminster but he had nothing to say on the central question.

In the interim between the end of the hearing and the issue of the judgement I attended a packed annual Mountbatten Lecture in the Playfair Library, Old College, part of my alma mater, Edinburgh University. The speaker was none other than the secretary-general of

NATO, Lord Robertson. I thought his speech was insipid, filled with dates and carefully chosen statistics, whilst ducking anything of real substance. The questions from the floor were being furiously fired and awkwardly answered until the principal, Lord Sutherland of Houndwood, who was in the chair, spotted me and invited mine. I asked, 'Should the Scottish High Court follow the World Court and pronounce the threat or use of Trident to be illegal, how long will decommissioning take?' The top brass with him shuffled and turned round uneasily in their front-row seats. Lord Robertson's stuttered answer was, 'They are not going to do that.' People were astonished and shouted, 'How do you know?' To their untrained ears that obviously sounded like he knew something in advance of the High Court judgement. I was silent, knowing the answer could only be just more bravado.

The High Court issued its answers in March 2001 to a muted public response. The decision was dead against the proposition that anyone had any right of any kind to interfere with nuclear weapons, and meant that the Gimblett judgement could no longer be used. The High Court judgement most unusually did not cite which legal books and cases were used. It drew immediate and voracious criticism from well-informed and ill-informed sources alike. But in all fairness to the judges, who never speak in public about their judgements, their last word was that they had 'grave misgivings' about being asked to judge matters of government defence policy and the deployment of Trident in the first place. That gave me the impression that the whole issue had been derailed by the faceless person who had drafted that badly worded question.

That derailment has left a feeling of limbo in the international ranks of those inclined to rid the planet of nuclear weapons, leaving just wars to be fought, so far as possible, without massive indiscriminate civilian deaths. But just as deeply felt amongst those world-wide ranks is that, for some weeks after the disarmament action aboard *Maytime* in Loch Goil, Scotland, on that balmy night in June 1999, whilst the British Ministry of Defence put the pieces back together again, it could truly be said that The Trident Three had created a state of nuclear peace.

Index

Acronym Institute 41

Action of Churches Together in
Scotland 47

Ainslie, John 33, 40, 57, 148, 202, 265

Aldermaston warhead assembly plant
35

Amnesty International 127

Anthorn intelligence-gathering site 35

Bedjaoui, Judge 73, 95

Berlow, Matthew 15, 20–21, 103,
126–27, 134, 191, 213–14
at bail hearing 30–31

Bernadotte, Count 69–70

Blair, Constable Donald 12–13, 159,
160, 198, 200

Blair, Tony 224

Bonomy, Ian 18

Boyle, Professor Francis 139, 143,
170–71, 181–83, 185–90, 249

British Aerospace 127–28

British government
Cold War mentality of 63
at World Court see Chapter 9
and World Court judgement 237

Brooks, Detective Constable Hazel
159, 173

Burghfield warhead assembly plant 35

Bush, President George W 56

Butch Cassidy and the Sundance Kid 66

Butler, General Lee 55–56

Byres, Constable James 12–13, 159,
160, 195–99

Cassidy, Detective Sergeant Peter
158–63, 164–68, 171–77

Chambers, PC Stuart 203

Chapman, Dr W Arthur 49

Chernobyl accident 65

CND 57, 67
see also Scottish CND; Scottish
Christian CND

Cold War 58
mentality, persistence of 63

Colman, John 203

Cornton Vale jail 1, 16
see also Chapter 3

Craig, Revd Maxwell 47

Criminal Law Act (England) 129

Crown Office, Edinburgh 45

Cuban missile crisis 55

Defence Evaluation Research Agency
(DERA) 5, 10, 37, 207–09

Index

Denmark, complaint to UN 111
Derby submarine-construction site 35
Dunoon Sheriff Court 28–29

East Timor 127–30
Echelon Programme 205, 242
Ecology Party 67
Elder, Dorothy Grace 226

Faculty of Advocates, library 101
Falklands War 53, 58
Fox, Stephen 181, 242
Fraser of Carmyllie, Lord 45–46, 48

Gaius 85
Gardner, PC Karen 201–02, 204
Genocide Act 1969 46
Gilchrist, W A 48
Gimblett, Sheriff Margaret 53, 135,
        142, 143–44, 150–51, 167, 215, 223
    judgement of 257–60
    and jury, address to 263–64
Greenham Common 39, 59, 69, 110
Greenock 101, 135
Greenpeace 57, 111

Hamilton, Archie 46
Hamilton, Ian 133–34, 268
Hardie of Blackford, Lord 269
Harper, Conrad K 73
Havel, Vaclev 68
Hayek, Professor F A 51
High Court judgement 273
    see also Scottish Law; The Trident
        Three; Zelter, Angie
Hiroshima 121–22
HMS Sheffield 58
HMS Torbay 60
HMS Vanguard 60, 243
Holy Loch, Scotland 60

House of Commons defence select
    committee 52

India-Pakistan dispute and possible
        nuclear threat 41
indictments, wording of 23–24
Indonesia 127–30
Ingham, Officer John 203
Inglis, John 20
Institute for Law and Peace (INLAP)
        220–21
International Court of Justice (World
        Court) vii, 1–2, 27, 45, 47, 50,
        69–83 passim
    advisory opinions of 69–70
    judgement of 94–95, 236–37, 249
    make-up of 73
    and Resolution 49/75 K, adoption of
        by General Assembly of UN
        70–71
    and territorial integrity 89–90
    see also Chapter 10; World Court
        Project
International Herald Tribune 41

Johnson, Rebecca 40–41, 235–40, 255

Kinloss Nimrod aircraft site 35
Kronlid, Lotta 127–28

Loch Goil 5, 16, 37, 179
Lockheed 115
Longson, Andrea 104, 106, 250
Louise Weiss Foundation 54
Lyell, Sir Nicholas 73, 76–79, 81–82

MacBride, Sean 67, 123
McAllion, John 226
McInnes, Ian 193
McKenzie, David 181, 265, 266

McKenzie, Fraser 191–95

McLaughlin, John 21, 102, 150,
      157–58, 173–77 *passim*, 201

McNamara, Robert 55

McPhee, Iain 13, 148, 151, 152, 177,
      193, 200–01
   at trial 202, 206–10

Malcolm, Dr Chris 205

Mandela, Nelson 120

Mason, Sir Ronald 51, 52

Mayer, Lizzie 15

Mayer, Sam 145

Maytime 5–11, 39, 173, 268
   indictments concerning 23–25
   O'Brian's evidence concerning 154
   see also Part Four

Menwith Hill intelligence-gathering
      site 35

Menzies, Lord 82

Minford, Professor Patrick 52

Ministry of Defence
   and Greenham Common 110
   and nuclear accidents, admissions of
      58
   police 12, 36

Mothersson, Keith 67–68

Mountbatten of Burma, Earl 54–55

Moxley, Ellen vii, 1, 21
   Cassidy's interview with 164–67
   joint initial consultation with 28
   and trial defence, giving of 243–44
   and Vietnam War 39, 153, 243
   see also Operation *Maytime*; trial of
      The Trident Three; The Trident
      Three

Moynihan, Gerry 271–72

Murray, Lord 104–07, 190, 249, 251

Nagasaki 121–22

National Ignition Facility 82, 238, 244

NATO 53, 268

necessity, defence of 108–09, 112–22,
      130

Needham, Andrea 127–28

Newt 5, 11, 173, 177

Niemoeller, Pastor Martin 109

nuclear capability of 56
   see also nuclear peace, world-wide
      efforts

nuclear materials, disposal of 59

nuclear peace, world-wide efforts
      110–11
   in Canada 120–21
   in Japan 121–22
   in Netherlands 122–25
   in USA 111–20

nuclear waste, contamination by 234

nuclear-related accidents, reporting of
      58

Nuremberg trials, defences in 252

O'Brian, PC Thomas 151–54, 157–58

O'Neil, Aiden 272

Operation *Maytime* 6–13
   ground rules for 37
   planning of *see* Chapter 5

Panzer, Judge Ulf 122, 213, 225, 227–29

Paton, PC David 200–01

Pax Legalis 220

Pentagon 267

Pershing missiles 227–29

plane crashes 59

Polaris nuclear submarines 49, 51

Prestwick anti-submarine helicopter
      base 35

Putin, President Vladimir 56

RAF Kinloss 59

RAF Wittering 60

Rainbow Warrior III

Reagan, Ronald 51, 118

Right Livelihood Award vii

Robertson of Port Ellen, Lord 78, 273

Robson, Air Vice-Marshal Bobby 53

Roder, Ulla vii, 1, 16

    Cassidy's interview with 167–68

    and Denmark, political action in 38

    and deportation order, threat of 140

    first consultation with 25–27, 31

    and illness during trial 215

    and trial defence, giving of 229–30

    see also Operation *Maytime*; trial of

        The Trident Three; The Trident

        Three

Rodger, Alan (later Lord) 48–50,

    254–55

Rogers, Professor Paul 139, 231–35

Rugby intelligence-gathering site 35

Russia 62

    bureaucracy and corruption within

      64

    and hijacked submarine 60

    hypothetical nuclear strike on

      64–65

    nuclear capability of 56

    people of 63

Salmond, Alex 267

Scottish Christian CND 45–49

    see also CND

Scottish CND 33–34, 49, 50

    see also CND

Scottish law 99

    and courts, types of 100

    criminal-case basics of 22

    and High Court 270

    and juries 148

    and necessity 108–09, 113

    sheriffs within 29

Sheridan, Tommy 268–69

South Africa 119–20

Steven, Helen 39, 160

Stewart, Andrew 203

Stockholm International Peace

    Research Institute 54

Stone of Destiny 133

strategic defence reviews 79–80

Sutherland of Houndwood, Lord 273

Tall, Commander Jeffrey 53

Tallents, Jane 107, 139, 154–55, 160,

    170, 181, 204, 226

Thatcher, Margaret 51–52

The Trident Three

    bail hearing for 28–31

    in Byres's evidence 197

    and expert witnesses 101

    at High Court 270–72

    and indictments 23–25

    and *Maytime* operation 6–13

    and media coverage 267

    MSPs' letter of support for 226, 244

    are not guilty 260, 263–64

    and post-trial press conference

      265–67

    see also Moxley, Ellen; Operation

        Maytime; Roder, Ulla; trial of The

        Trident Three; Zelter, Angie

Thomas, Hugh 186–87

Thompson, Robert 177–79

Three Mile Island 115

trial of The Trident Three

    aftermath of 267–68

    and joint statement 173–76, 244

    jury in 148–50

    and Mayer's submission on aspects of

      law 247–55

    moved to Greenock 101

    and not-guilty decision 260, 263–64

pleas in 143
police interviews played at 161–68
and written joint minutes 202–04
see also Moxley, Ellen; Operation
  Maytime; Parts Four, Five; Roder,
  Ulla; The Trident Three; Zelter,
  Angie
Trident 5–6, 10, 16–17, 79
  anechoic secrecy of 37
  constant preparedness of 53
  infrastructure system of 34–36
  and Polaris, substitute for 49, 51–52
  protests against 100
  and safety-control systems, vulnera-
    bility of 233
  Spearhead torpedoes for 36
  and warheads, firing of 60–61
Trident Ploughshares 2000 (TP 2000)
  2, 6, 7, 15, 34, 181, 222
  at bail hearing 29
  pledgers' ground rules 36–37
  and submarine movements, pledgers'
    observations of 38
  at trial 136, 142, 167, 183, 214, 235,
    264

United Nations vii, 68–69, 77–78, 81,
  86
  and East Timor 128
  and Resolution 49/75 K, adoption of
    by General Assembly 70–71
USA
  and Cuba crisis, misjudgement over
    55
  and UK's Trident decision, delighted
    with 52
USS *Holland* 60
USS *Los Angeles* 60
USS *Scorpion* 58–59

Walker, Pia 141
Washington Post 41
Webster, David L 138–39, 146, 148,
  152–53, 159–61, 164, 171–73, 178,
  184, 192–94, 201, 255–56
  and Boyle cross-examination
    189–90
  and Johnson cross-examination 240
  and Zelter cross-examination
    223–25
Wilson, Joanna 127–28
World Court *see* International Court
  of Justice
World Court Project 48, 70–73,
  102–03, 221
  goes international 68
  launched in UK 67–68
  and Resolution 49/75 K, adoption of
    by General Assembly of UN
    70–71
  see also International Court of Justice
World Health Organisation 68

Yugoslavia 92

Zelter, Angie vii, 1, 16, 122, 213,
  268–69
  Cassidy's interview with 161–63
  cross-examination of 223–25
  and daughter's visit to courtroom
    168–69
  and Greenham Common 39
  and Hawk case 127, 129, 130
  at High Court 271, 272
  and Johnson, questions to 239–40
  and trial defence, giving of 215–23
  and witnesses, cross-examination of
    158
  see also Operation *Maytime*; trial of
    The Trident Three